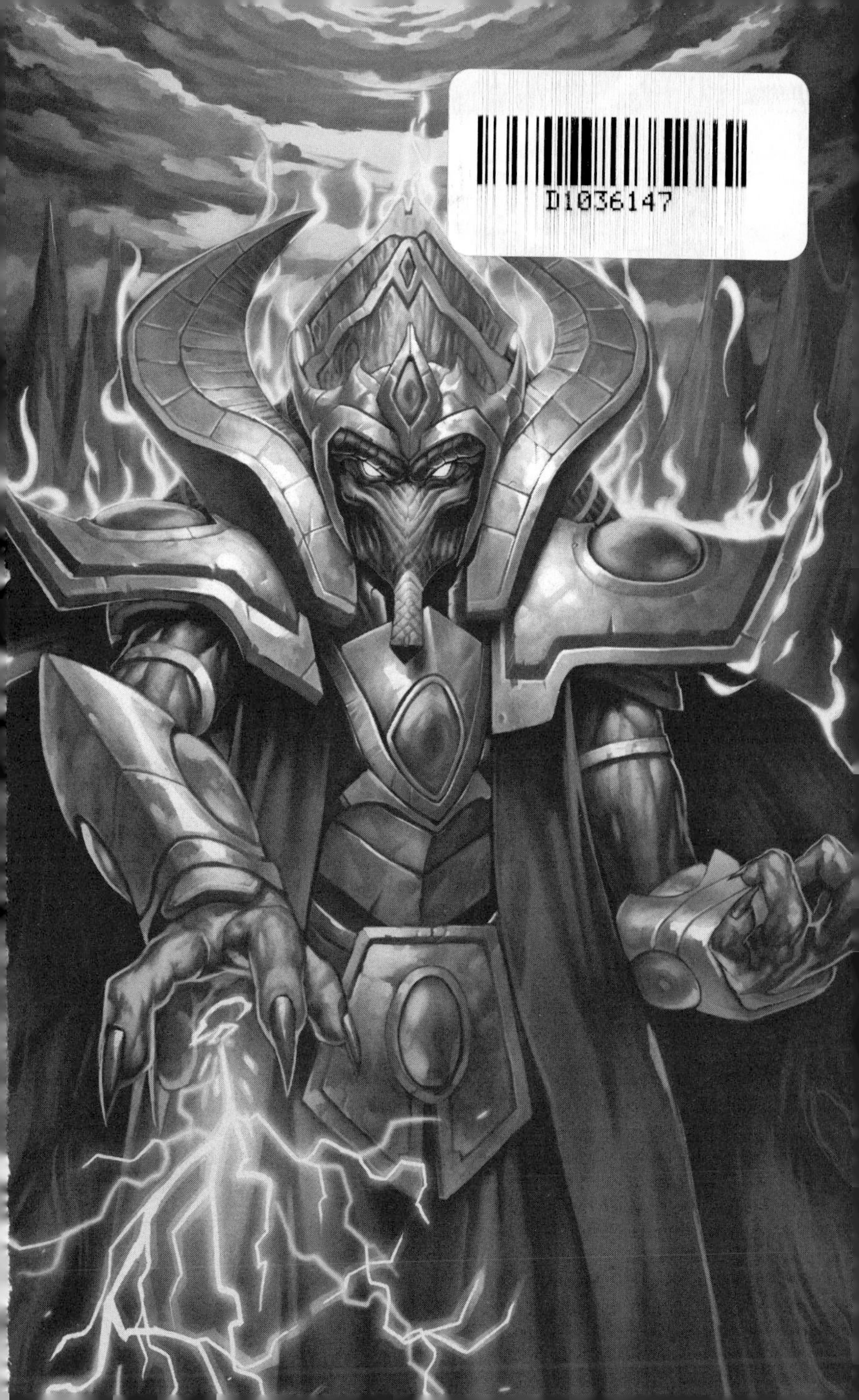

StarCraft: Frontline Vol. 3

Contributing Editor - Troy Lewter
Layout and Lettering - Michael Paolilli
Creative Consultant - Michael Paolilli
Graphic Designer - Louis Csontos
Cover Artist - UDON with Saejin Oh

Editor - Hope Donovan
Print Production Manager - Lucas Rivera
Managing Editor - Vy Nguyen
Senior Designer - Louis Csontos
Director of Sales and Manufacturing - Allyson De Simone
Associate Publisher - Marco F. Pavia
President and C.O.O. - John Parker
C.E.O. and Chief Creative Officer - Stu Levy

BLIZZARD ENTERTAINMENT

Senior Vice President,
Story and Franchise Development - Lydia Bottegoni
Director, Creative Development - Ralph Sanchez
Lead Editor, Publishing - Paul Morrissey
Senior Editor - Cate Gary
Copy Editor - Allison Irons
Producer - Brianne M Loftis
Vice President, Global Consumer Products - Matt Beecher
Senior Manager, Global Licensing - Byron Parnell
Special Thanks - Sean Copeland, Evelyn Fredericksen, Phillip Hillenbrand, Christi Kugler, Alix Nicholaeff, Justin Parker

BLIZZARD ENTERTAINMENT

gear.blizzard.com

This book contains material originally published by TOKYOPOP Inc.

First Blizzard Entertainment printing: March 2019

ISBN: 978-1-9456834-9-7

10 9 8 7 6 5 4 3 2 1

Printed in the USA

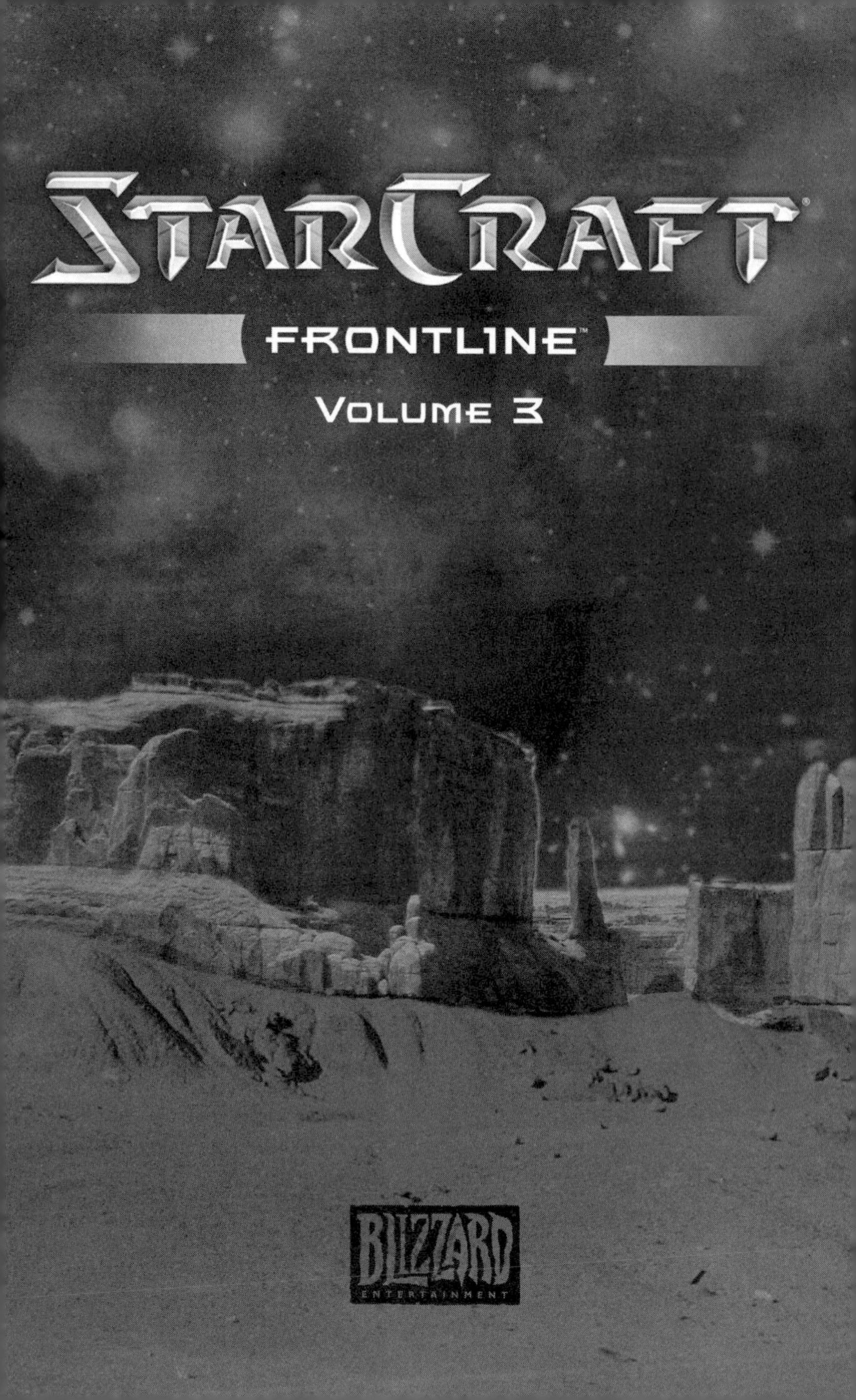
StarCraft
FRONTLINE
Volume 3

STARCRAFT

FRONTLINE
VOLUME 3

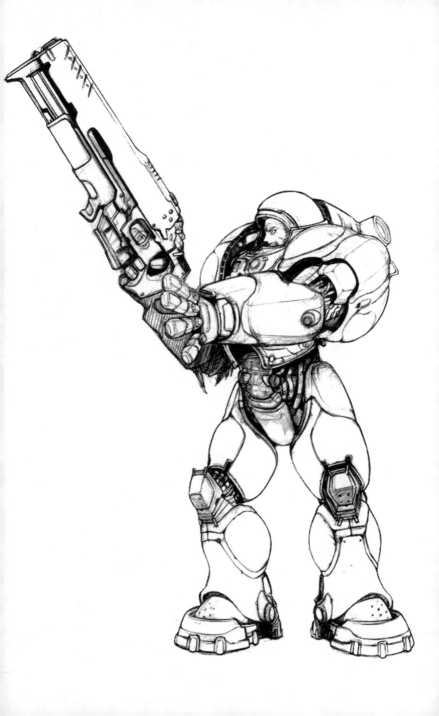

StarCraft

Frontline™
Volume 3

War-Torn

Written by Paul Benjamin & Dave Shramek

Art by Hector Sevilla

Letterer: Michael Paolilli

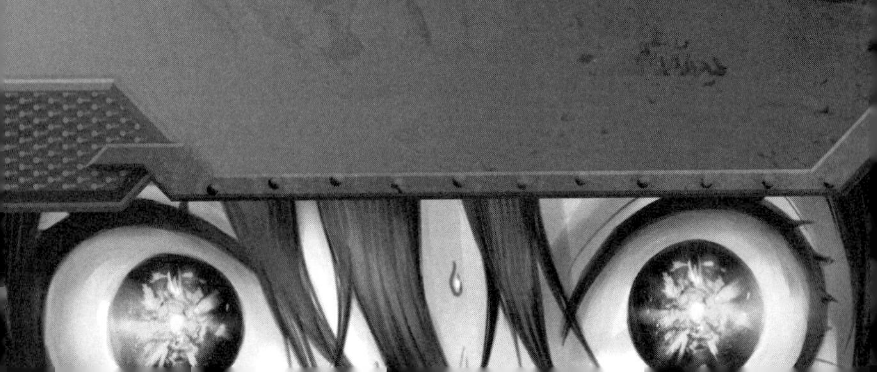

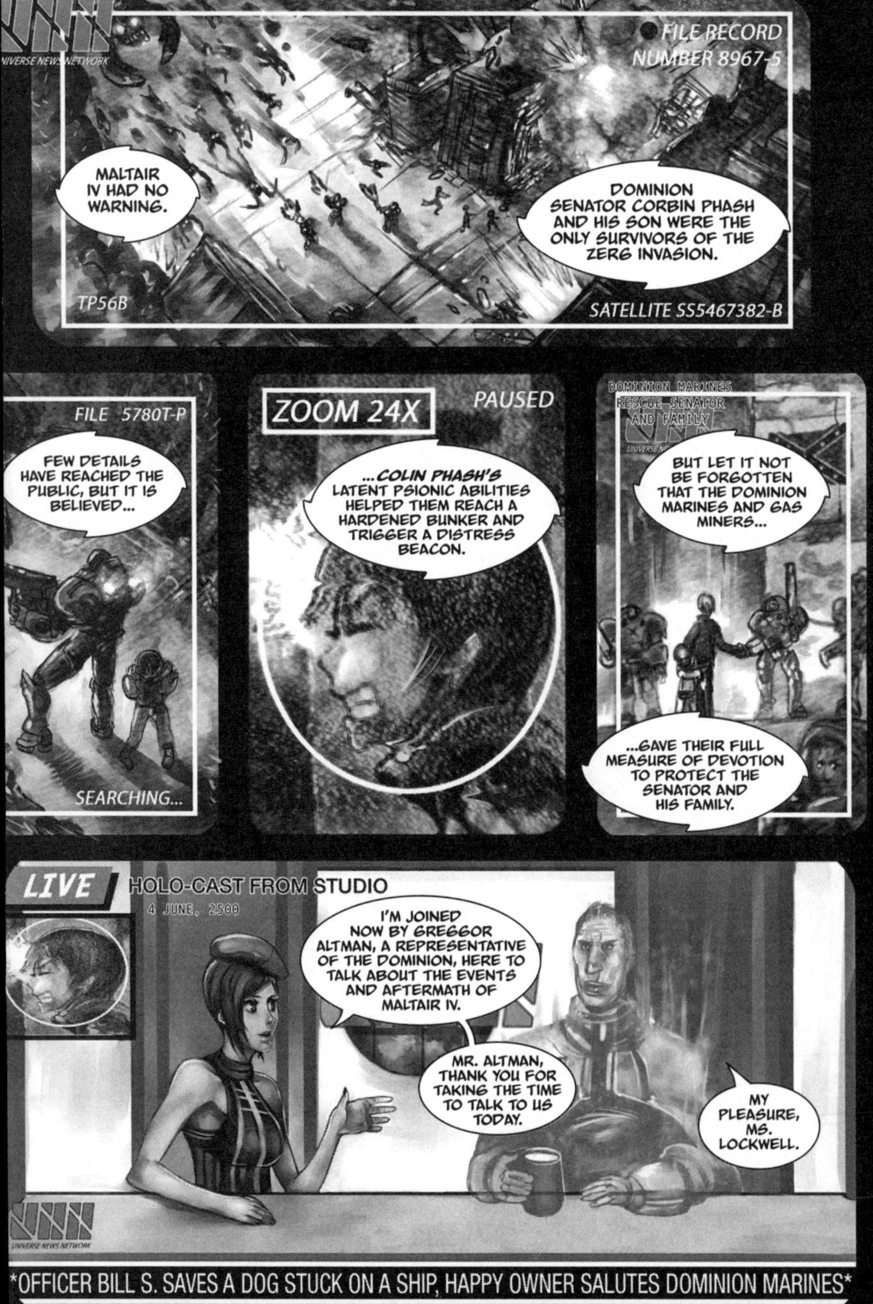
UNIVERSE NEWS NETWORK
FILE RECORD
NUMBER 8967-5
MALTAIR IV HAD NO WARNING.
DOMINION SENATOR CORBIN PHASH AND HIS SON WERE THE ONLY SURVIVORS OF THE ZERG INVASION.
TP56B
SATELLITE SS5467382-B
FILE 5780T-P
FEW DETAILS HAVE REACHED THE PUBLIC, BUT IT IS BELIEVED...
SEARCHING...
ZOOM 24X
PAUSED
...COLIN PHASH'S LATENT PSIONIC ABILITIES HELPED THEM REACH A HARDENED BUNKER AND TRIGGER A DISTRESS BEACON.
DOMINION MARINES RESCUE SENATOR AND FAMILY
BUT LET IT NOT BE FORGOTTEN THAT THE DOMINION MARINES AND GAS MINERS...
...GAVE THEIR FULL MEASURE OF DEVOTION TO PROTECT THE SENATOR AND HIS FAMILY.
LIVE
HOLO-CAST FROM STUDIO
4 JUNE, 2500
I'M JOINED NOW BY GREGGOR ALTMAN, A REPRESENTATIVE OF THE DOMINION, HERE TO TALK ABOUT THE EVENTS AND AFTERMATH OF MALTAIR IV.
MR. ALTMAN, THANK YOU FOR TAKING THE TIME TO TALK TO US TODAY.
MY PLEASURE, MS. LOCKWELL.
UNIVERSE NEWS NETWORK
OFFICER BILL S. SAVES A DOG STUCK ON A SHIP, HAPPY OWNER SALUTES DOMINION MARINES

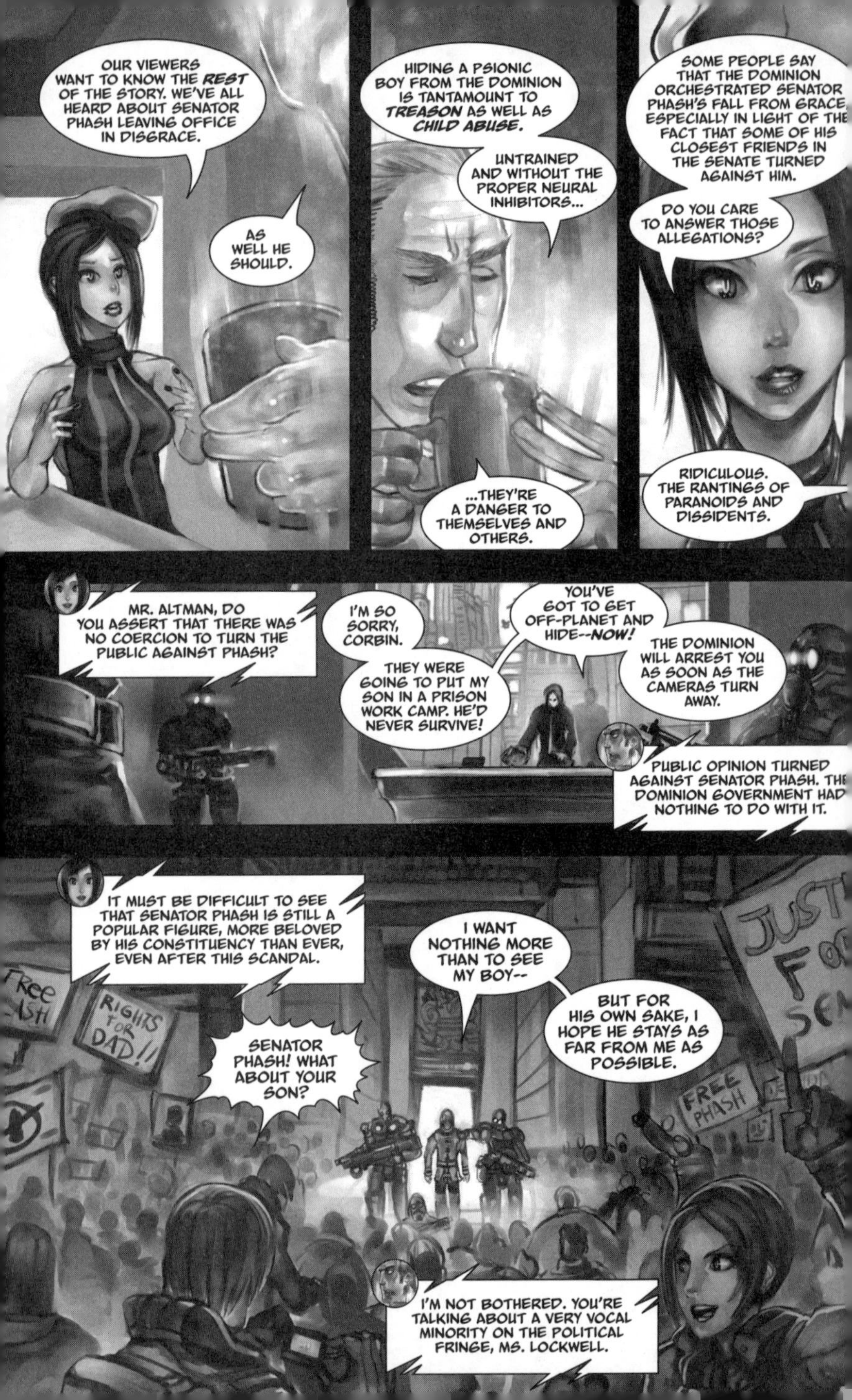
OUR VIEWERS WANT TO KNOW THE REST OF THE STORY. WE'VE ALL HEARD ABOUT SENATOR PHASH LEAVING OFFICE IN DISGRACE.
AS WELL HE SHOULD.
HIDING A PSIONIC BOY FROM THE DOMINION IS TANTAMOUNT TO TREASON AS WELL AS CHILD ABUSE.
UNTRAINED AND WITHOUT THE PROPER NEURAL INHIBITORS...
...THEY'RE A DANGER TO THEMSELVES AND OTHERS.
SOME PEOPLE SAY THAT THE DOMINION ORCHESTRATED SENATOR PHASH'S FALL FROM GRACE, ESPECIALLY IN LIGHT OF THE FACT THAT SOME OF HIS CLOSEST FRIENDS IN THE SENATE TURNED AGAINST HIM.
DO YOU CARE TO ANSWER THOSE ALLEGATIONS?
RIDICULOUS. THE RANTINGS OF PARANOIDS AND DISSIDENTS.
MR. ALTMAN, DO YOU ASSERT THAT THERE WAS NO COERCION TO TURN THE PUBLIC AGAINST PHASH?
I'M SO SORRY, CORBIN.
THEY WERE GOING TO PUT MY SON IN A PRISON WORK CAMP. HE'D NEVER SURVIVE!
YOU'VE GOT TO GET OFF-PLANET AND HIDE--NOW!
THE DOMINION WILL ARREST YOU AS SOON AS THE CAMERAS TURN AWAY.
PUBLIC OPINION TURNED AGAINST SENATOR PHASH. THE DOMINION GOVERNMENT HAD NOTHING TO DO WITH IT.
IT MUST BE DIFFICULT TO SEE THAT SENATOR PHASH IS STILL A POPULAR FIGURE, MORE BELOVED BY HIS CONSTITUENCY THAN EVER, EVEN AFTER THIS SCANDAL.
RIGHTS FOR DAD!!
SENATOR PHASH! WHAT ABOUT YOUR SON?
I WANT NOTHING MORE THAN TO SEE MY BOY--
BUT FOR HIS OWN SAKE, I HOPE HE STAYS AS FAR FROM ME AS POSSIBLE.
FREE PHASH
I'M NOT BOTHERED. YOU'RE TALKING ABOUT A VERY VOCAL MINORITY ON THE POLITICAL FRINGE, MS. LOCKWELL.

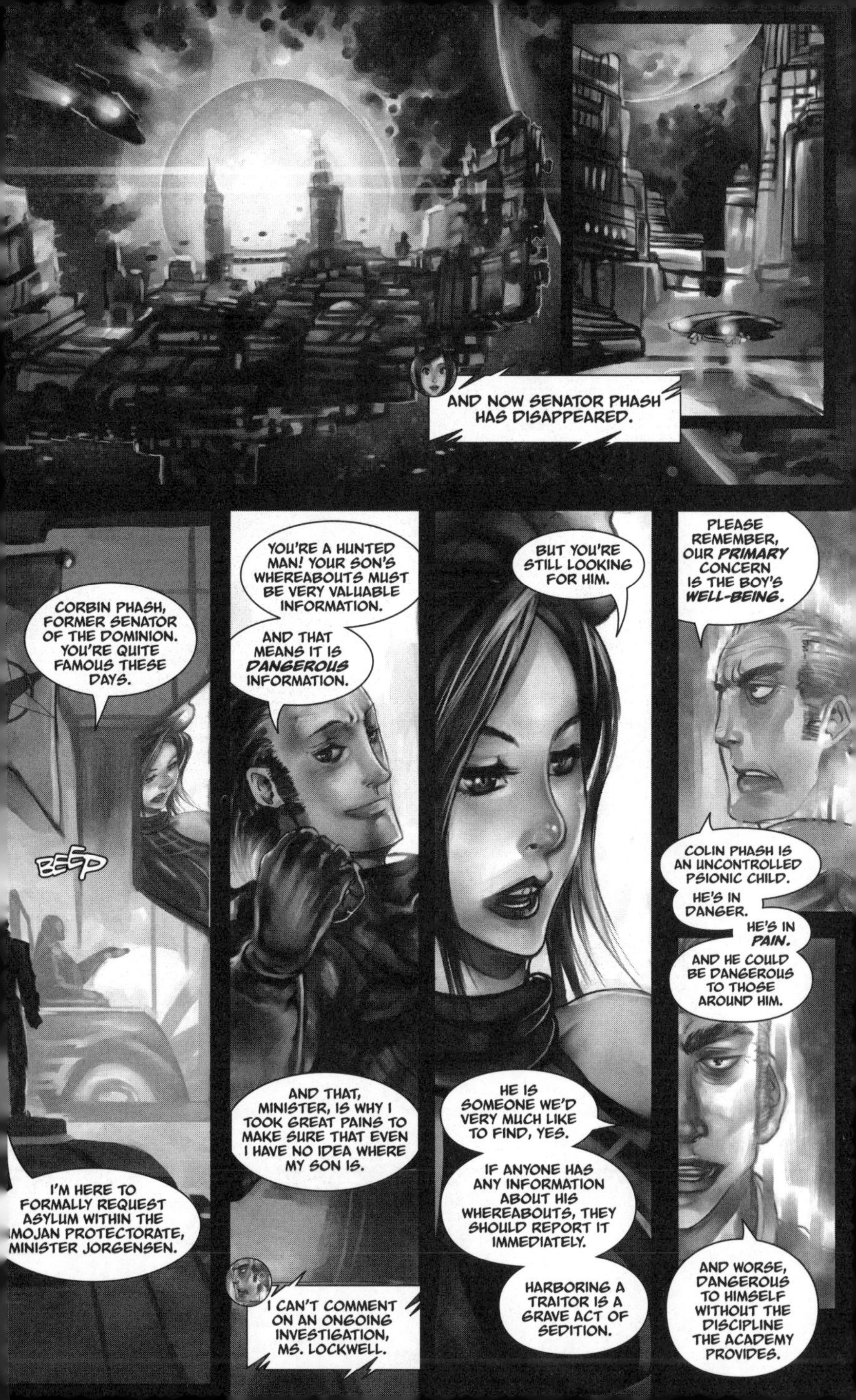

AND NOW SENATOR PHASH HAS DISAPPEARED.
CORBIN PHASH, FORMER SENATOR OF THE DOMINION. YOU'RE QUITE FAMOUS THESE DAYS.
BEEP
I'M HERE TO FORMALLY REQUEST ASYLUM WITHIN THE IMOJAN PROTECTORATE, MINISTER JORGENSEN.
YOU'RE A HUNTED MAN! YOUR SON'S WHEREABOUTS MUST BE VERY VALUABLE INFORMATION.
AND THAT MEANS IT IS *DANGEROUS* INFORMATION.
AND THAT, MINISTER, IS WHY I TOOK GREAT PAINS TO MAKE SURE THAT EVEN I HAVE NO IDEA WHERE MY SON IS.
I CAN'T COMMENT ON AN ONGOING INVESTIGATION, MS. LOCKWELL.
BUT YOU'RE STILL LOOKING FOR HIM.
HE IS SOMEONE WE'D VERY MUCH LIKE TO FIND, YES.
IF ANYONE HAS ANY INFORMATION ABOUT HIS WHEREABOUTS, THEY SHOULD REPORT IT IMMEDIATELY.
HARBORING A TRAITOR IS A GRAVE ACT OF SEDITION.
PLEASE REMEMBER, OUR *PRIMARY* CONCERN IS THE BOY'S *WELL-BEING.*
COLIN PHASH IS AN UNCONTROLLED PSIONIC CHILD.
HE'S IN DANGER.
HE'S IN *PAIN.*
AND HE COULD BE DANGEROUS TO THOSE AROUND HIM.
AND WORSE, DANGEROUS TO HIMSELF WITHOUT THE DISCIPLINE THE ACADEMY PROVIDES.

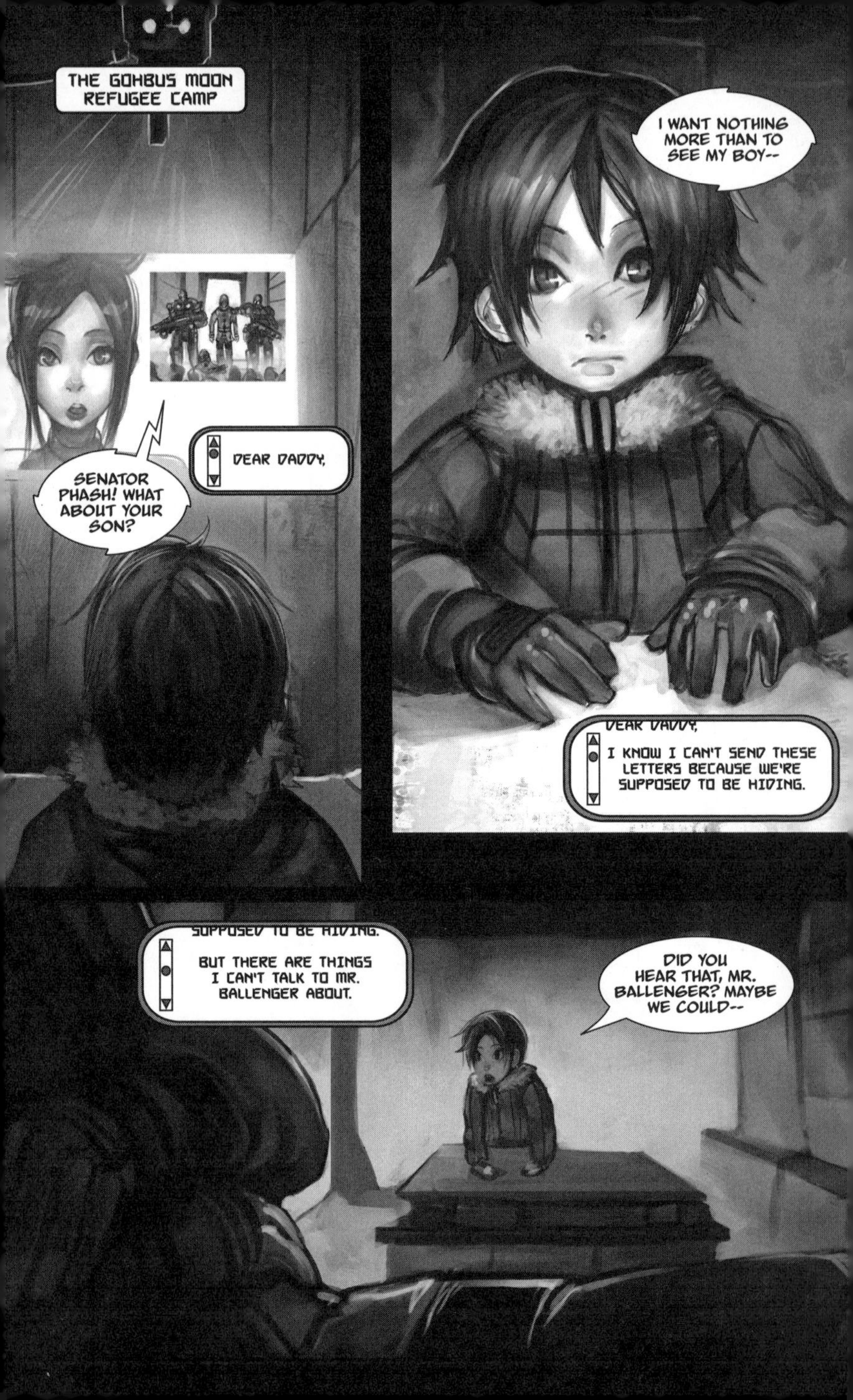
THE GOHBUS MOON REFUGEE CAMP
SENATOR PHASH! WHAT ABOUT YOUR SON?
DEAR DADDY,
I WANT NOTHING MORE THAN TO SEE MY BOY--
DEAR DADDY,
I KNOW I CAN'T SEND THESE LETTERS BECAUSE WE'RE SUPPOSED TO BE HIDING.
SUPPOSED TO BE HIDING.
BUT THERE ARE THINGS I CAN'T TALK TO MR. BALLENGER ABOUT.
DID YOU HEAR THAT, MR. BALLENGER? MAYBE WE COULD--

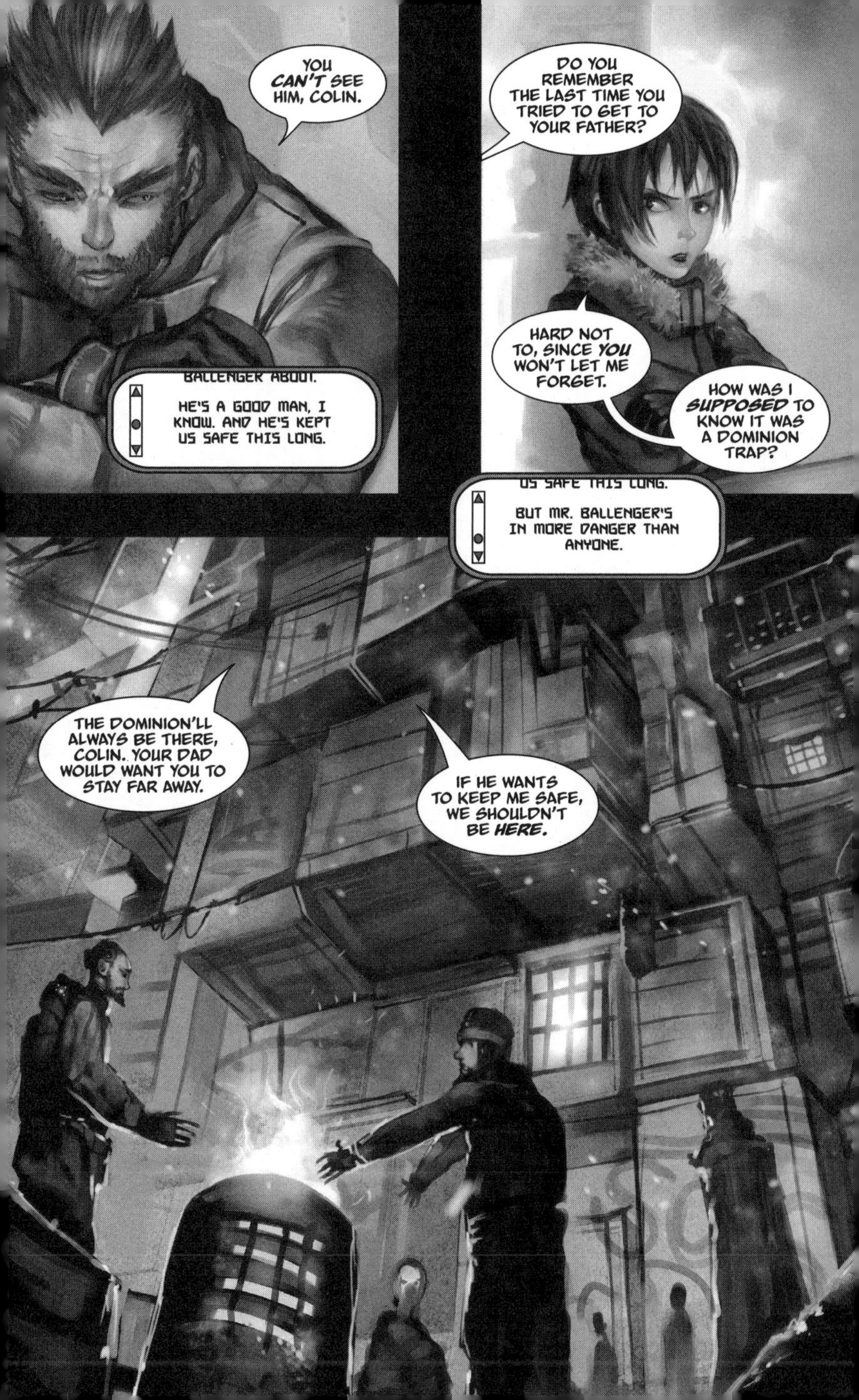
YOU CAN'T SEE HIM, COLIN.
BALLENGER ABOUT.
HE'S A GOOD MAN, I KNOW. AND HE'S KEPT US SAFE THIS LONG.
DO YOU REMEMBER THE LAST TIME YOU TRIED TO GET TO YOUR FATHER?
HARD NOT TO, SINCE YOU WON'T LET ME FORGET.
HOW WAS I SUPPOSED TO KNOW IT WAS A DOMINION TRAP?
US SAFE THIS LONG.
BUT MR. BALLENGER'S IN MORE DANGER THAN ANYONE.
THE DOMINION'LL ALWAYS BE THERE, COLIN. YOUR DAD WOULD WANT YOU TO STAY FAR AWAY.
IF HE WANTS TO KEEP ME SAFE, WE SHOULDN'T BE HERE.

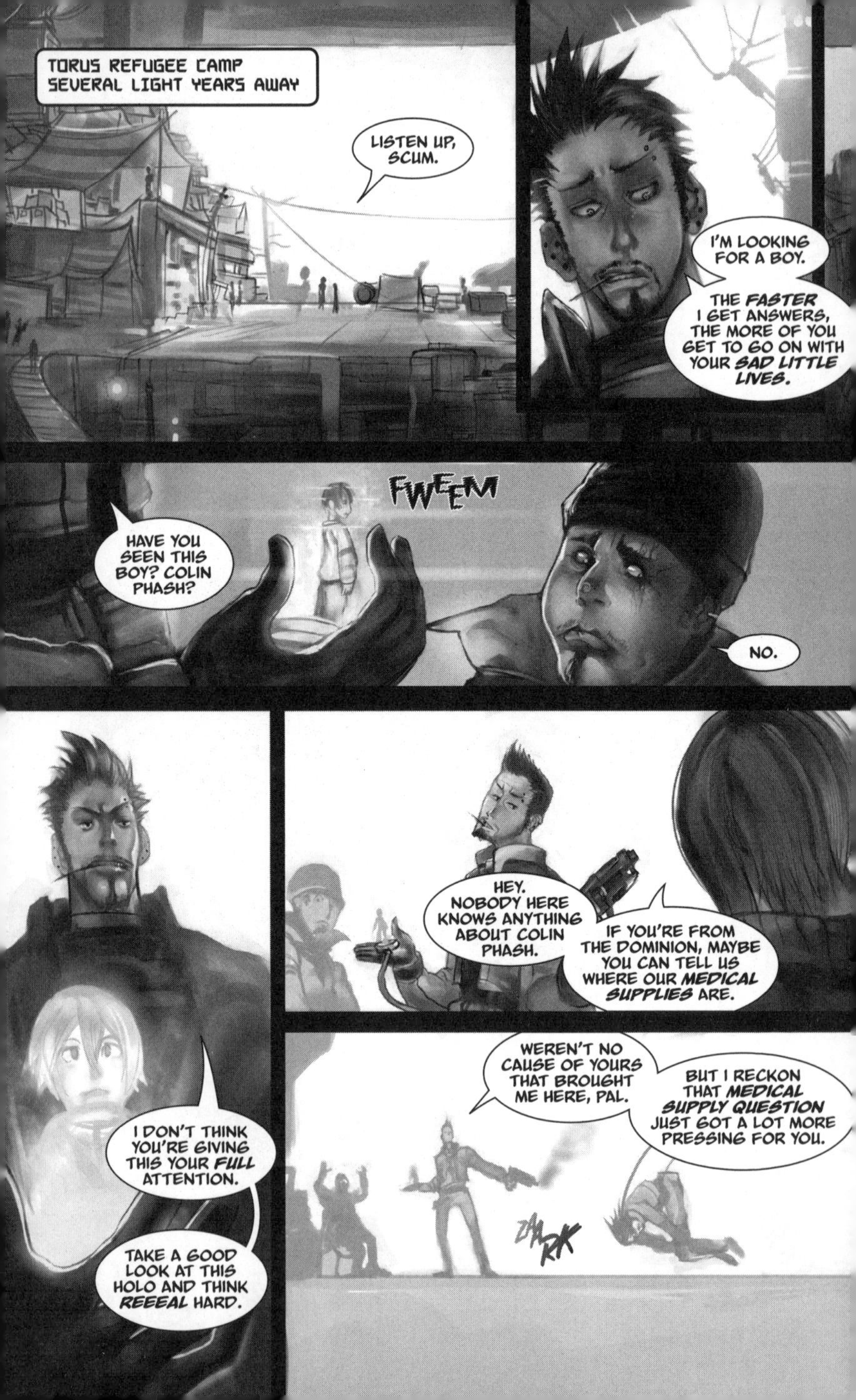
TORUS REFUGEE CAMP
SEVERAL LIGHT YEARS AWAY
LISTEN UP, SCUM.
I'M LOOKING FOR A BOY.
THE FASTER I GET ANSWERS, THE MORE OF YOU GET TO GO ON WITH YOUR SAD LITTLE LIVES.
FWEEM
HAVE YOU SEEN THIS BOY? COLIN PHASH?
NO.
I DON'T THINK YOU'RE GIVING THIS YOUR FULL ATTENTION.
TAKE A GOOD LOOK AT THIS HOLO AND THINK REEEAL HARD.
HEY. NOBODY HERE KNOWS ANYTHING ABOUT COLIN PHASH.
IF YOU'RE FROM THE DOMINION, MAYBE YOU CAN TELL US WHERE OUR MEDICAL SUPPLIES ARE.
WEREN'T NO CAUSE OF YOURS THAT BROUGHT ME HERE, PAL.
BUT I RECKON THAT MEDICAL SUPPLY QUESTION JUST GOT A LOT MORE PRESSING FOR YOU.
ZAKRK

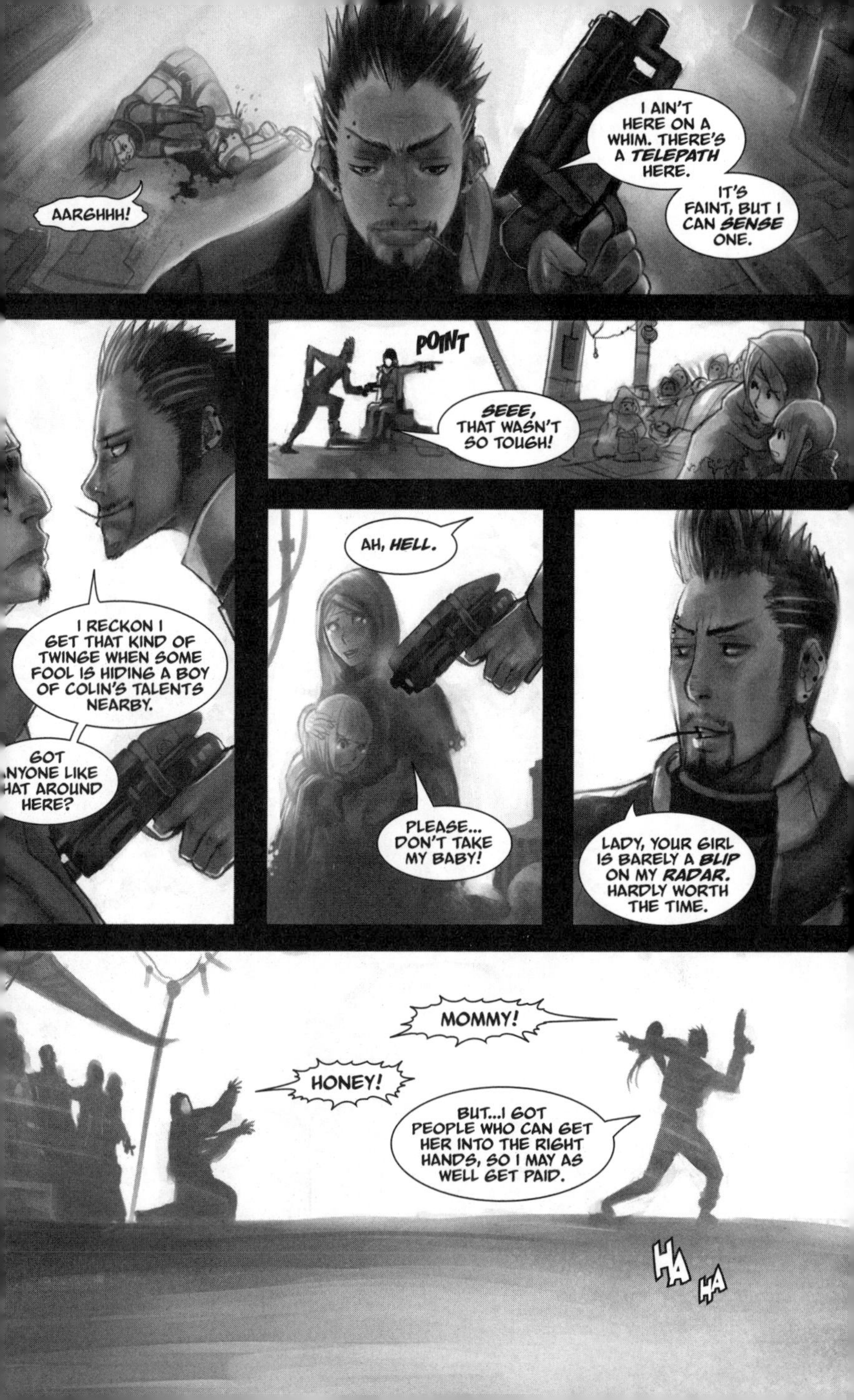
AARGHHH!
I AIN'T HERE ON A WHIM. THERE'S A TELEPATH HERE.
IT'S FAINT, BUT I CAN SENSE ONE.
I RECKON I GET THAT KIND OF TWINGE WHEN SOME FOOL IS HIDING A BOY OF COLIN'S TALENTS NEARBY.
GOT ANYONE LIKE THAT AROUND HERE?
POINT
SEEE, THAT WASN'T SO TOUGH!
AH, HELL.
PLEASE... DON'T TAKE MY BABY!
LADY, YOUR GIRL IS BARELY A BLIP ON MY RADAR. HARDLY WORTH THE TIME.
MOMMY!
HONEY!
BUT...I GOT PEOPLE WHO CAN GET HER INTO THE RIGHT HANDS, SO I MAY AS WELL GET PAID.
HA
HA

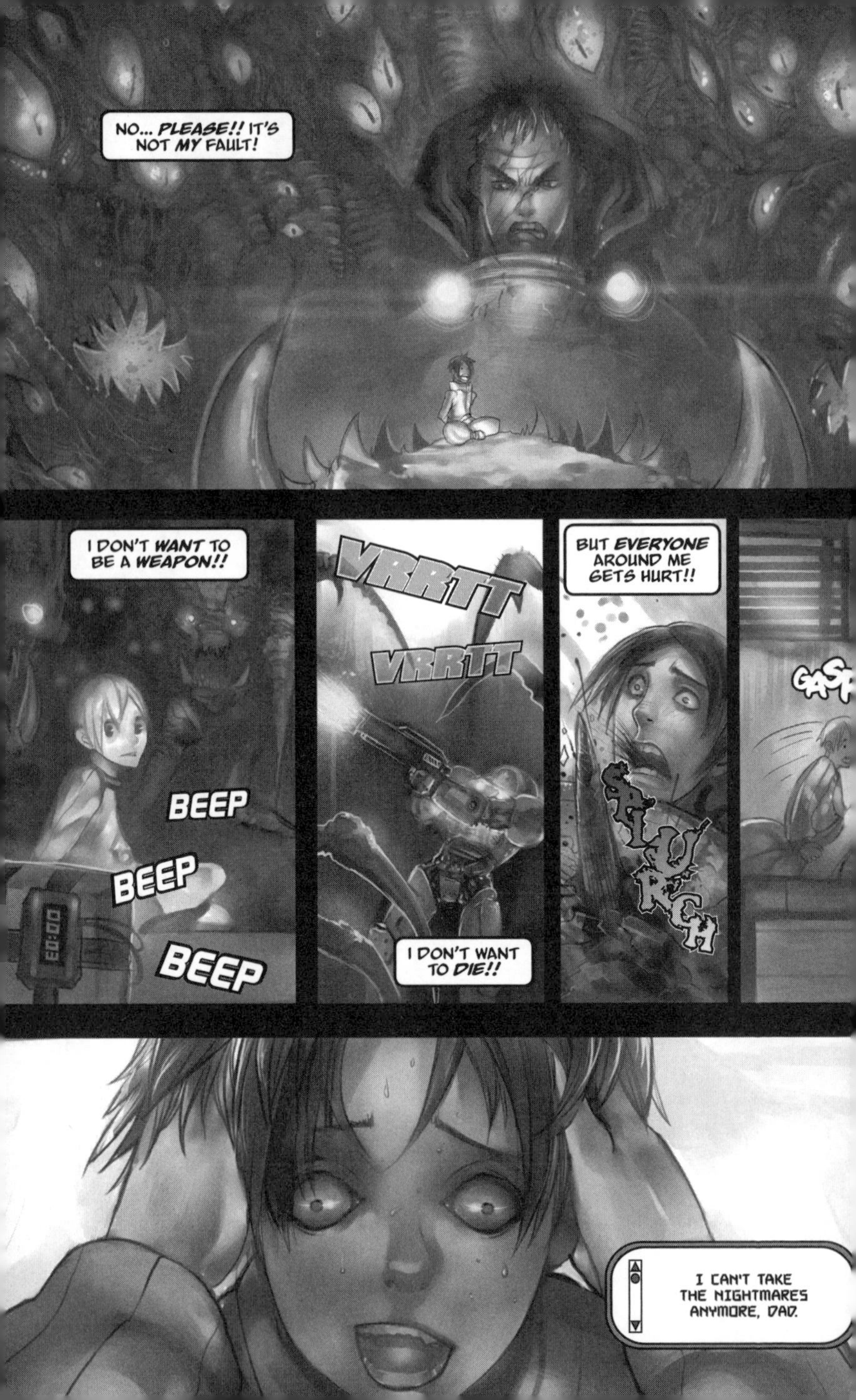
NO... PLEASE!! IT'S NOT MY FAULT!
I DON'T WANT TO BE A WEAPON!!
BEEP
BEEP
BEEP
VRRTT
VRRTT
I DON'T WANT TO DIE!!
BUT EVERYONE AROUND ME GETS HURT!!
SPLURCH
I CAN'T TAKE THE NIGHTMARES ANYMORE, DAD.

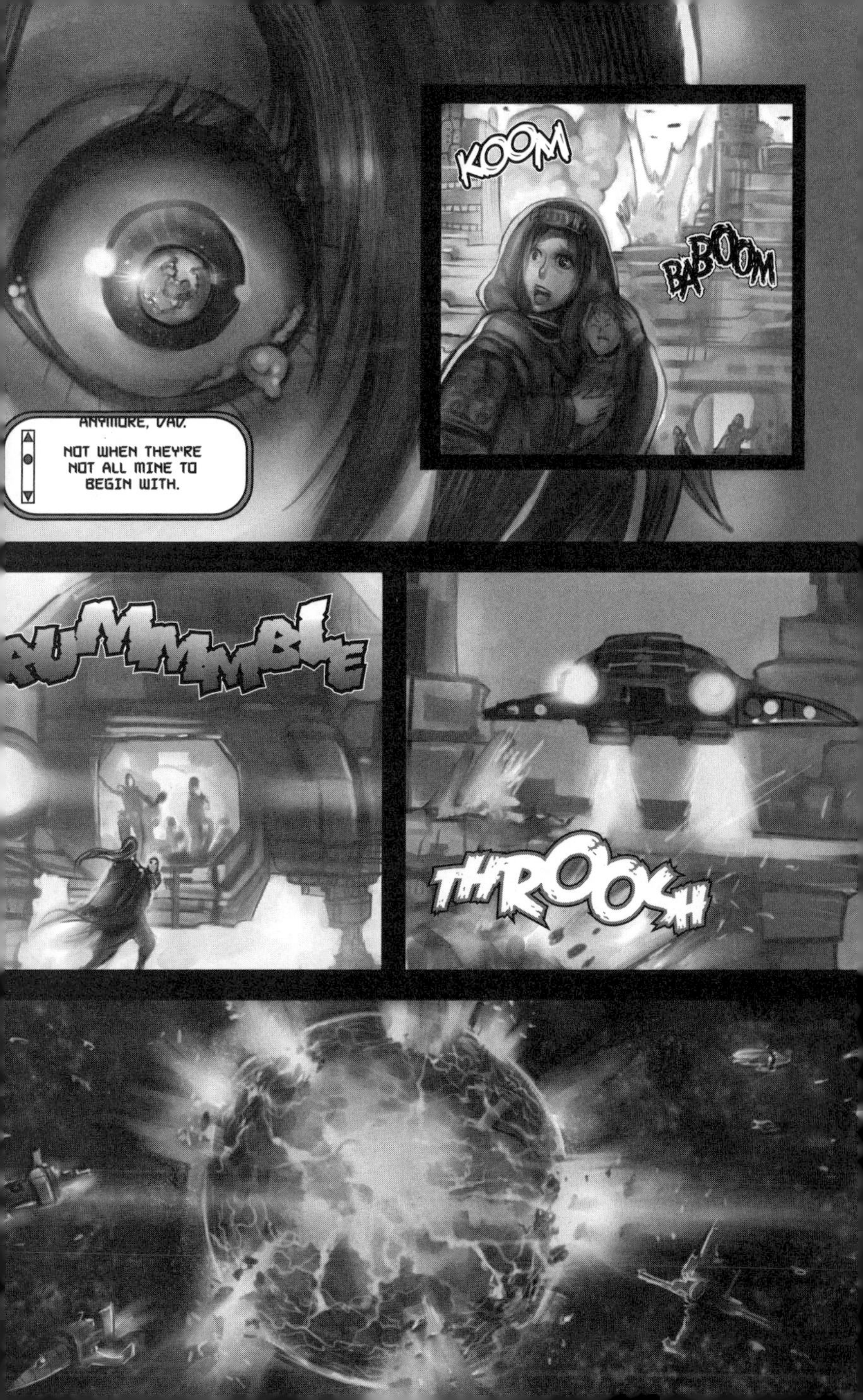
ANYMORE, DAD.
NOT WHEN THEY'RE NOT ALL MINE TO BEGIN WITH.
KOOM
BABOOM
UMMMBLE
THROOSH

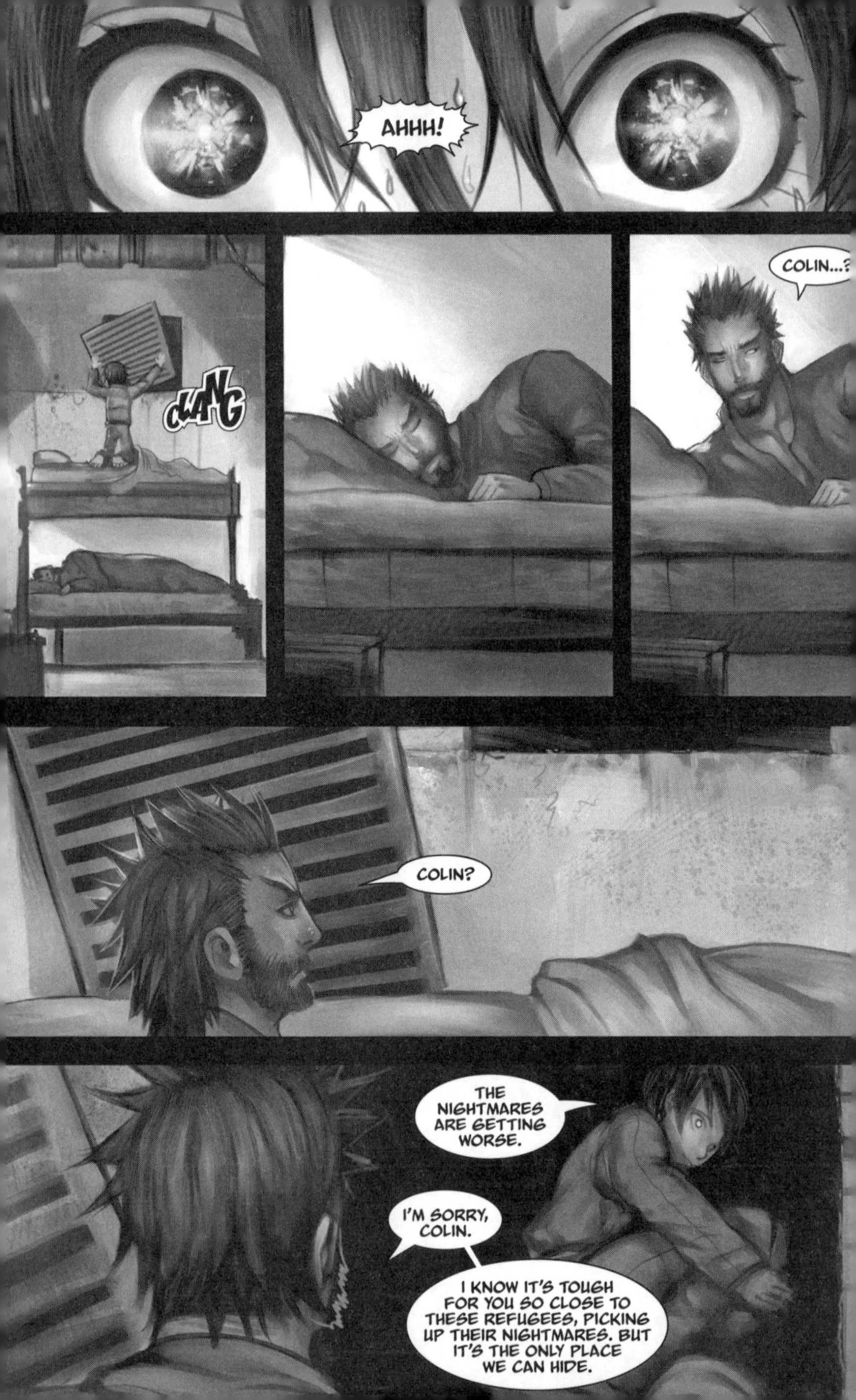
AHHH!
CLANG
COLIN...?
COLIN?
THE NIGHTMARES ARE GETTING WORSE.
I'M SORRY, COLIN.
I KNOW IT'S TOUGH FOR YOU SO CLOSE TO THESE REFUGEES, PICKING UP THEIR NIGHTMARES. BUT IT'S THE ONLY PLACE WE CAN HIDE.

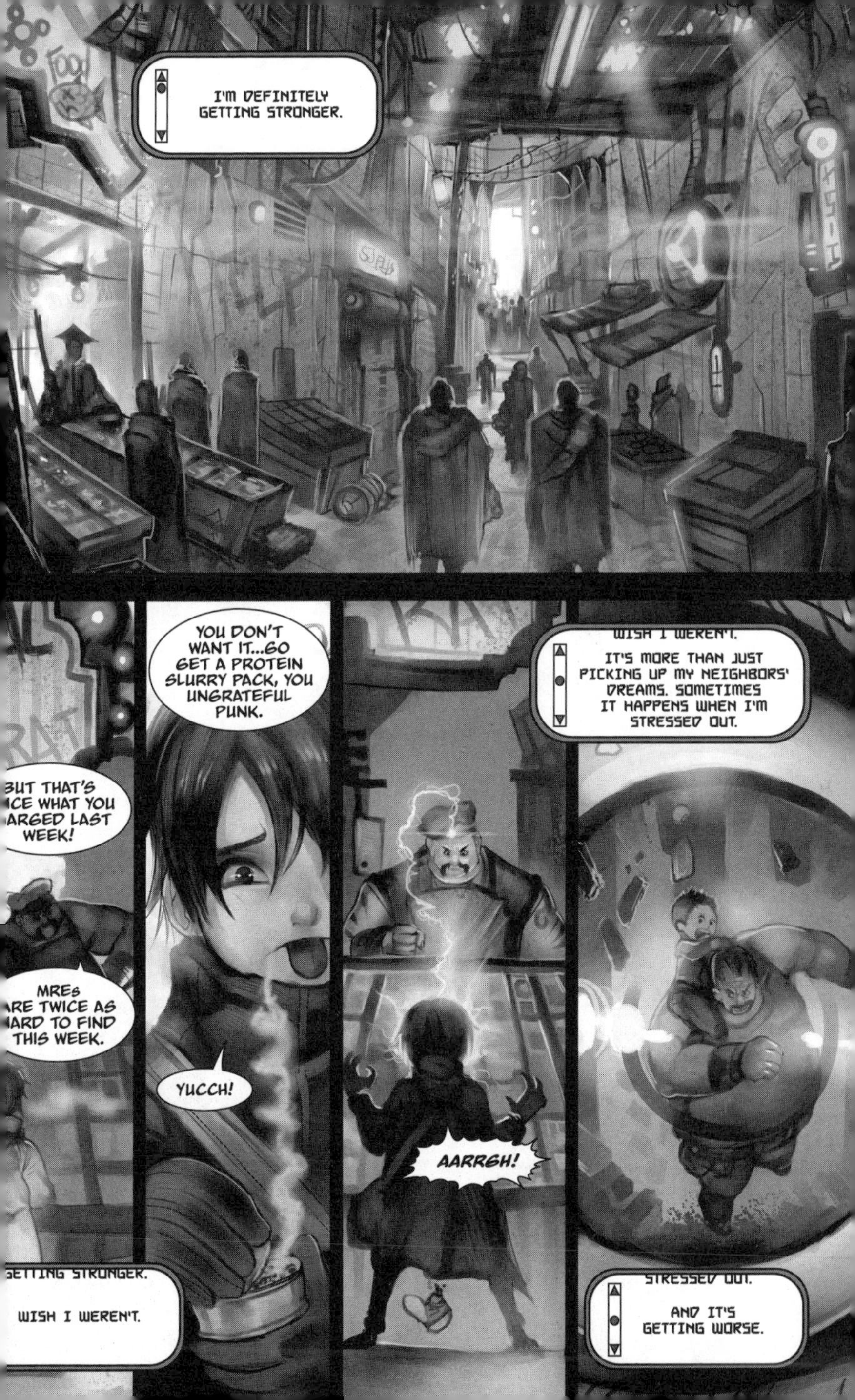
I'M DEFINITELY GETTING STRONGER.
UT THAT'S CE WHAT YOU ARGED LAST WEEK!
MREs RE TWICE AS ARD TO FIND THIS WEEK.
YOU DON'T WANT IT...GO GET A PROTEIN SLURRY PACK, YOU UNGRATEFUL PUNK.
YUCCH!
WISH I WEREN'T.
AARRGH!
IT'S MORE THAN JUST PICKING UP MY NEIGHBORS' DREAMS. SOMETIMES IT HAPPENS WHEN I'M STRESSED OUT.
AND IT'S GETTING WORSE.

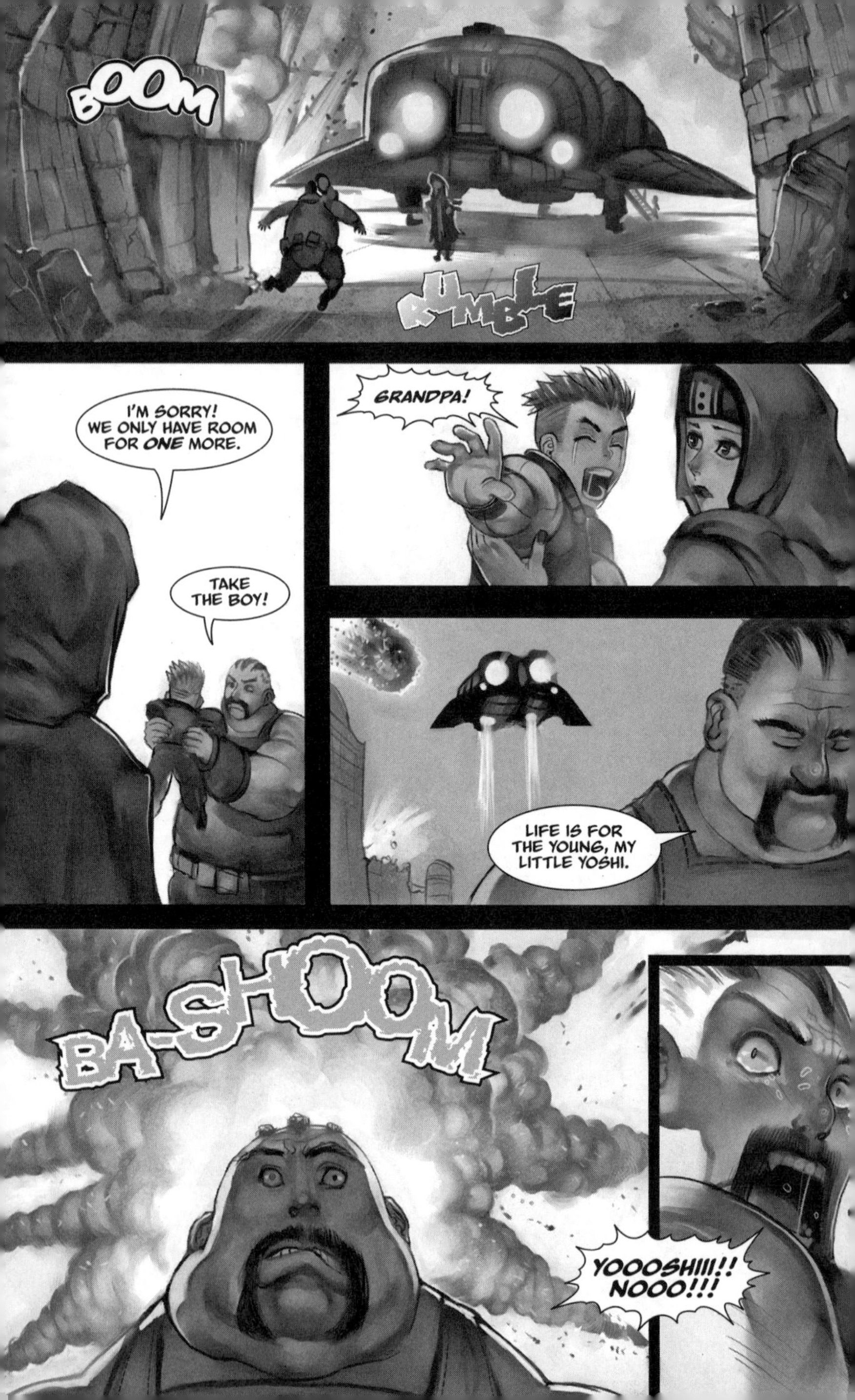
BOOM
RUMBLE
I'M SORRY! WE ONLY HAVE ROOM FOR *ONE* MORE.
TAKE THE BOY!
GRANDPA!
LIFE IS FOR THE YOUNG, MY LITTLE YOSHI.
BA-SHOOM
YOOOSHIII!! NOOO!!!

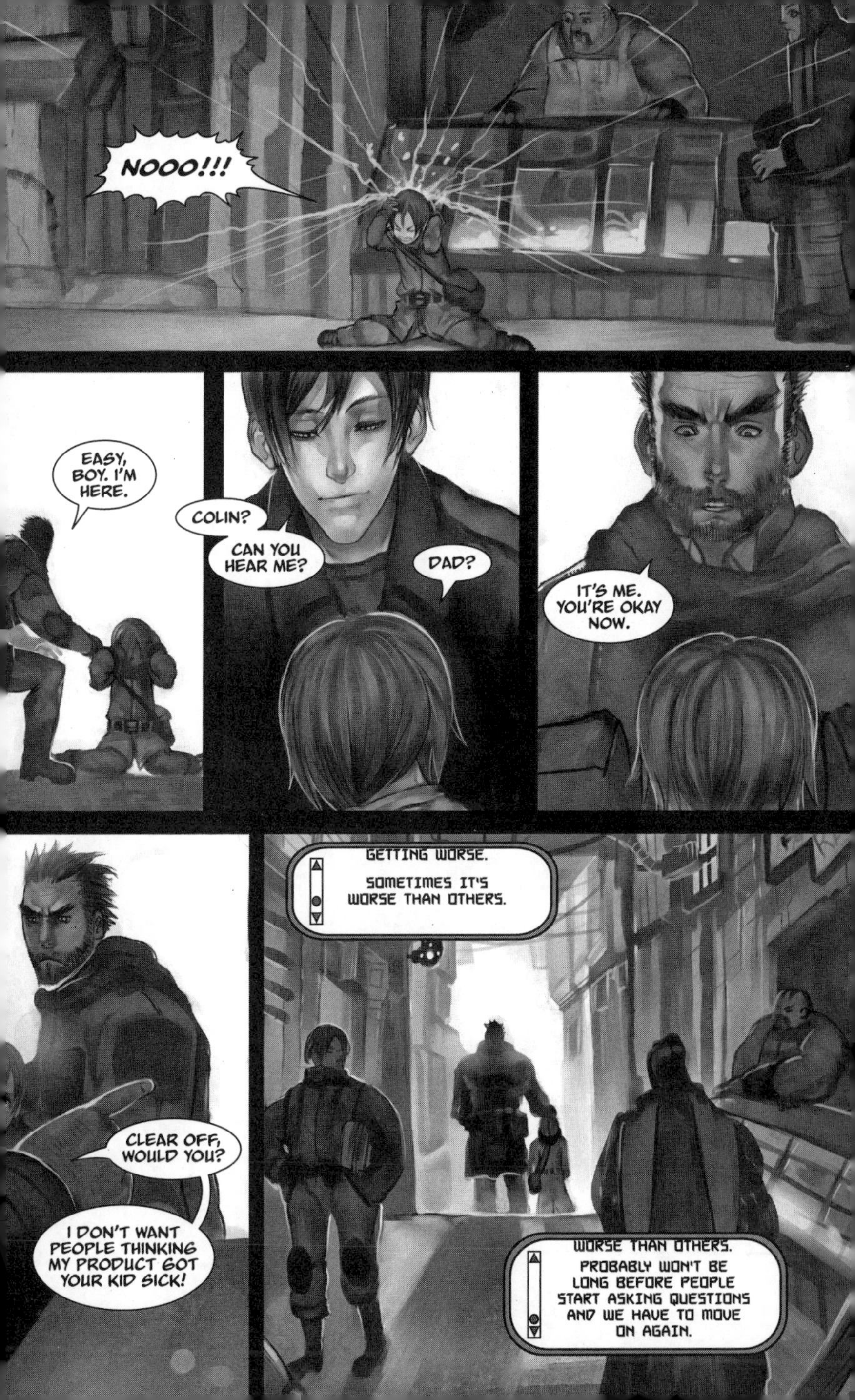
NOOO!!!
EASY, BOY. I'M HERE.
COLIN?
CAN YOU HEAR ME?
DAD?
IT'S ME. YOU'RE OKAY NOW.
CLEAR OFF, WOULD YOU?
I DON'T WANT PEOPLE THINKING MY PRODUCT GOT YOUR KID SICK!
GETTING WORSE.
SOMETIMES IT'S WORSE THAN OTHERS.
WORSE THAN OTHERS.
PROBABLY WON'T BE LONG BEFORE PEOPLE START ASKING QUESTIONS AND WE HAVE TO MOVE ON AGAIN.

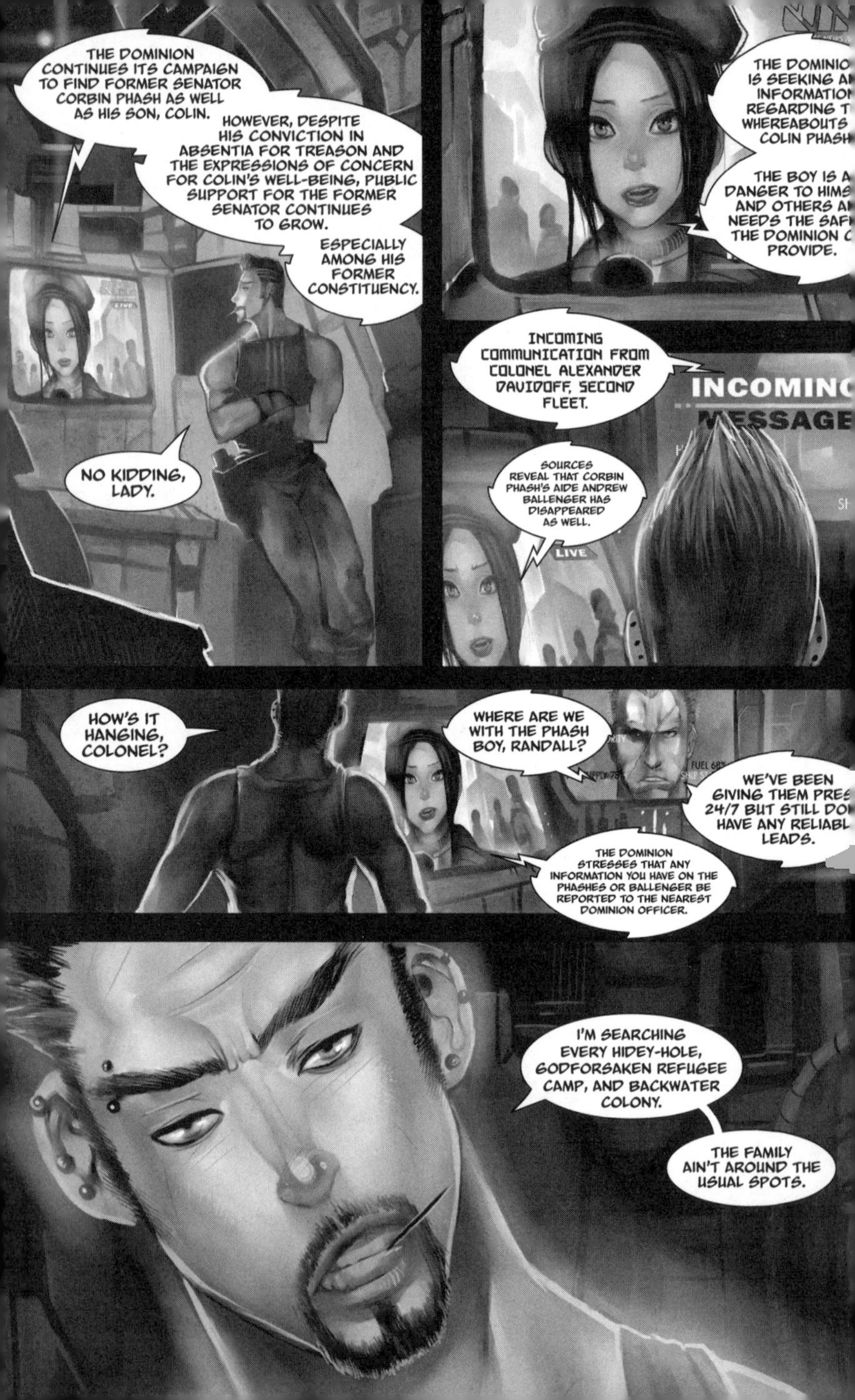

THE DOMINION CONTINUES ITS CAMPAIGN TO FIND FORMER SENATOR CORBIN PHASH AS WELL AS HIS SON, COLIN.
HOWEVER, DESPITE HIS CONVICTION IN ABSENTIA FOR TREASON AND THE EXPRESSIONS OF CONCERN FOR COLIN'S WELL-BEING, PUBLIC SUPPORT FOR THE FORMER SENATOR CONTINUES TO GROW.
ESPECIALLY AMONG HIS FORMER CONSTITUENCY.
NO KIDDING, LADY.
THE DOMINIO IS SEEKING A INFORMATIO REGARDING T WHEREABOUTS COLIN PHAS
THE BOY IS A DANGER TO HIMS AND OTHERS A NEEDS THE SAF THE DOMINION C PROVIDE.
INCOMING COMMUNICATION FROM COLONEL ALEXANDER DAVIDOFF, SECOND FLEET.
INCOMIN MESSAGE
SOURCES REVEAL THAT CORBIN PHASH'S AIDE ANDREW BALLENGER HAS DISAPPEARED AS WELL.
LIVE
HOW'S IT HANGING, COLONEL?
WHERE ARE WE WITH THE PHASH BOY, RANDALL?
WE'VE BEEN GIVING THEM PRES 24/7 BUT STILL DO HAVE ANY RELIAB LEADS.
THE DOMINION STRESSES THAT ANY INFORMATION YOU HAVE ON THE PHASHES OR BALLENGER BE REPORTED TO THE NEAREST DOMINION OFFICER.
I'M SEARCHING EVERY HIDEY-HOLE, GODFORSAKEN REFUGEE CAMP, AND BACKWATER COLONY.
THE FAMILY AIN'T AROUND THE USUAL SPOTS.

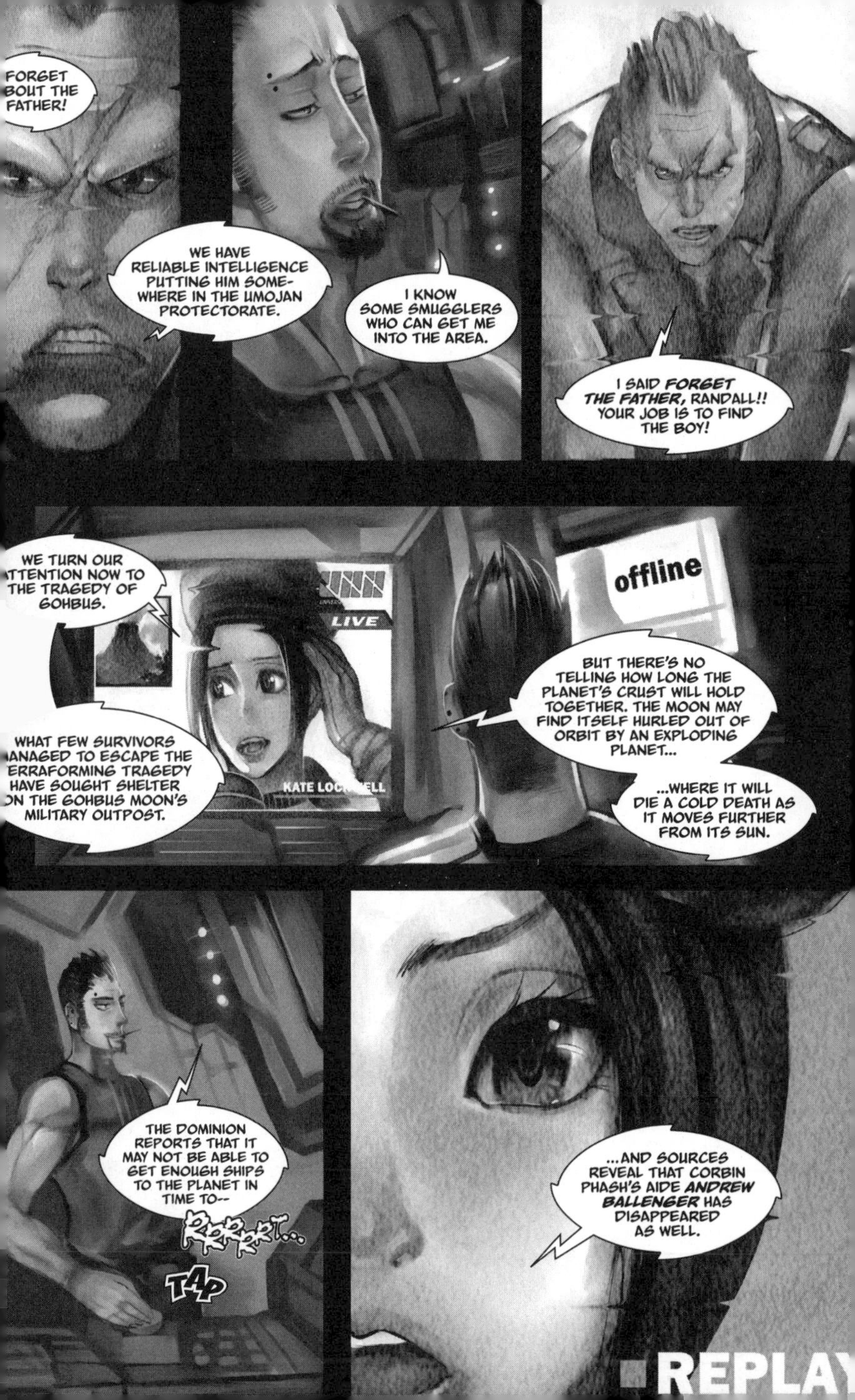
FORGET 'BOUT THE FATHER!
WE HAVE RELIABLE INTELLIGENCE PUTTING HIM SOME-WHERE IN THE UMOJAN PROTECTORATE.
I KNOW SOME SMUGGLERS WHO CAN GET ME INTO THE AREA.
I SAID FORGET THE FATHER, RANDALL!! YOUR JOB IS TO FIND THE BOY!
WE TURN OUR ATTENTION NOW TO THE TRAGEDY OF GOHBUS.
LIVE
offline
WHAT FEW SURVIVORS MANAGED TO ESCAPE THE TERRAFORMING TRAGEDY HAVE SOUGHT SHELTER ON THE GOHBUS MOON'S MILITARY OUTPOST.
KATE LOCKWELL
BUT THERE'S NO TELLING HOW LONG THE PLANET'S CRUST WILL HOLD TOGETHER. THE MOON MAY FIND ITSELF HURLED OUT OF ORBIT BY AN EXPLODING PLANET...
...WHERE IT WILL DIE A COLD DEATH AS IT MOVES FURTHER FROM ITS SUN.
THE DOMINION REPORTS THAT IT MAY NOT BE ABLE TO GET ENOUGH SHIPS TO THE PLANET IN TIME TO--
TAP
...AND SOURCES REVEAL THAT CORBIN PHASH'S AIDE ANDREW BALLENGER HAS DISAPPEARED AS WELL.
REPLAY

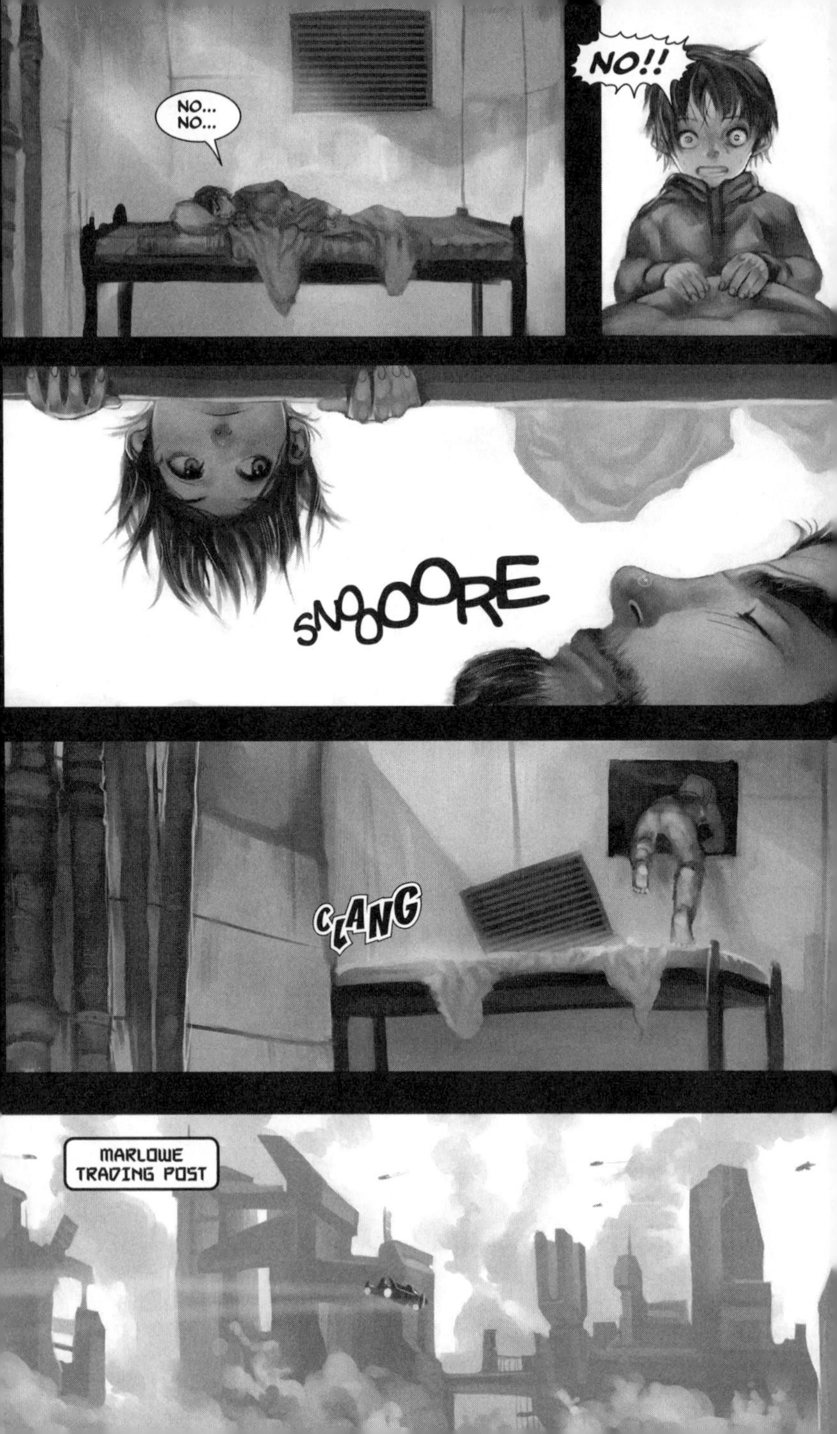
NO...
NO...
NO!!
SNOOOORE
CLANG
MARLOWE
TRADING POST

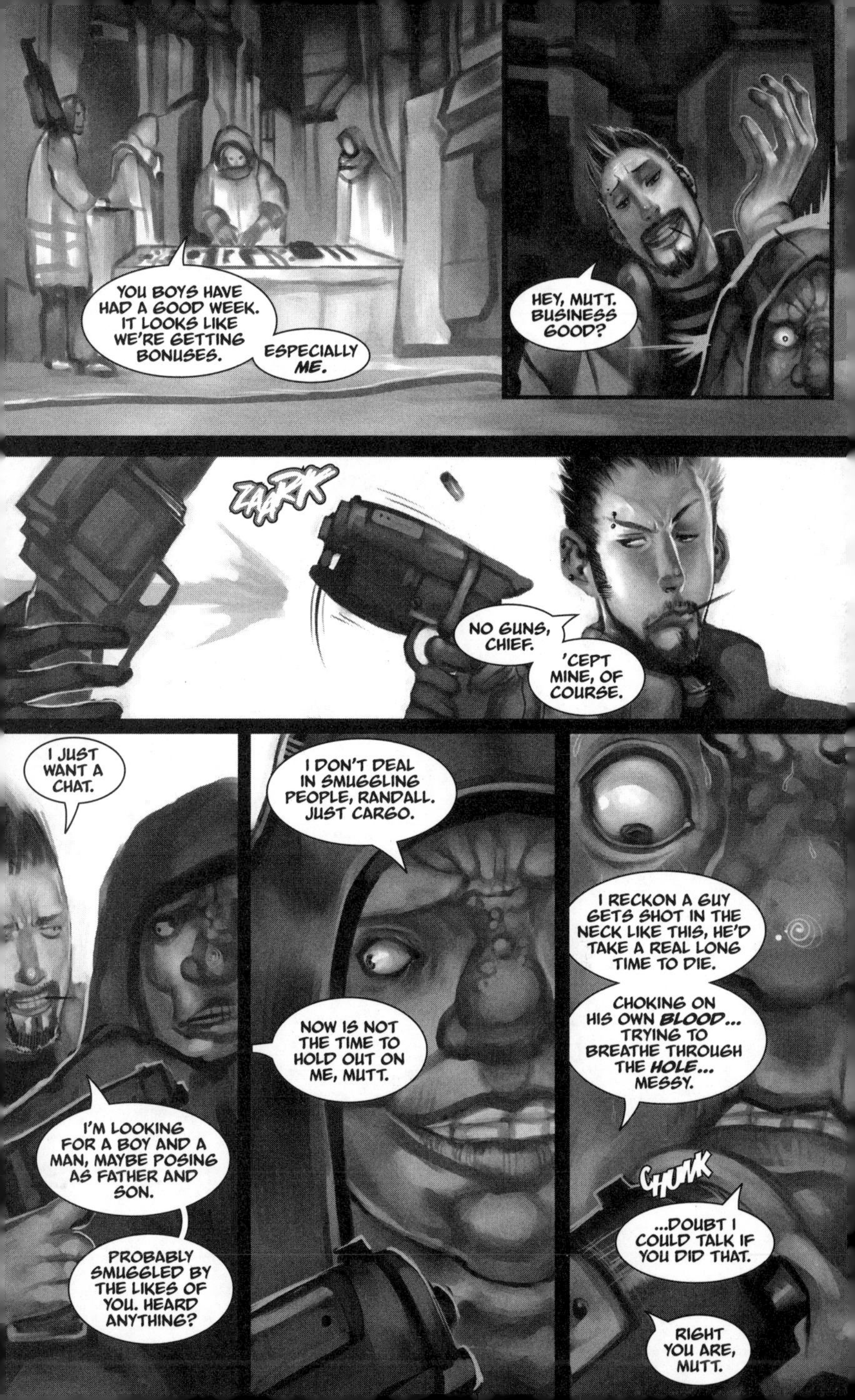
YOU BOYS HAVE HAD A GOOD WEEK. IT LOOKS LIKE WE'RE GETTING BONUSES.
ESPECIALLY *ME.*
HEY, MUTT. BUSINESS GOOD?
ZAARK
NO GUNS, CHIEF.
'CEPT MINE, OF COURSE.
I JUST WANT A CHAT.
I'M LOOKING FOR A BOY AND A MAN, MAYBE POSING AS FATHER AND SON.
PROBABLY SMUGGLED BY THE LIKES OF YOU. HEARD ANYTHING?
I DON'T DEAL IN SMUGGLING PEOPLE, RANDALL. JUST CARGO.
NOW IS NOT THE TIME TO HOLD OUT ON ME, MUTT.
I RECKON A GUY GETS SHOT IN THE NECK LIKE THIS, HE'D TAKE A REAL LONG TIME TO DIE.
CHOKING ON HIS OWN *BLOOD...* TRYING TO BREATHE THROUGH THE *HOLE...* MESSY.
CHUNK
...DOUBT I COULD TALK IF YOU DID THAT.
RIGHT YOU ARE, MUTT.

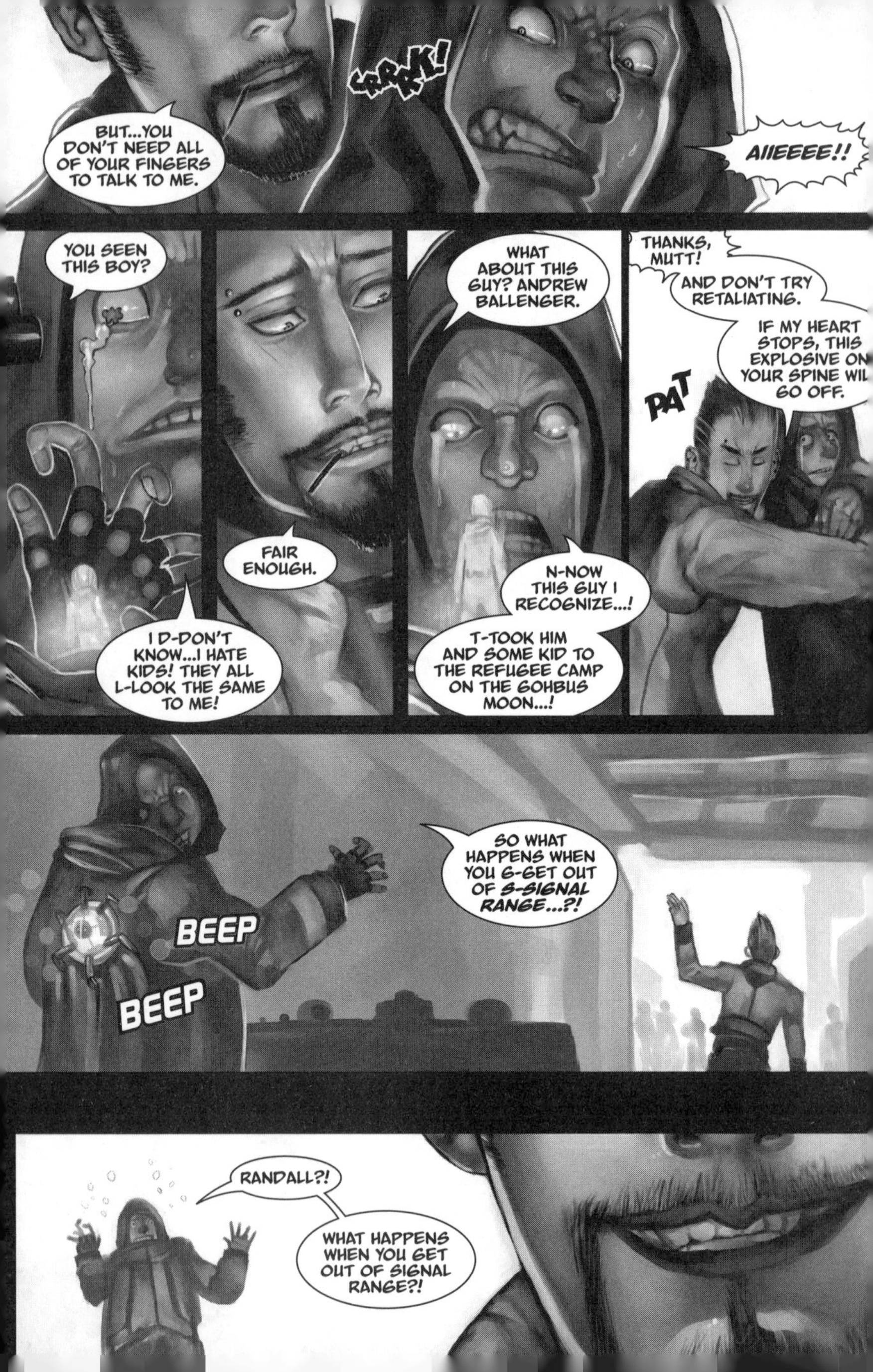
BUT...YOU DON'T NEED ALL OF YOUR FINGERS TO TALK TO ME.
CRRRK!
AIIEEEE!!
YOU SEEN THIS BOY?
I D-DON'T KNOW...I HATE KIDS! THEY ALL L-LOOK THE SAME TO ME!
FAIR ENOUGH.
WHAT ABOUT THIS GUY? ANDREW BALLENGER.
N-NOW THIS GUY I RECOGNIZE...!
T-TOOK HIM AND SOME KID TO THE REFUGEE CAMP ON THE GOHBUS MOON...!
THANKS, MUTT!
AND DON'T TRY RETALIATING.
IF MY HEART STOPS, THIS EXPLOSIVE ON YOUR SPINE WIL GO OFF.
PAT
SO WHAT HAPPENS WHEN YOU G-GET OUT OF *S-SIGNAL RANGE...?!*
BEEP
BEEP
RANDALL?!
WHAT HAPPENS WHEN YOU GET OUT OF SIGNAL RANGE?!

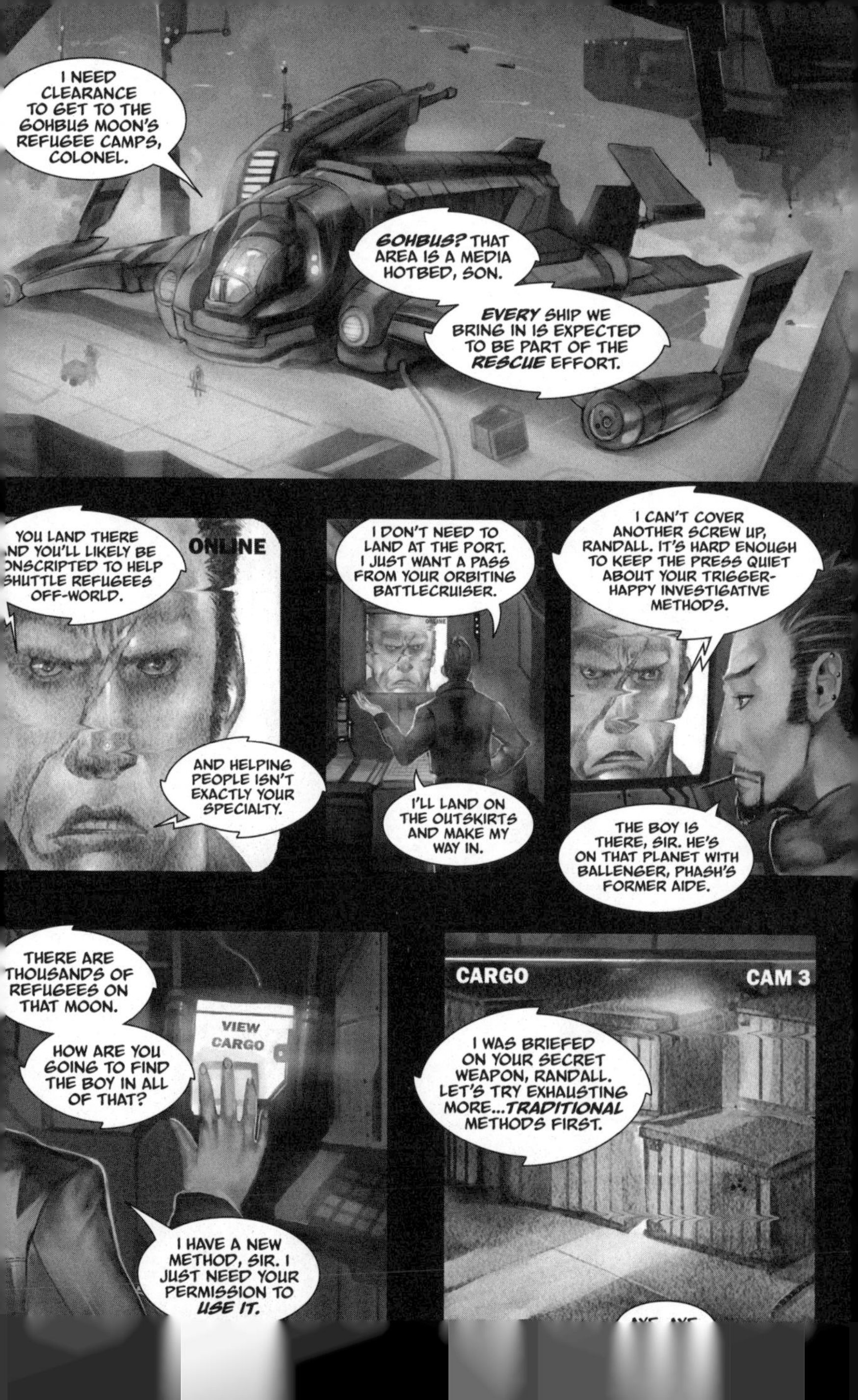
I NEED CLEARANCE TO GET TO THE GOHBUS MOON'S REFUGEE CAMPS, COLONEL.
GOHBUS? THAT AREA IS A MEDIA HOTBED, SON.
EVERY SHIP WE BRING IN IS EXPECTED TO BE PART OF THE RESCUE EFFORT.
ONLINE
YOU LAND THERE
ND YOU'LL LIKELY BE
ONSCRIPTED TO HELP
SHUTTLE REFUGEES
OFF-WORLD.
AND HELPING PEOPLE ISN'T EXACTLY YOUR SPECIALTY.
I DON'T NEED TO LAND AT THE PORT. I JUST WANT A PASS FROM YOUR ORBITING BATTLECRUISER.
I'LL LAND ON THE OUTSKIRTS AND MAKE MY WAY IN.
I CAN'T COVER ANOTHER SCREW UP, RANDALL. IT'S HARD ENOUGH TO KEEP THE PRESS QUIET ABOUT YOUR TRIGGER-HAPPY INVESTIGATIVE METHODS.
THE BOY IS THERE, SIR. HE'S ON THAT PLANET WITH BALLENGER, PHASH'S FORMER AIDE.
THERE ARE THOUSANDS OF REFUGEES ON THAT MOON.
HOW ARE YOU GOING TO FIND THE BOY IN ALL OF THAT?
VIEW CARGO
I HAVE A NEW METHOD, SIR. I JUST NEED YOUR PERMISSION TO USE IT.
CARGO
CAM 3
I WAS BRIEFED ON YOUR SECRET WEAPON, RANDALL. LET'S TRY EXHAUSTING MORE...TRADITIONAL METHODS FIRST.

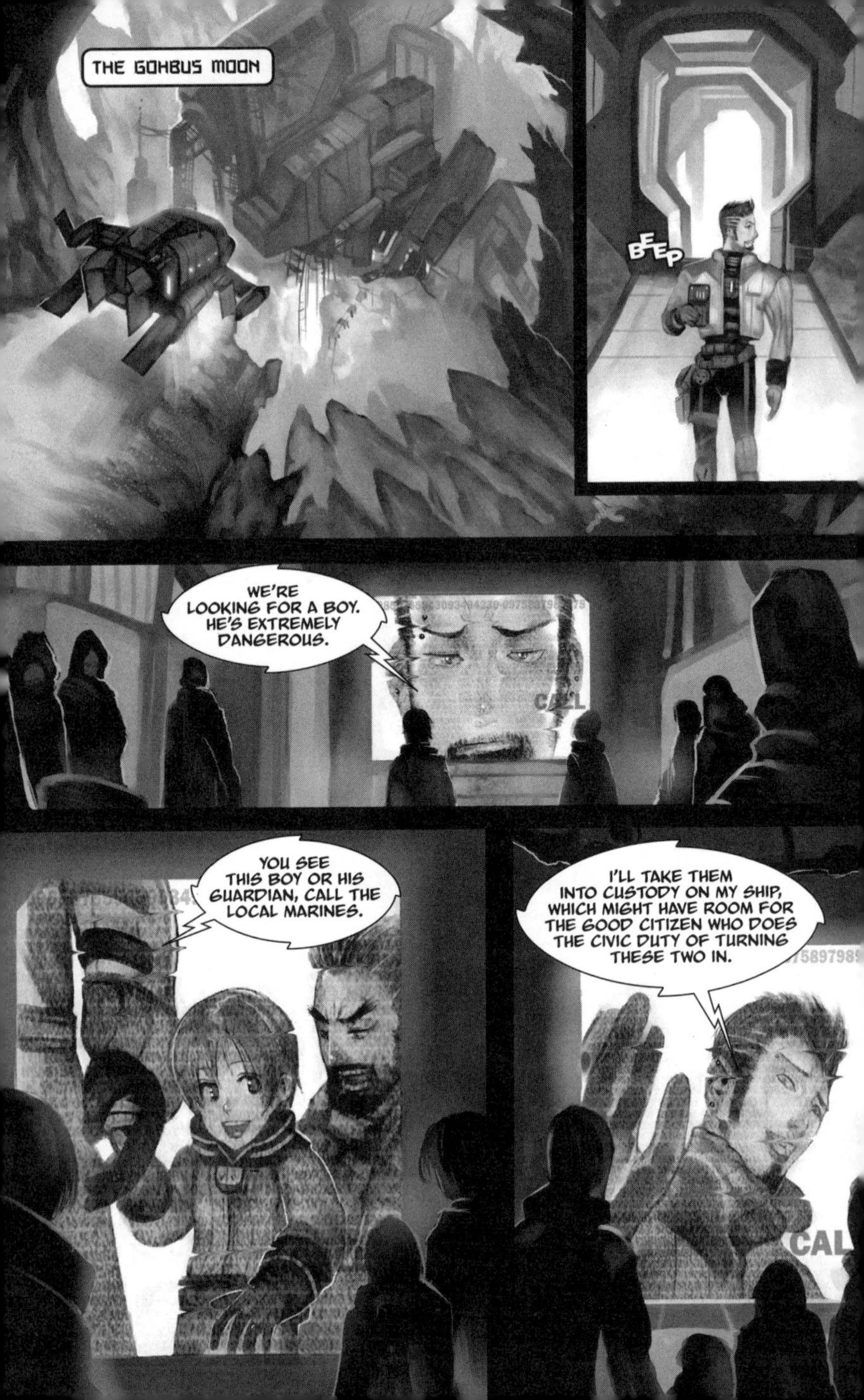
THE GOHBUS MOON
BEEP
WE'RE LOOKING FOR A BOY. HE'S EXTREMELY DANGEROUS.
CALL
YOU SEE THIS BOY OR HIS GUARDIAN, CALL THE LOCAL MARINES.
I'LL TAKE THEM INTO CUSTODY ON MY SHIP, WHICH MIGHT HAVE ROOM FOR THE GOOD CITIZEN WHO DOES THE CIVIC DUTY OF TURNING THESE TWO IN.
CAL

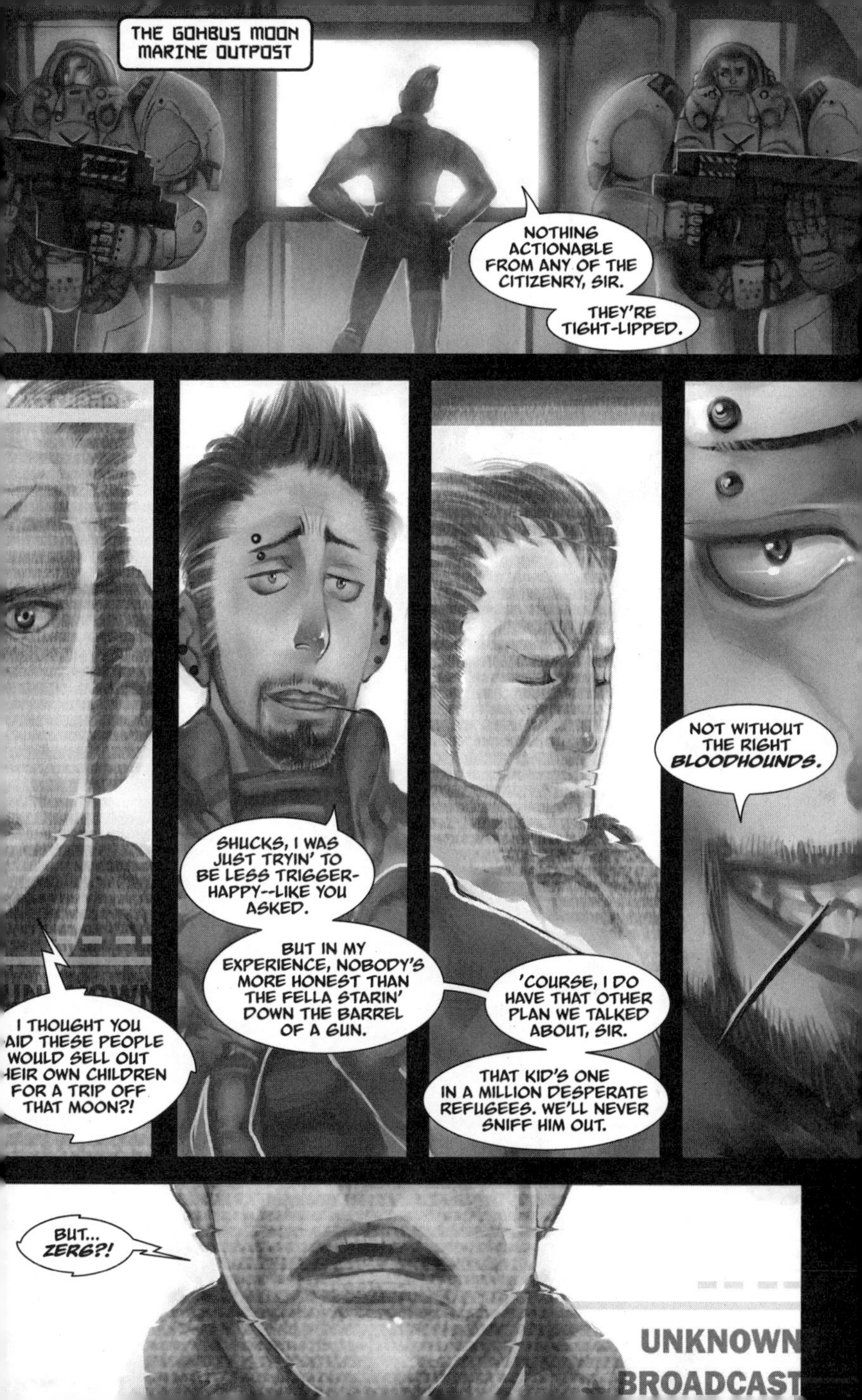
THE GOHBUS MOON MARINE OUTPOST
NOTHING ACTIONABLE FROM ANY OF THE CITIZENRY, SIR.
THEY'RE TIGHT-LIPPED.
I THOUGHT YOU AID THESE PEOPLE WOULD SELL OUT HEIR OWN CHILDREN FOR A TRIP OFF THAT MOON?!
SHUCKS, I WAS JUST TRYIN' TO BE LESS TRIGGER-HAPPY--LIKE YOU ASKED.
BUT IN MY EXPERIENCE, NOBODY'S MORE HONEST THAN THE FELLA STARIN' DOWN THE BARREL OF A GUN.
'COURSE, I DO HAVE THAT OTHER PLAN WE TALKED ABOUT, SIR.
THAT KID'S ONE IN A MILLION DESPERATE REFUGEES. WE'LL NEVER SNIFF HIM OUT.
NOT WITHOUT THE RIGHT BLOODHOUNDS.
BUT... ZERG?!
UNKNOWN BROADCAST

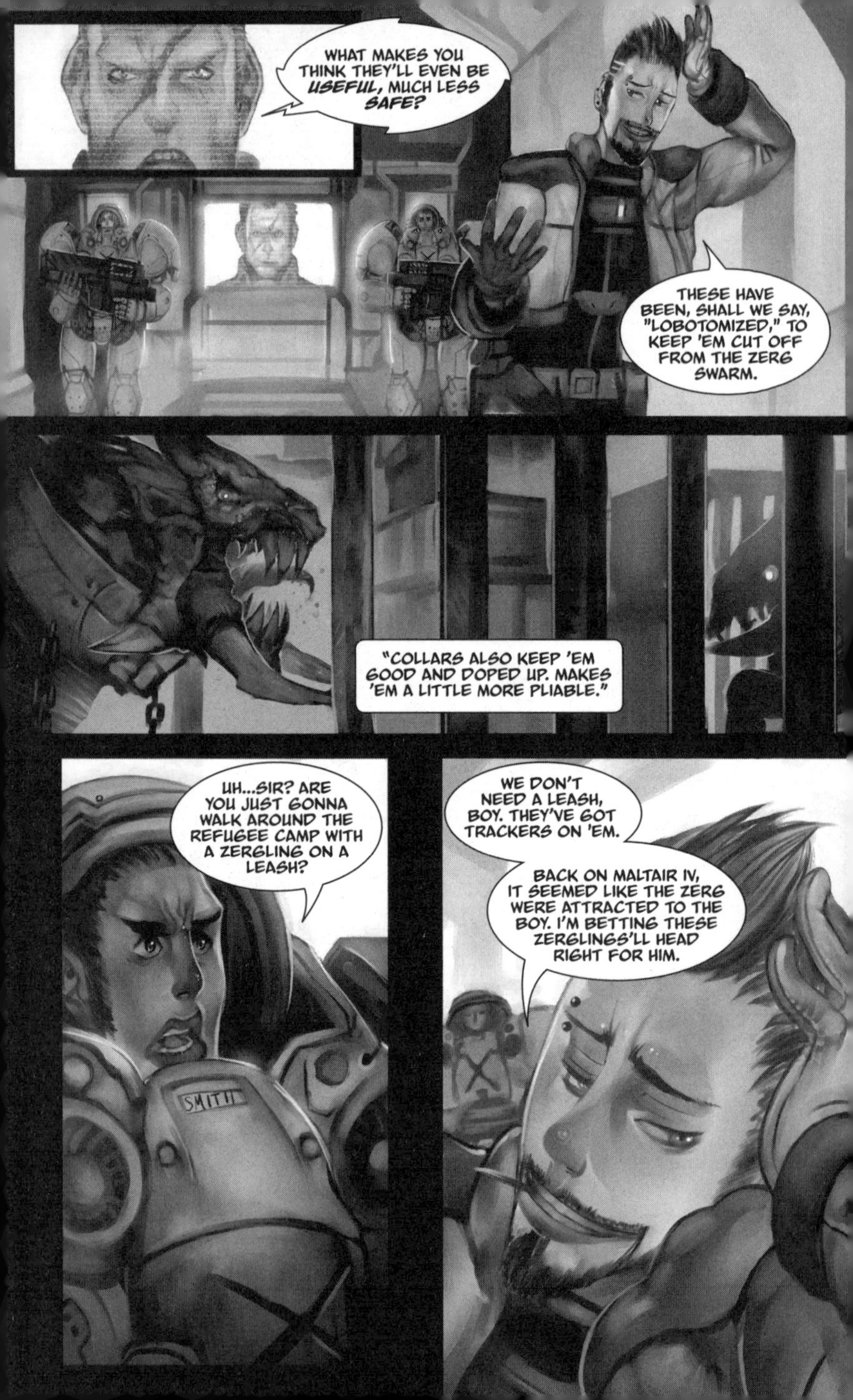
WHAT MAKES YOU THINK THEY'LL EVEN BE *USEFUL*, MUCH LESS *SAFE*?
THESE HAVE BEEN, SHALL WE SAY, "LOBOTOMIZED," TO KEEP 'EM CUT OFF FROM THE ZERG SWARM.
"COLLARS ALSO KEEP 'EM GOOD AND DOPED UP. MAKES 'EM A LITTLE MORE PLIABLE."
UH...SIR? ARE YOU JUST GONNA WALK AROUND THE REFUGEE CAMP WITH A ZERGLING ON A LEASH?
SMITH
WE DON'T NEED A LEASH, BOY. THEY'VE GOT TRACKERS ON 'EM.
BACK ON MALTAIR IV, IT SEEMED LIKE THE ZERG WERE ATTRACTED TO THE BOY. I'M BETTING THESE ZERGLINGS'LL HEAD RIGHT FOR HIM.

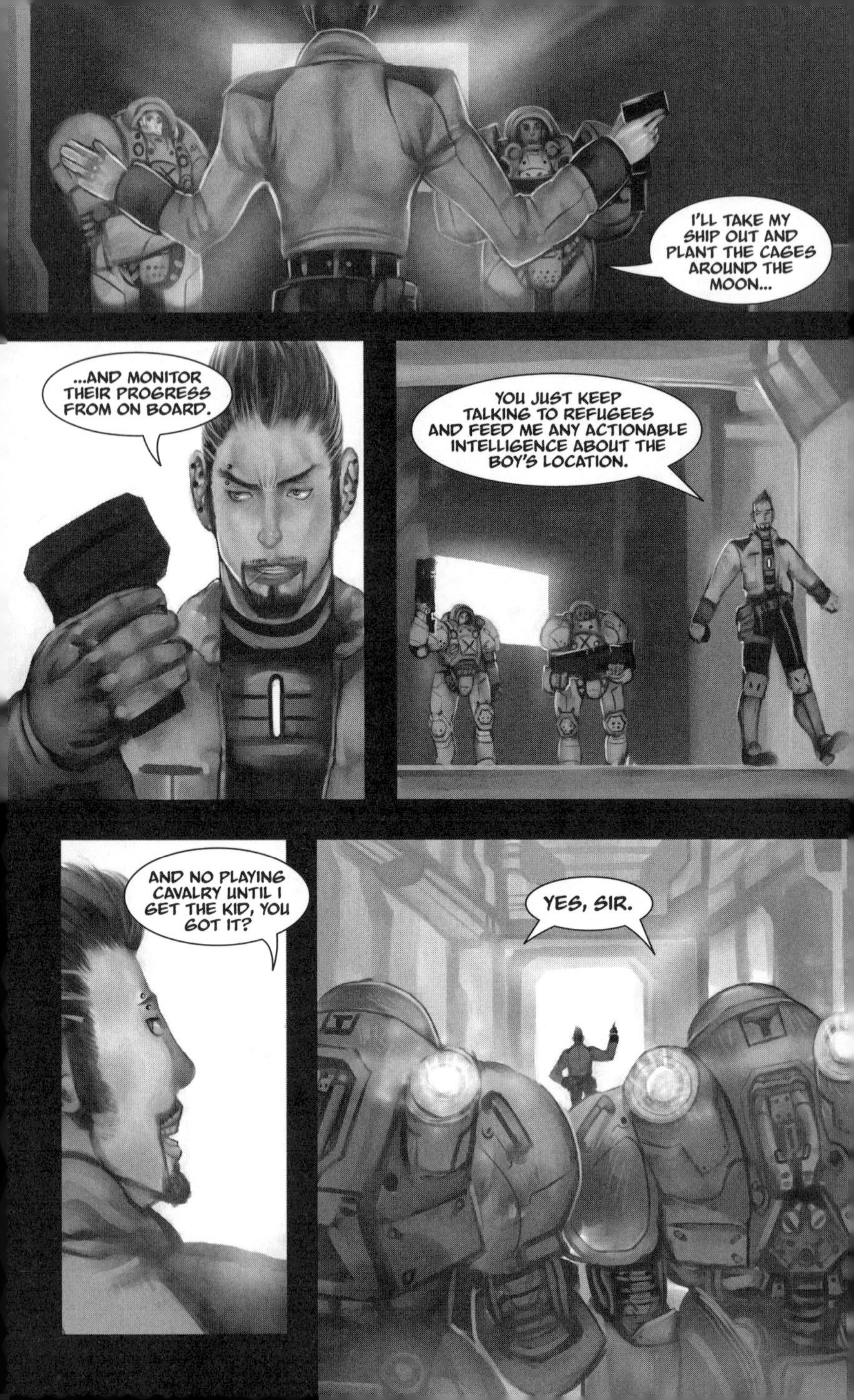
I'LL TAKE MY SHIP OUT AND PLANT THE CAGES AROUND THE MOON...
...AND MONITOR THEIR PROGRESS FROM ON BOARD.
YOU JUST KEEP TALKING TO REFUGEES AND FEED ME ANY ACTIONABLE INTELLIGENCE ABOUT THE BOY'S LOCATION.
AND NO PLAYING CAVALRY UNTIL I GET THE KID, YOU GOT IT?
YES, SIR.

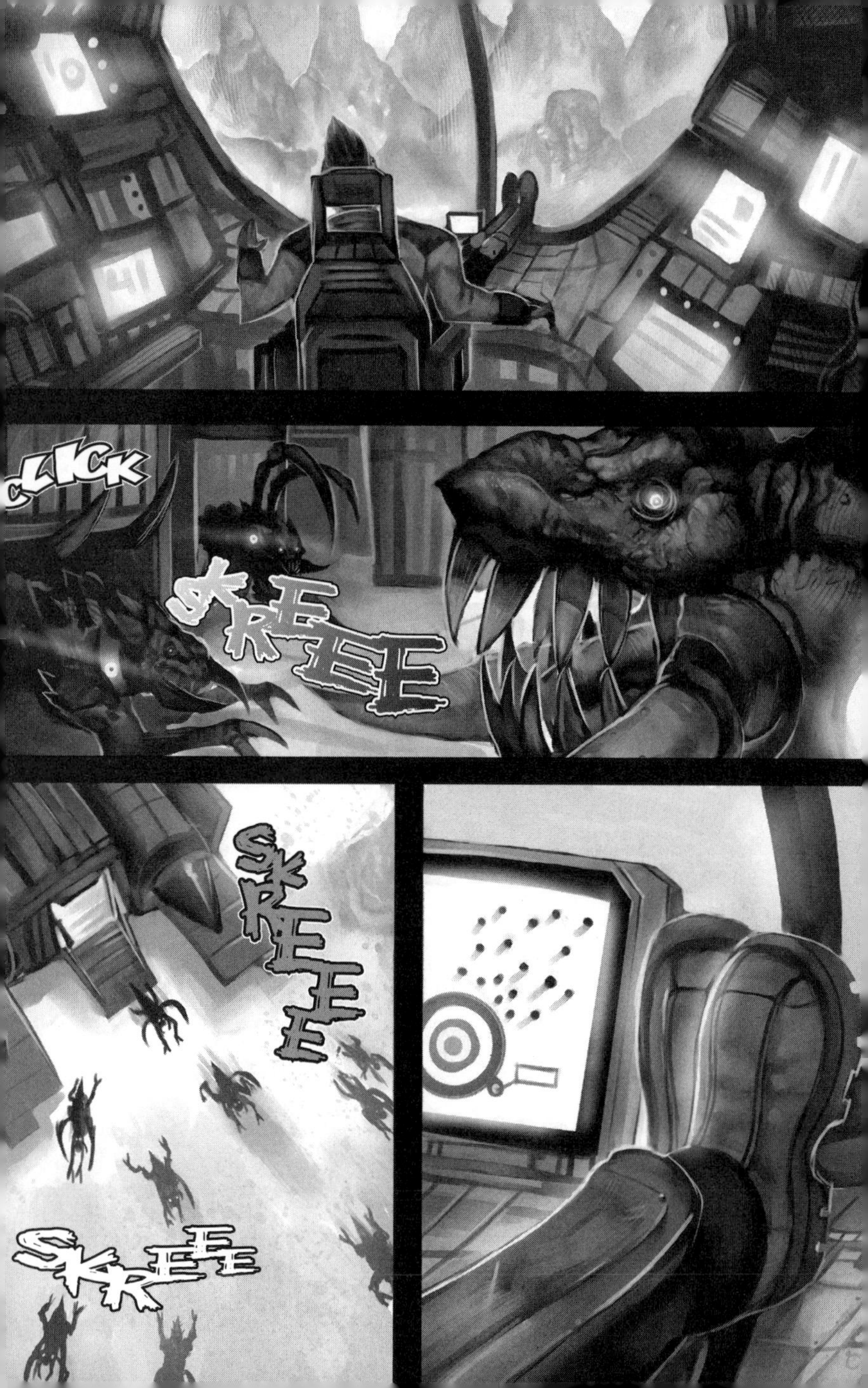
CLICK
SKREEEE
SKREEEE
SKREEE

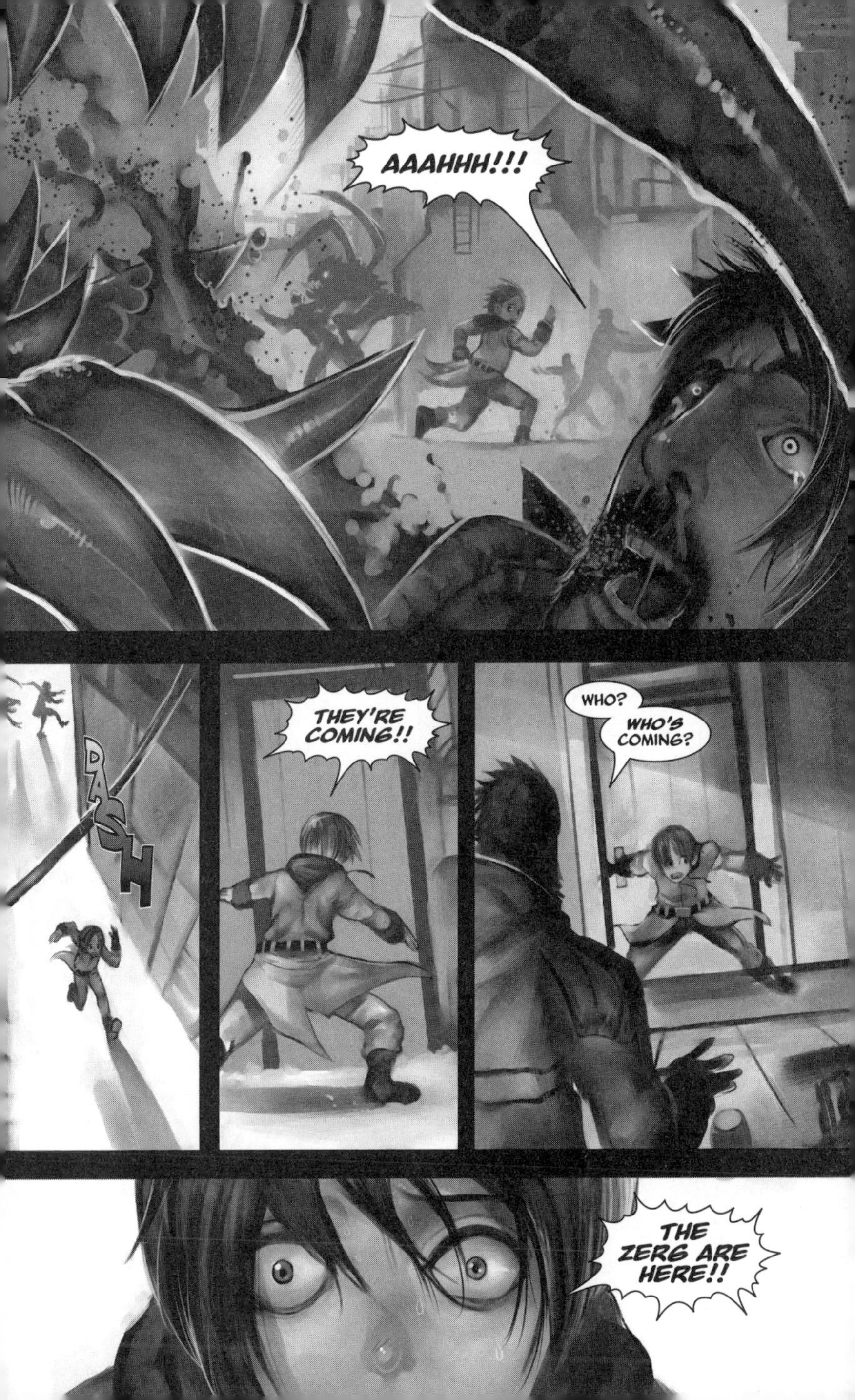
AAAHHH!!!
DASH
THEY'RE COMING!!
WHO?
WHO'S COMING?
THE ZERG ARE HERE!!

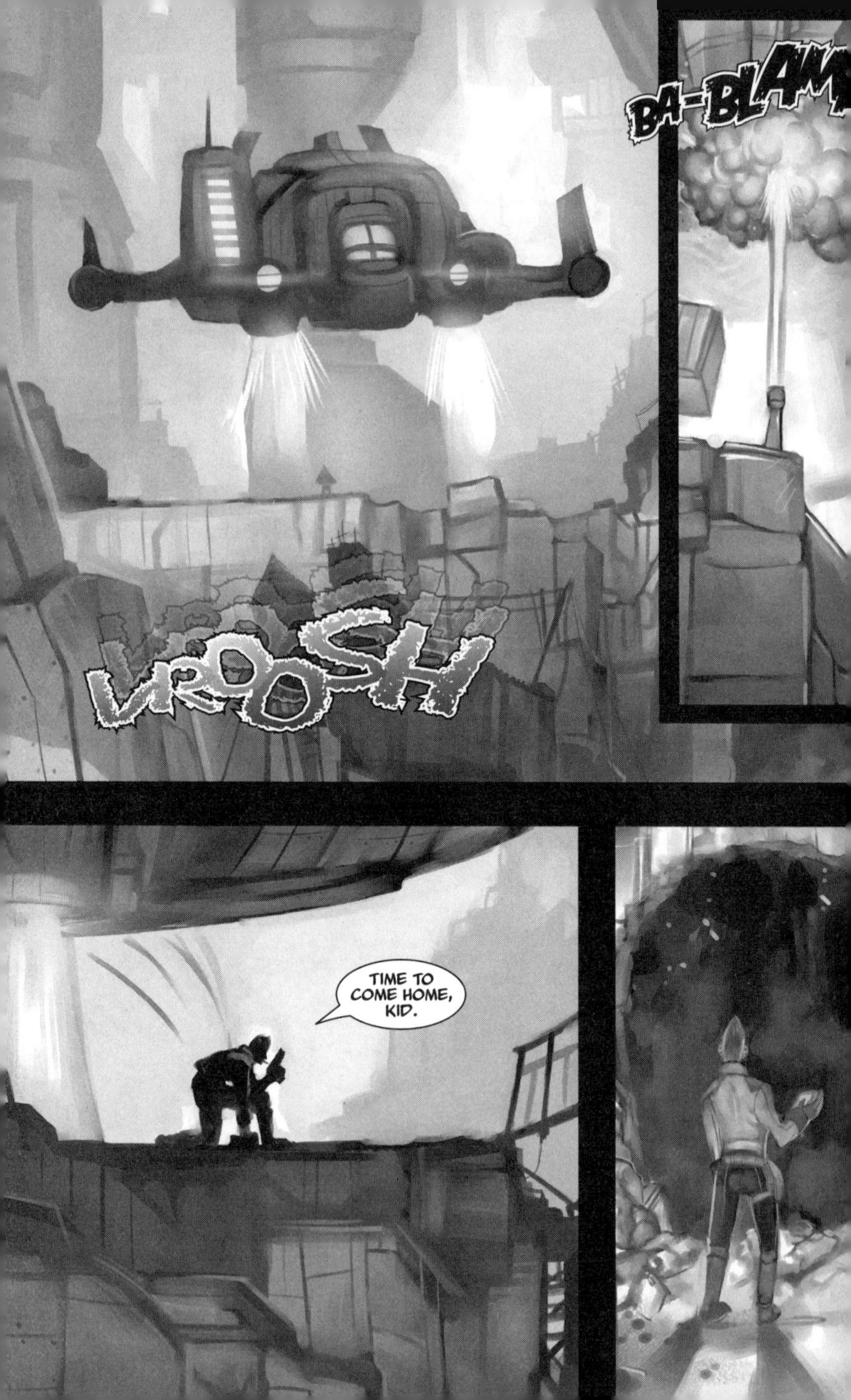
VROOSH
BA-BLAM
TIME TO COME HOME, KID.

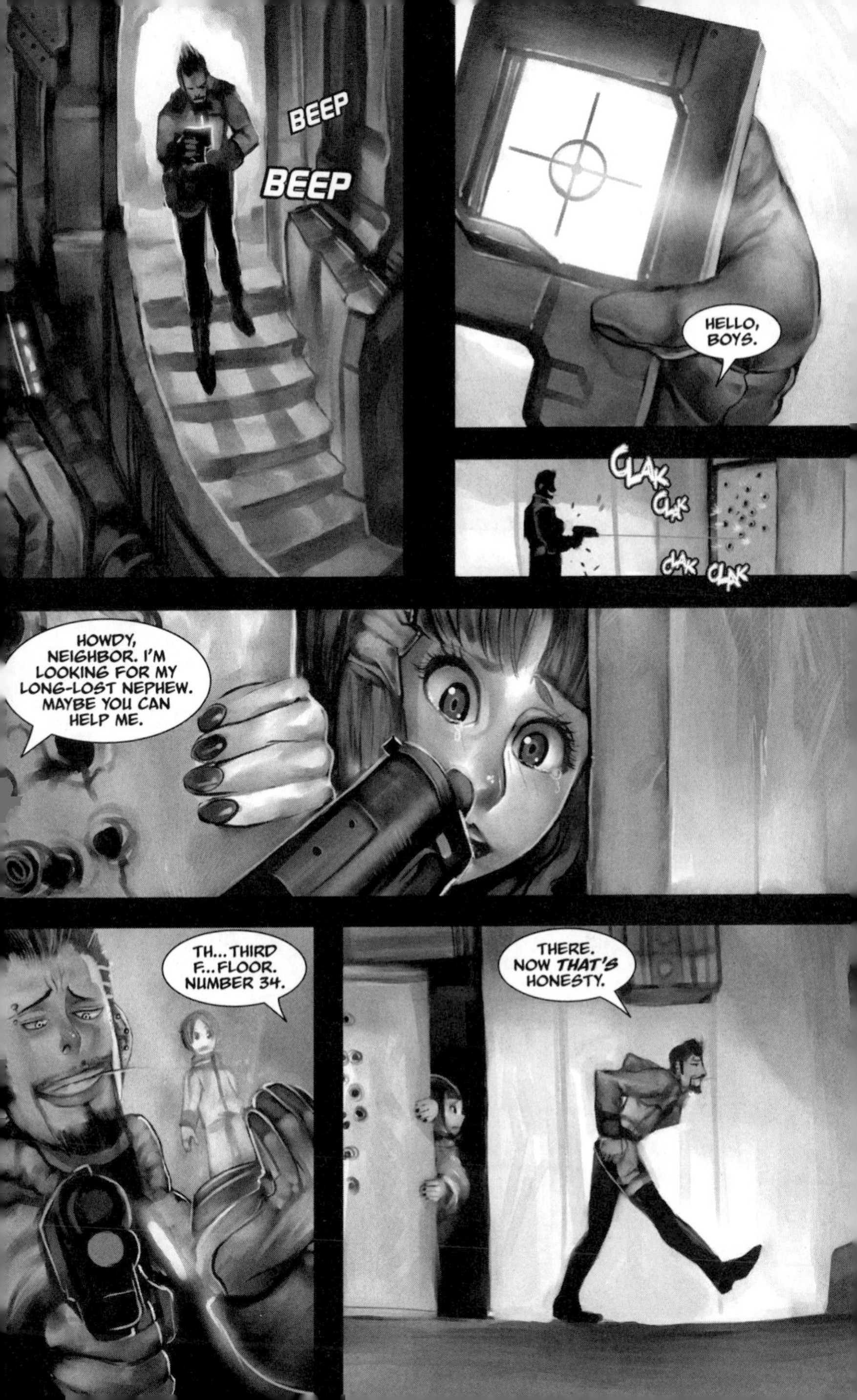
BEEP
BEEP
HELLO, BOYS.
CLAK
CLAK
CLAK
CLAK
HOWDY, NEIGHBOR. I'M LOOKING FOR MY LONG-LOST NEPHEW. MAYBE YOU CAN HELP ME.
TH...THIRD F...FLOOR. NUMBER 34.
THERE. NOW THAT'S HONESTY.

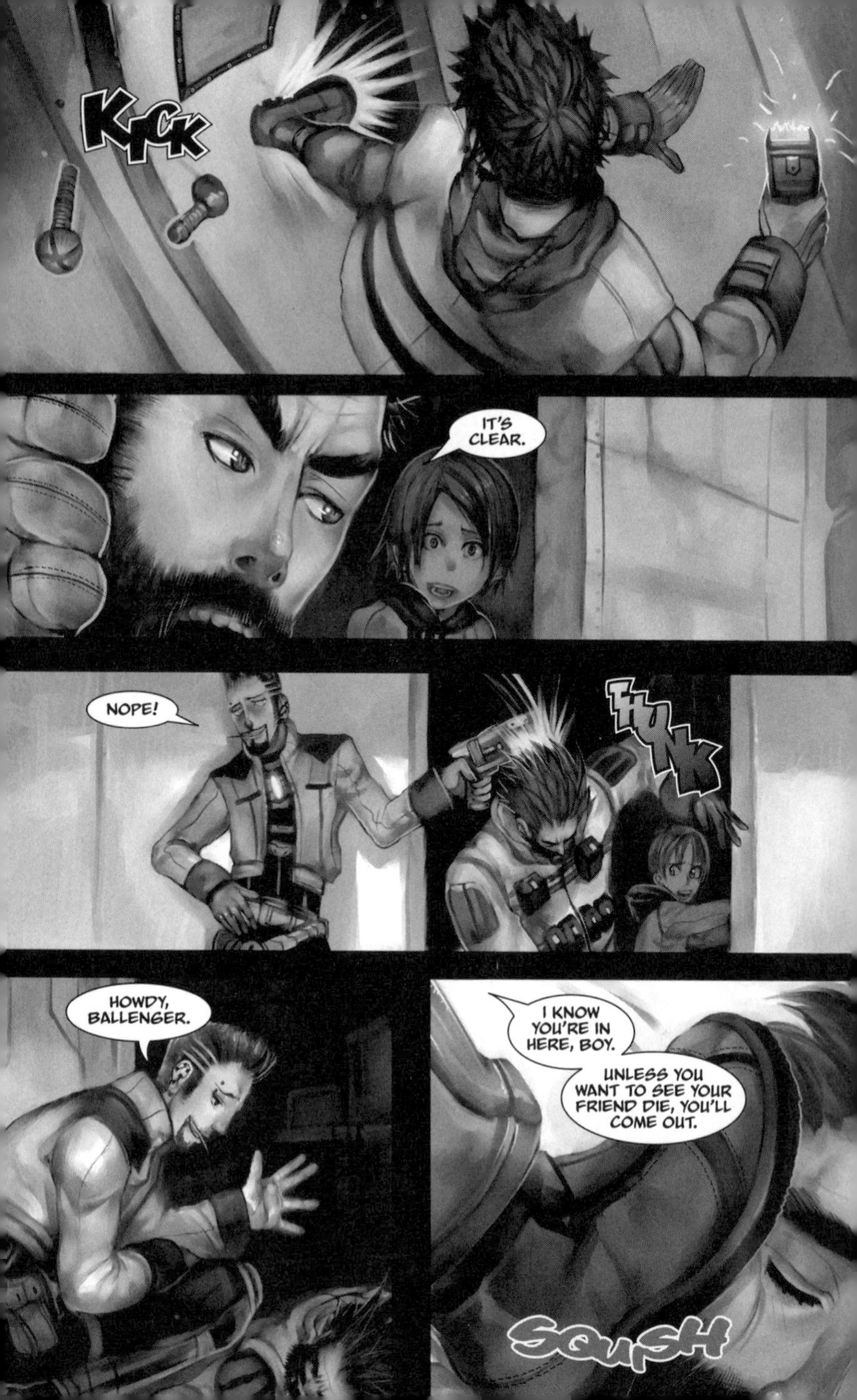
KLICK
IT'S CLEAR.
NOPE!
THUNK
HOWDY, BALLENGER.
I KNOW YOU'RE IN HERE, BOY.
UNLESS YOU WANT TO SEE YOUR FRIEND DIE, YOU'LL COME OUT.
SQUISH

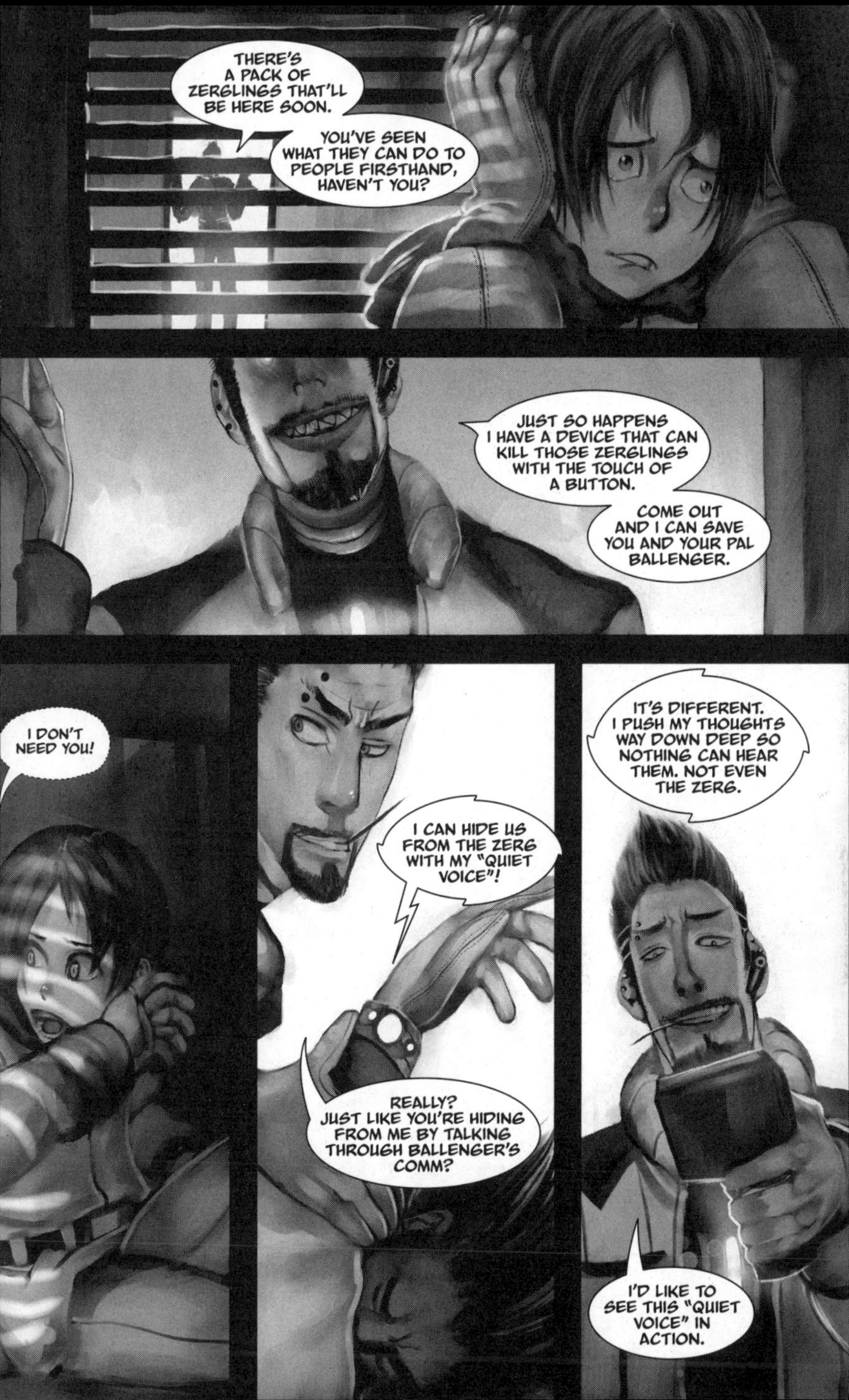
THERE'S A PACK OF ZERGLINGS THAT'LL BE HERE SOON.
YOU'VE SEEN WHAT THEY CAN DO TO PEOPLE FIRSTHAND, HAVEN'T YOU?
JUST SO HAPPENS I HAVE A DEVICE THAT CAN KILL THOSE ZERGLINGS WITH THE TOUCH OF A BUTTON.
COME OUT AND I CAN SAVE YOU AND YOUR PAL BALLENGER.
I DON'T NEED YOU!
I CAN HIDE US FROM THE ZERG WITH MY "QUIET VOICE"!
REALLY? JUST LIKE YOU'RE HIDING FROM ME BY TALKING THROUGH BALLENGER'S COMM?
IT'S DIFFERENT. I PUSH MY THOUGHTS WAY DOWN DEEP SO NOTHING CAN HEAR THEM. NOT EVEN THE ZERG.
I'D LIKE TO SEE THIS "QUIET VOICE" IN ACTION.

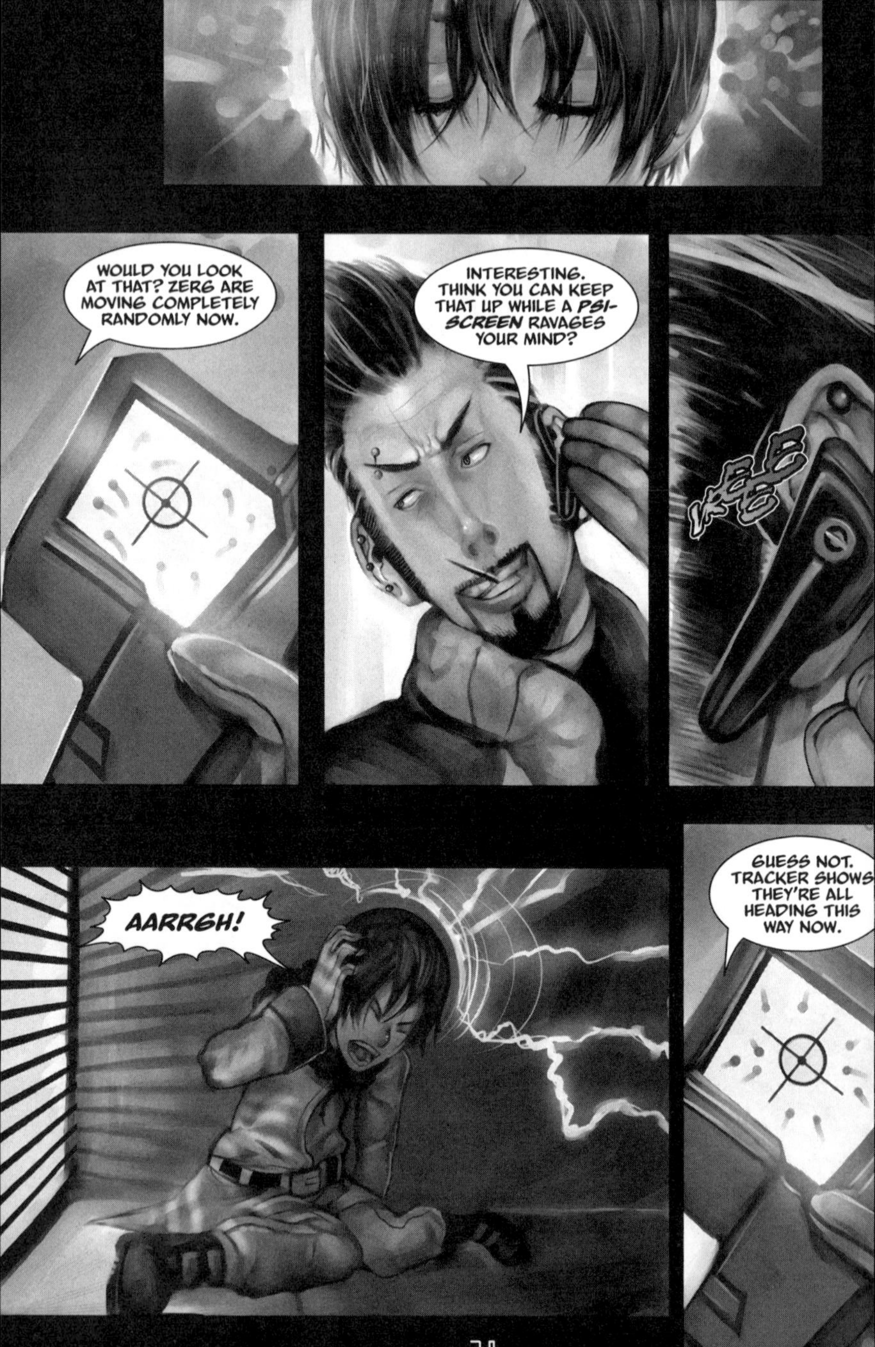
WOULD YOU LOOK AT THAT? ZERG ARE MOVING COMPLETELY RANDOMLY NOW.
INTERESTING. THINK YOU CAN KEEP THAT UP WHILE A *PSI-SCREEN* RAVAGES YOUR MIND?
AARRGH!
GUESS NOT. TRACKER SHOWS THEY'RE ALL HEADING THIS WAY NOW.

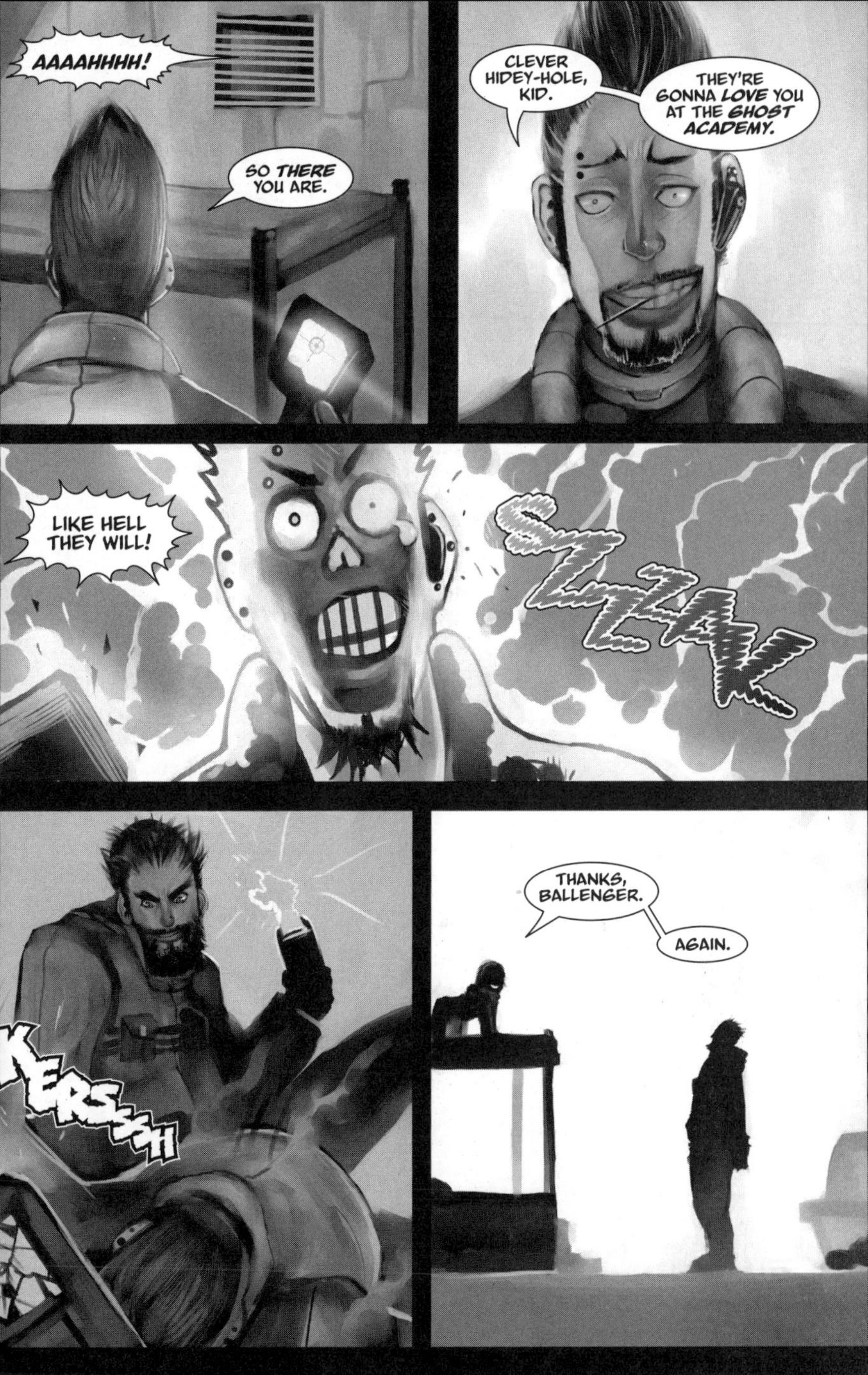
AAAAHHHH!
SO THERE YOU ARE.
CLEVER HIDEY-HOLE, KID.
THEY'RE GONNA LOVE YOU AT THE GHOST ACADEMY.
LIKE HELL THEY WILL!
SZZZAK
KERSSSH
THANKS, BALLENGER.
AGAIN.

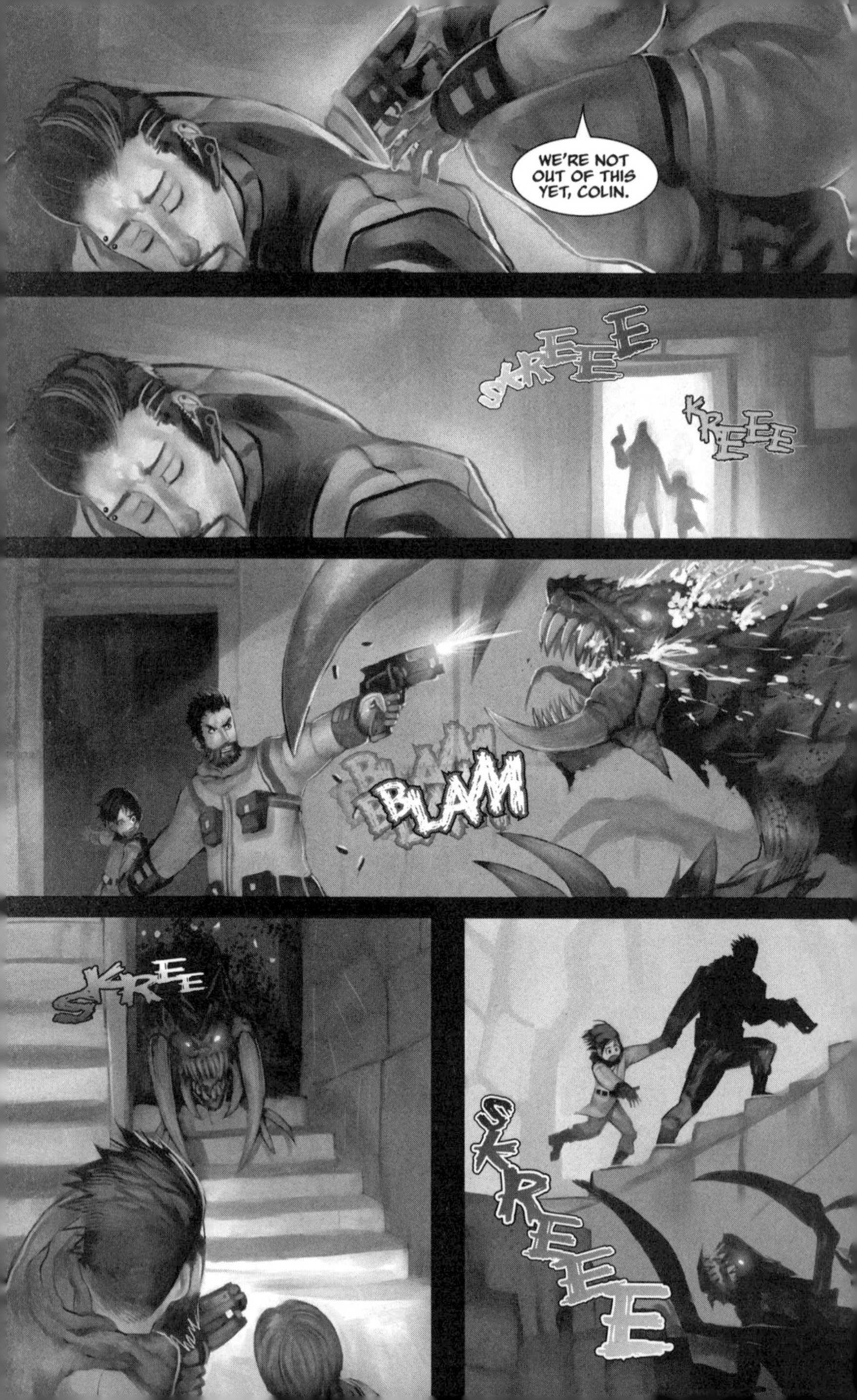
WE'RE NOT OUT OF THIS YET, COLIN.
SKREEEE
KREEE
BLAM
BLAM
SKREE
SKREEEE

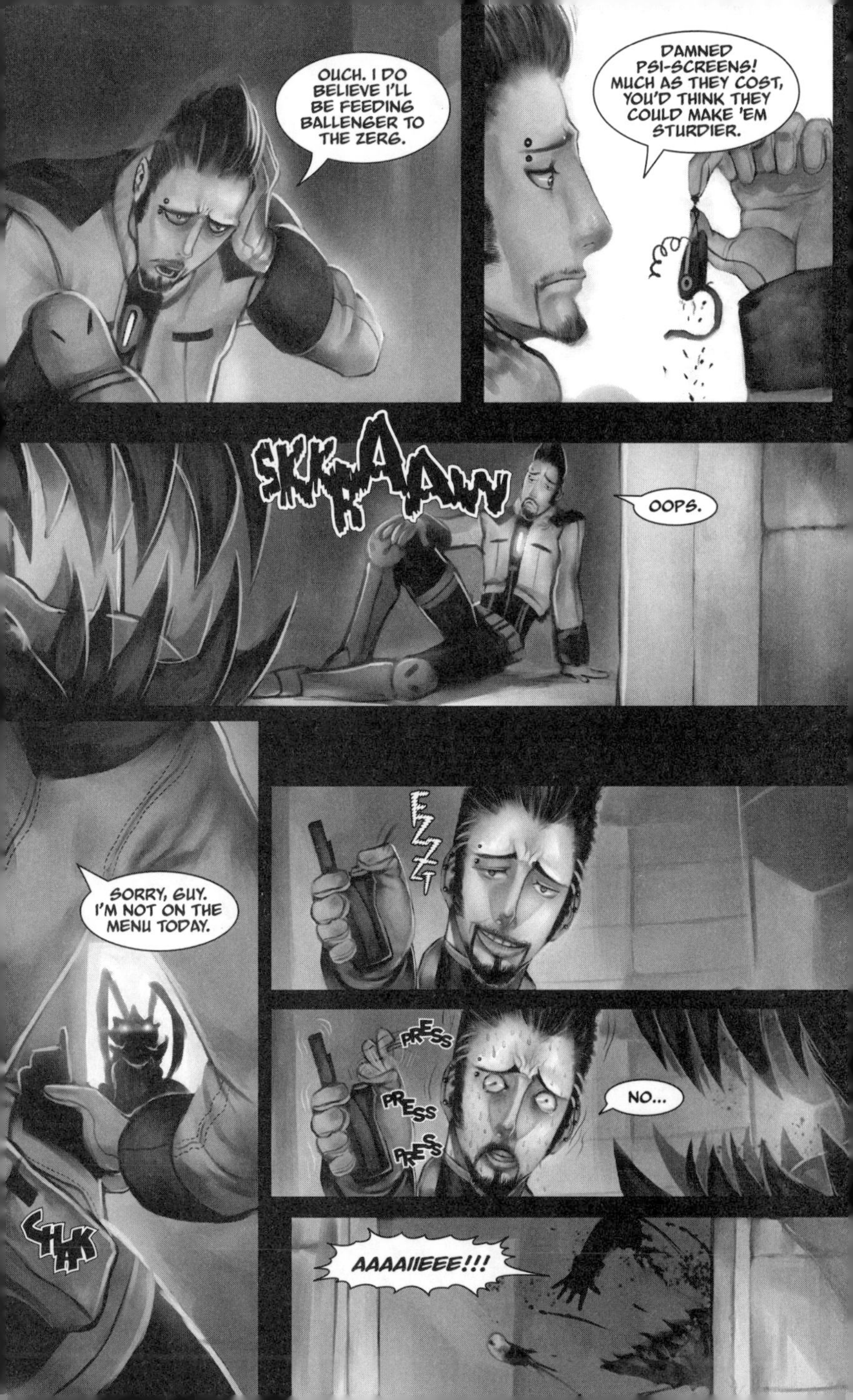
OUCH. I DO BELIEVE I'LL BE FEEDING BALLENGER TO THE ZERG.
DAMNED PSI-SCREENS! MUCH AS THEY COST, YOU'D THINK THEY COULD MAKE 'EM STURDIER.
SKKRAAWW
OOPS.
SORRY, GUY. I'M NOT ON THE MENU TODAY.
EZZZT
PRESS
PRESS
PRESS
NO...
CHAK
AAAAIIEEE!!!

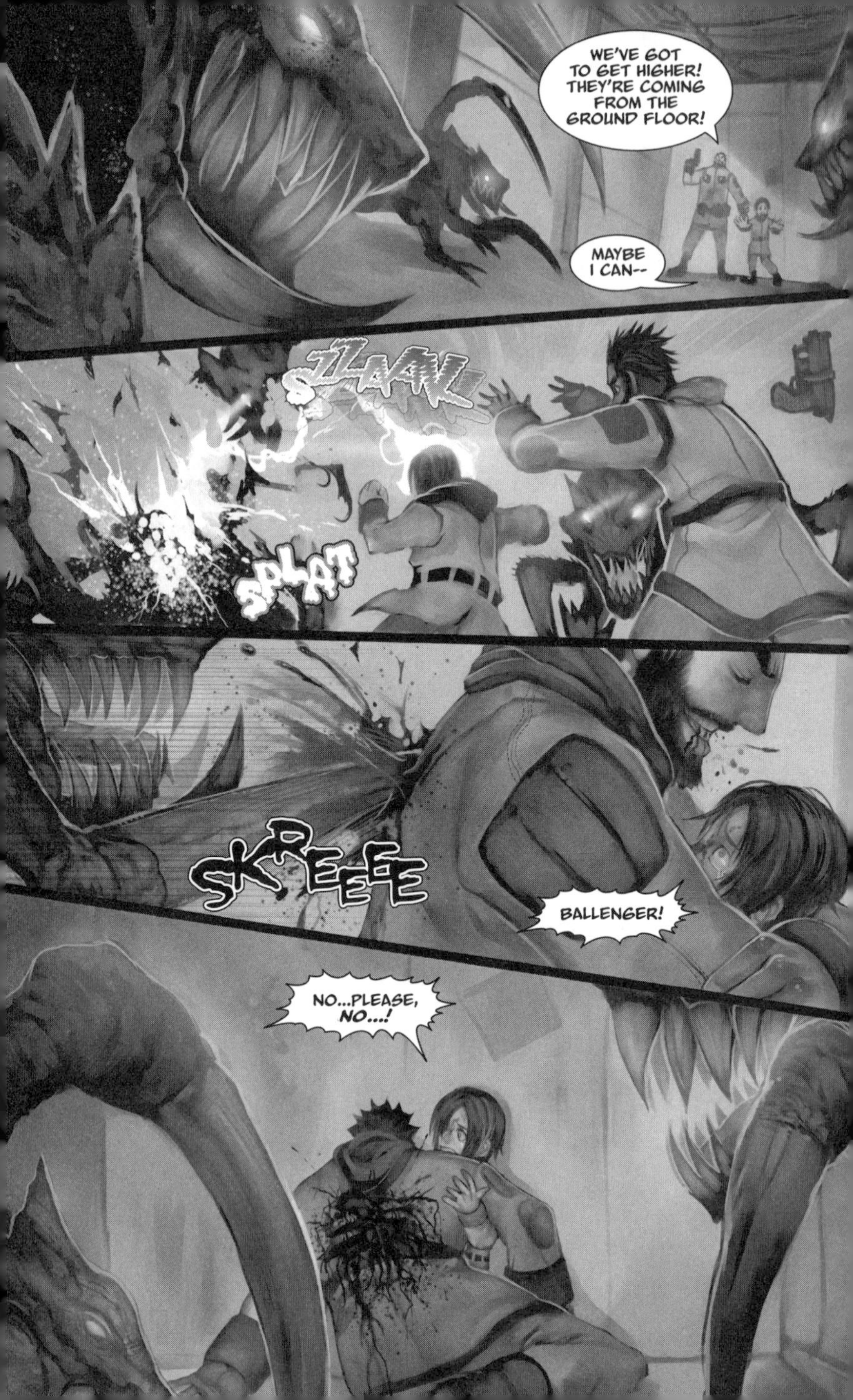
WE'VE GOT TO GET HIGHER! THEY'RE COMING FROM THE GROUND FLOOR!
MAYBE I CAN--
SPLAT
SKREEEE
BALLENGER!
NO...PLEASE, NO...!

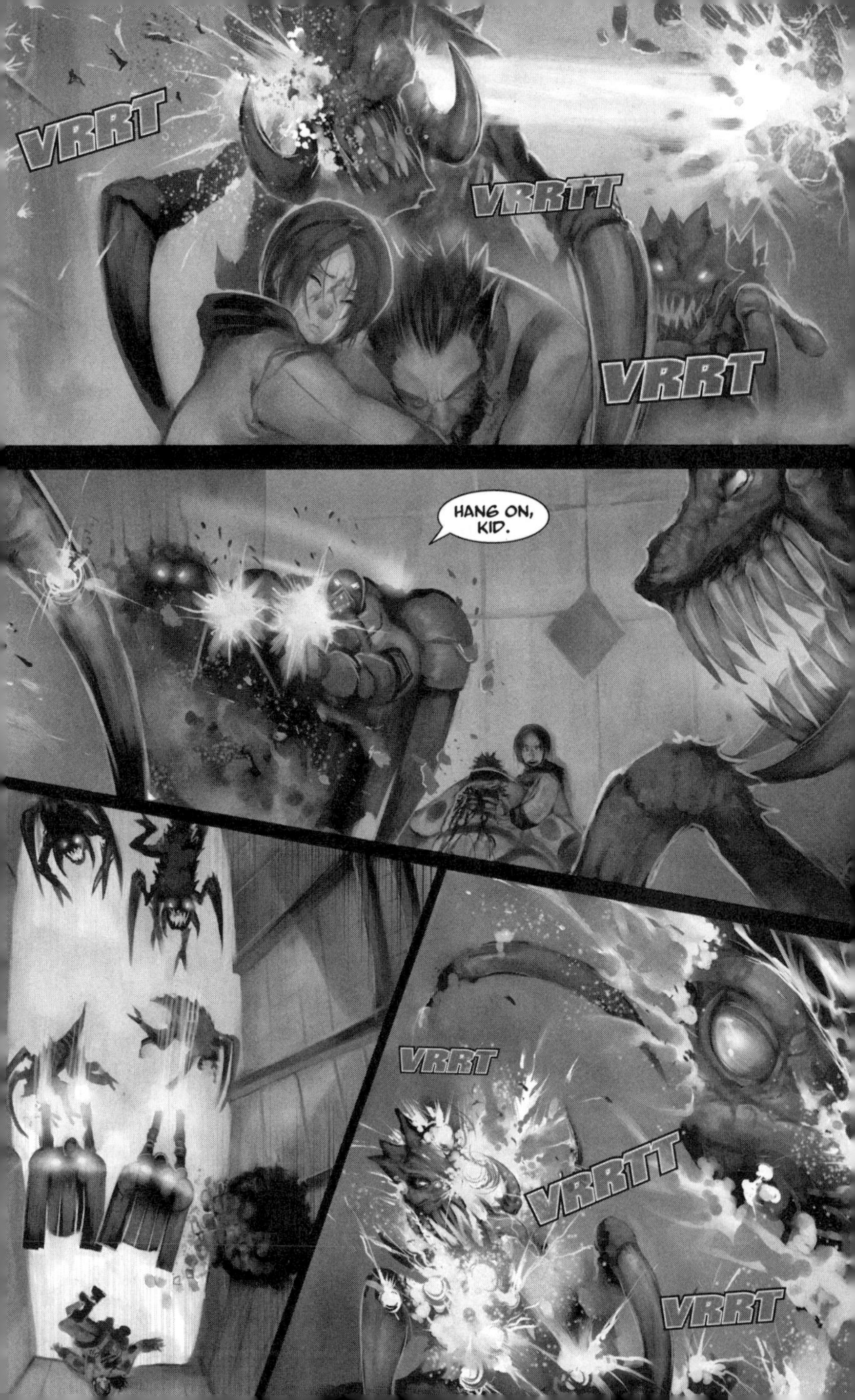
VRRT
VRRTT
VRRT
HANG ON, KID.
VRRT
VRRTT
VRRT

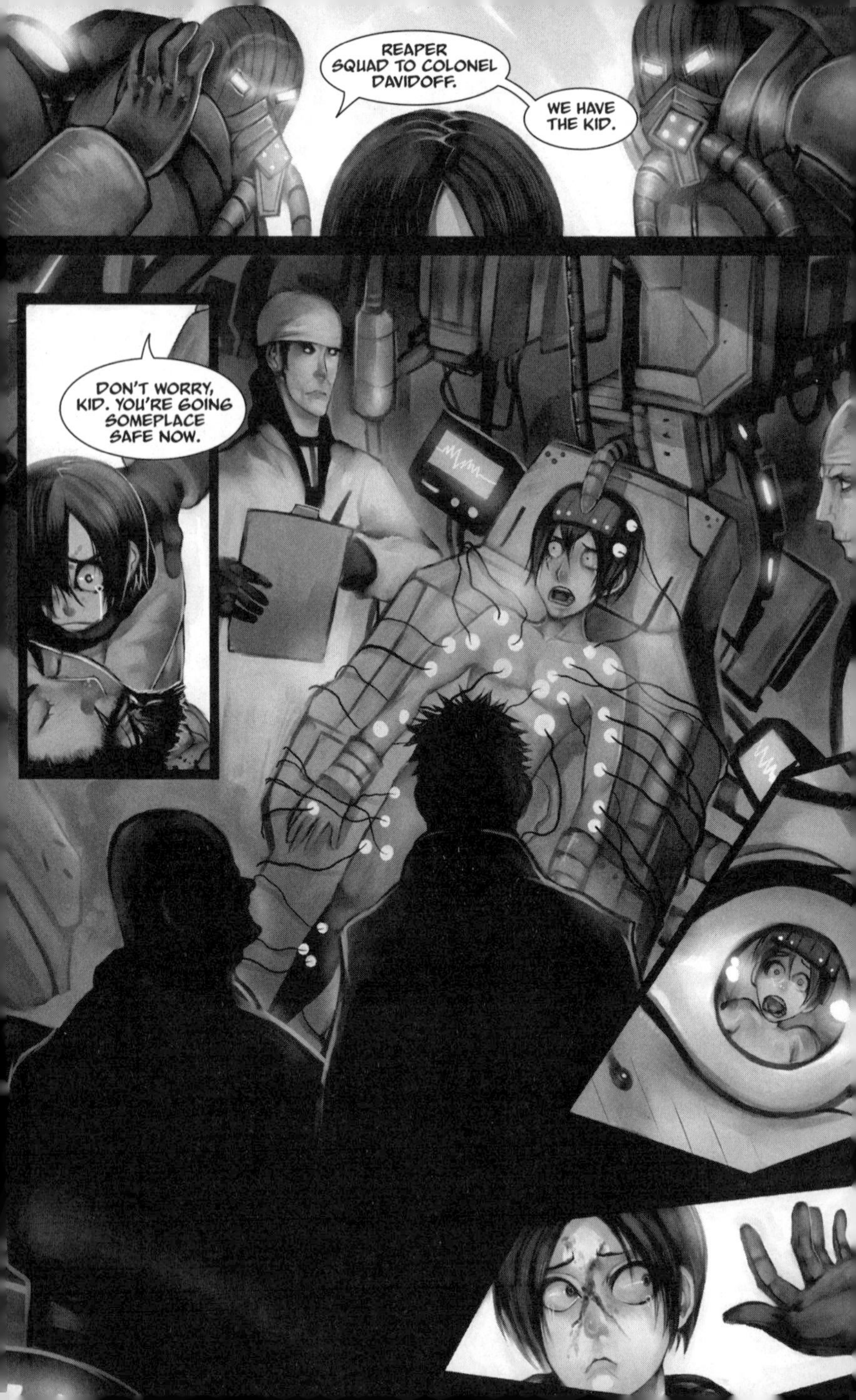
REAPER SQUAD TO COLONEL DAVIDOFF.
WE HAVE THE KID.
DON'T WORRY, KID. YOU'RE GOING SOMEPLACE SAFE NOW.

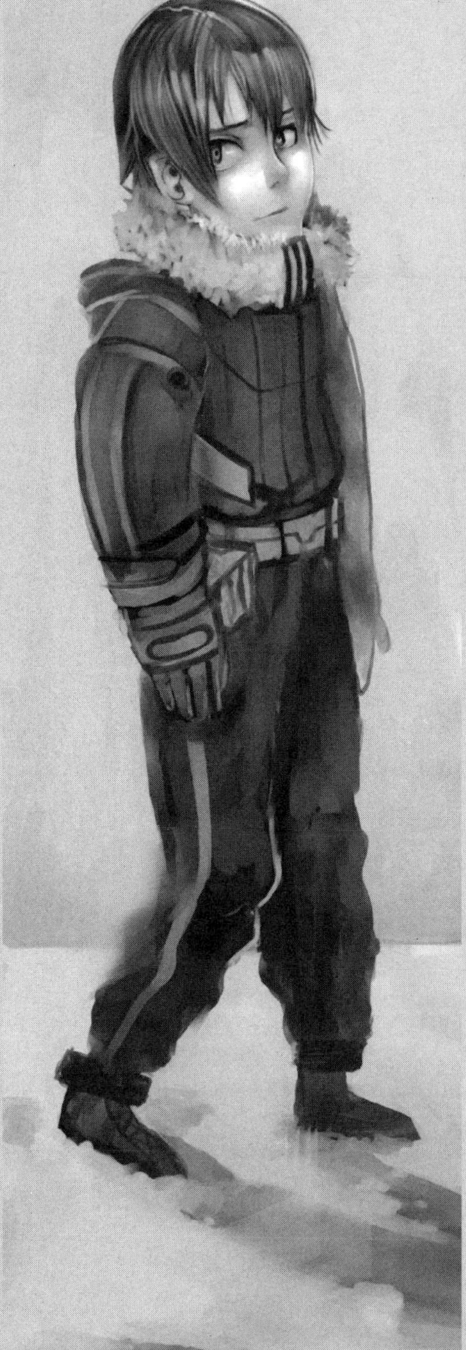

STARCRAFT

FRONTLINE
VOLUME 3

DO NO HARM

Written by Josh Elder

Pencils by Ramanda Kamarga

Inks by Angie Nathalia and Junaidi of Caravan Studio

Tones by Erfian Asafat of Caravan Studio and Beatusvir

Letterer: Michael Paolilli

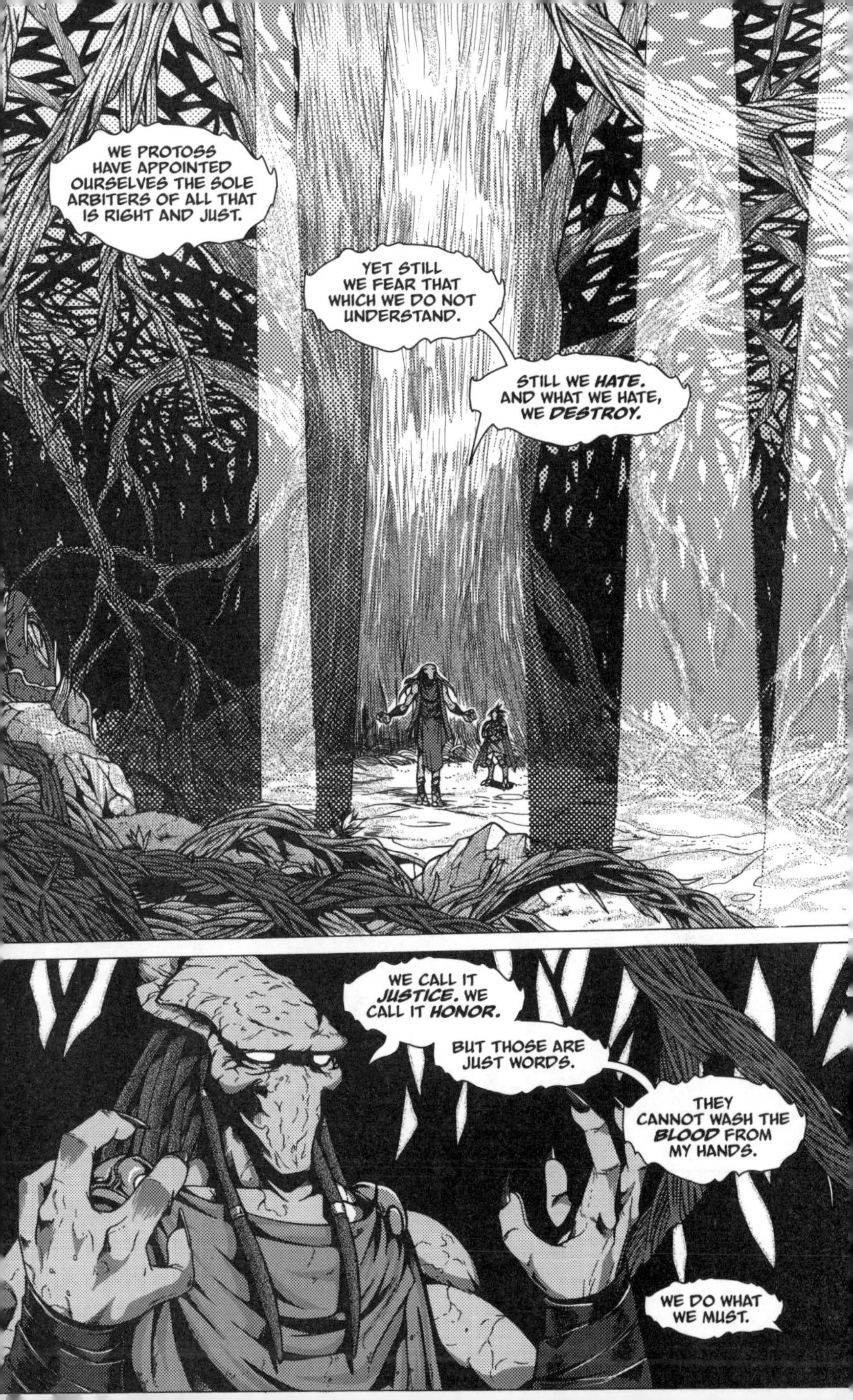
WE PROTOSS HAVE APPOINTED OURSELVES THE SOLE ARBITERS OF ALL THAT IS RIGHT AND JUST.
YET STILL WE FEAR THAT WHICH WE DO NOT UNDERSTAND.
STILL WE *HATE*. AND WHAT WE HATE, WE *DESTROY*.
WE CALL IT *JUSTICE*. WE CALL IT *HONOR*.
BUT THOSE ARE JUST WORDS.
THEY CANNOT WASH THE *BLOOD* FROM MY HANDS.
WE DO WHAT WE MUST.

YES, OR SO WE *TELL* OURSELVES.

I HAVE SERVED THE DAE'UHL MY ENTIRE LIFE.

ON ARTIKA, ON CHAR...

...ON WORLDS WITH NAMES THERE ARE NONE LEFT ALIVE TO REMEMBER.

I HAVE *KNOWN* WAR. NOW I WISH TO AT LAST KNOW *PEACE*.

THERE CAN BE NO PEACE WHILE OUR ENEMIES GATHER.

WHAT ENEMIES?

THE ZERG ARE CONTAINED ON CHAR, WHILE THE TERRANS HAVE *NEVER* TRULY BEEN A THREAT TO US.

THE ZERG CANNOT BE CONTAINED, AND THE HUMANS ARE MORE *DANGEROUS* THAN YOU KNOW.

THERE ARE EVEN RUMORS OF THEM *ABDUCTING* MEMBERS OF YOUR KHALAI CASTE FROM THE COLONY WORLDS.

THAT IS TRAGIC, BUT NO LONGER MY RESPONSIBILITY.

THESE ARE MY CHARGES NOW.

THE *ALAVASH* EVOLVED ALONGSIDE OUR PEOPLE ON AIUR...

...AND, LIKE US, SENSE THE THOUGHT AND FEELINGS OF OTHERS.

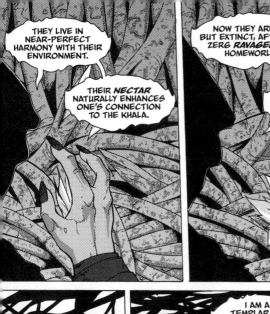

THEY LIVE IN NEAR-PERFECT HARMONY WITH THEIR ENVIRONMENT.

THEIR *NECTAR* NATURALLY ENHANCES ONE'S CONNECTION TO THE KHALA.

NOW THEY ARE ALL BUT EXTINCT, AFTER THE ZERG *RAVAGED* OUR HOMEWORLD.

I HAVE DEDICATED MYSELF TO THE PRESERVATION OF THESE LAST SPECIMENS...

...SO THAT FUTURE GENERATIONS MAY KNOW THEIR BEAUTY.

THERE IS HONOR IN THAT.

BUT YOU ARE A *WARRIOR*, AND YOU HAVE A DUTY TO *DEFEND* SUCH BEAUTY AGAINST THOSE WHO WOULD SEEK ITS RUIN.

I AM A TEMPLAR NO MORE. MY PLACE-- MY *DUTY*--IS HERE.

...SO BE IT.

TARO RUUL ASZ, MUADUN.

VAR'UM RUUL ASZ, AZIMAR.

AND ADUN GUIDE YOU.

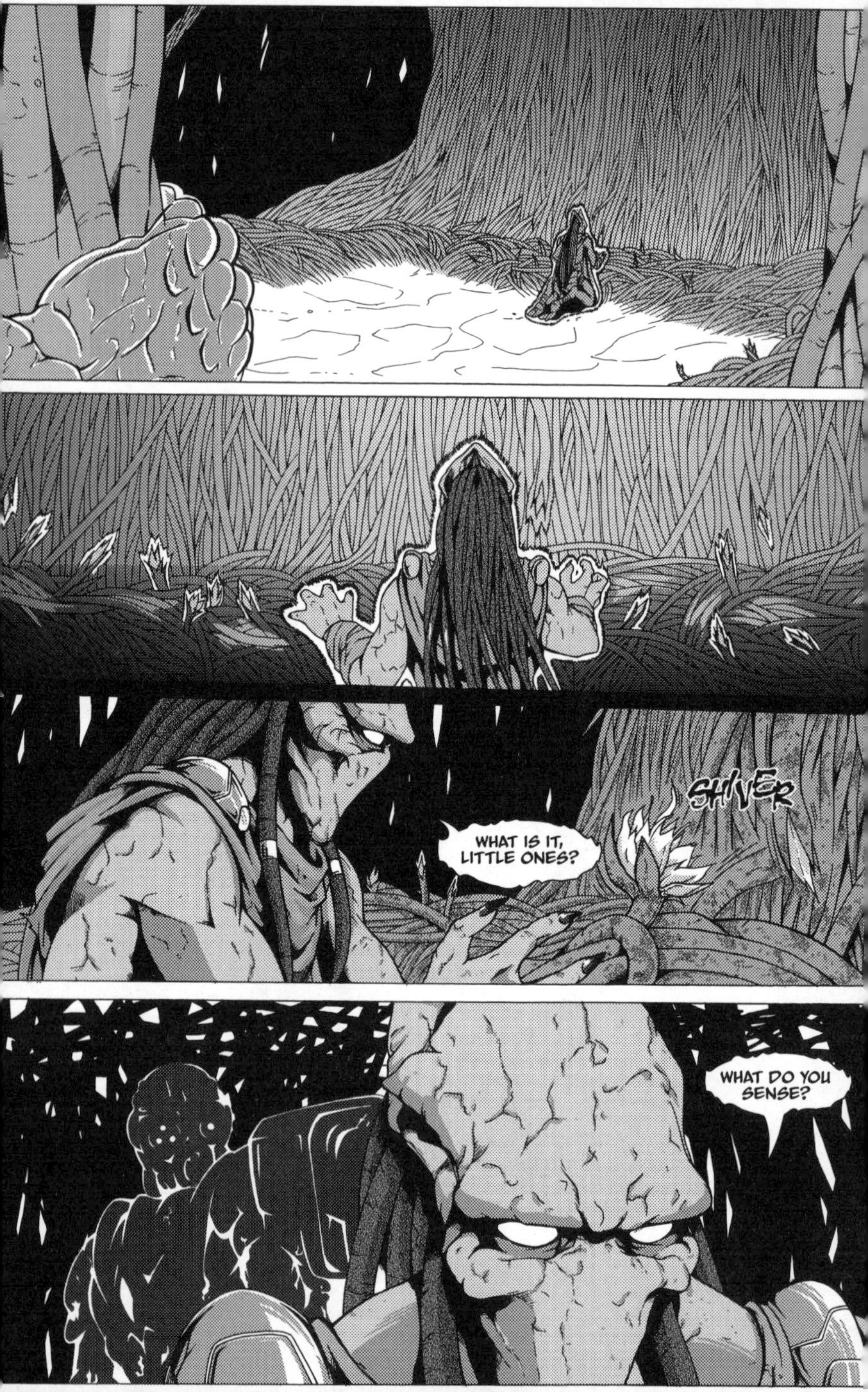
SHIVER
WHAT IS IT, LITTLE ONES?
WHAT DO YOU SENSE?

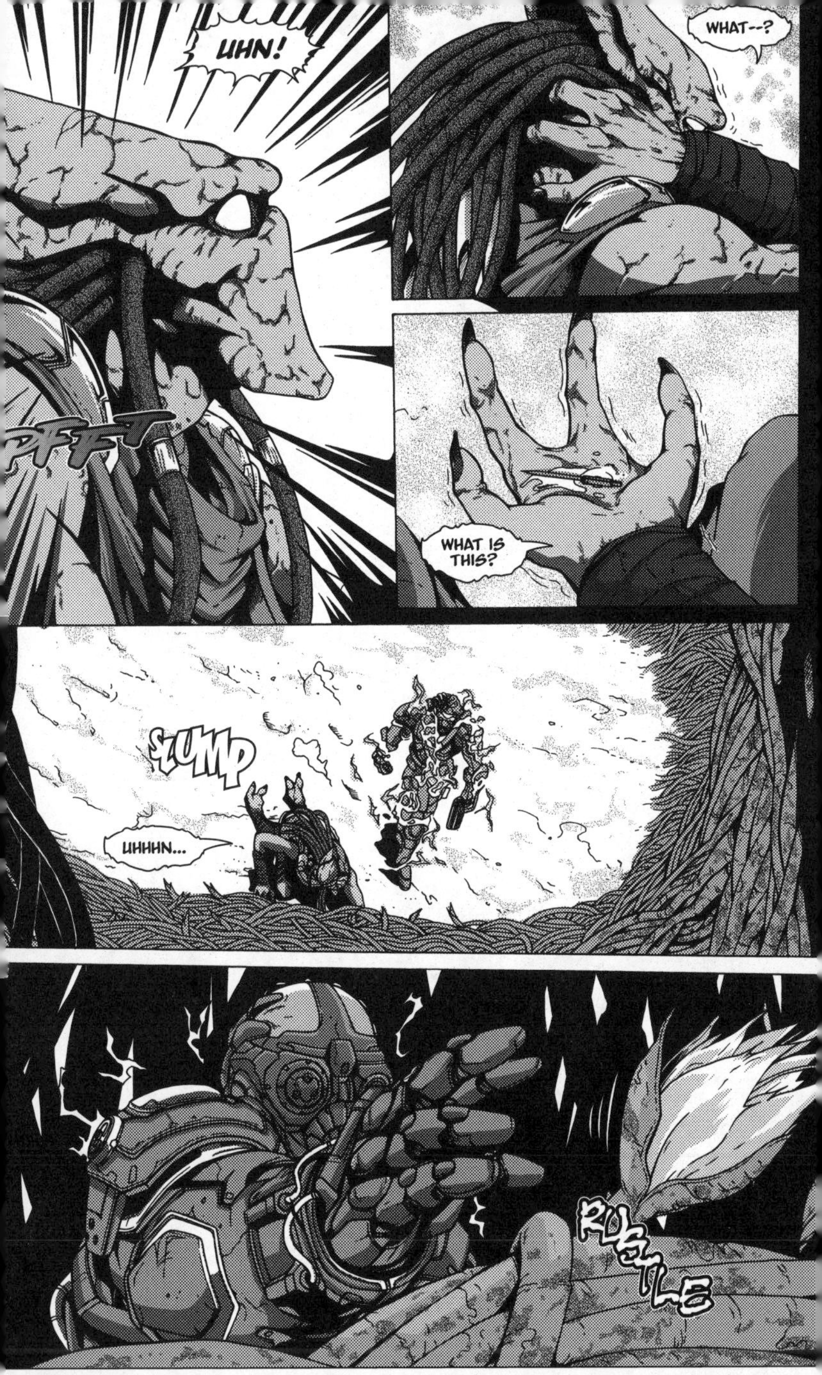
UHN!
PFFT
WHAT--?
WHAT IS THIS?
SLUMP
UHHHN...
RUSTLE

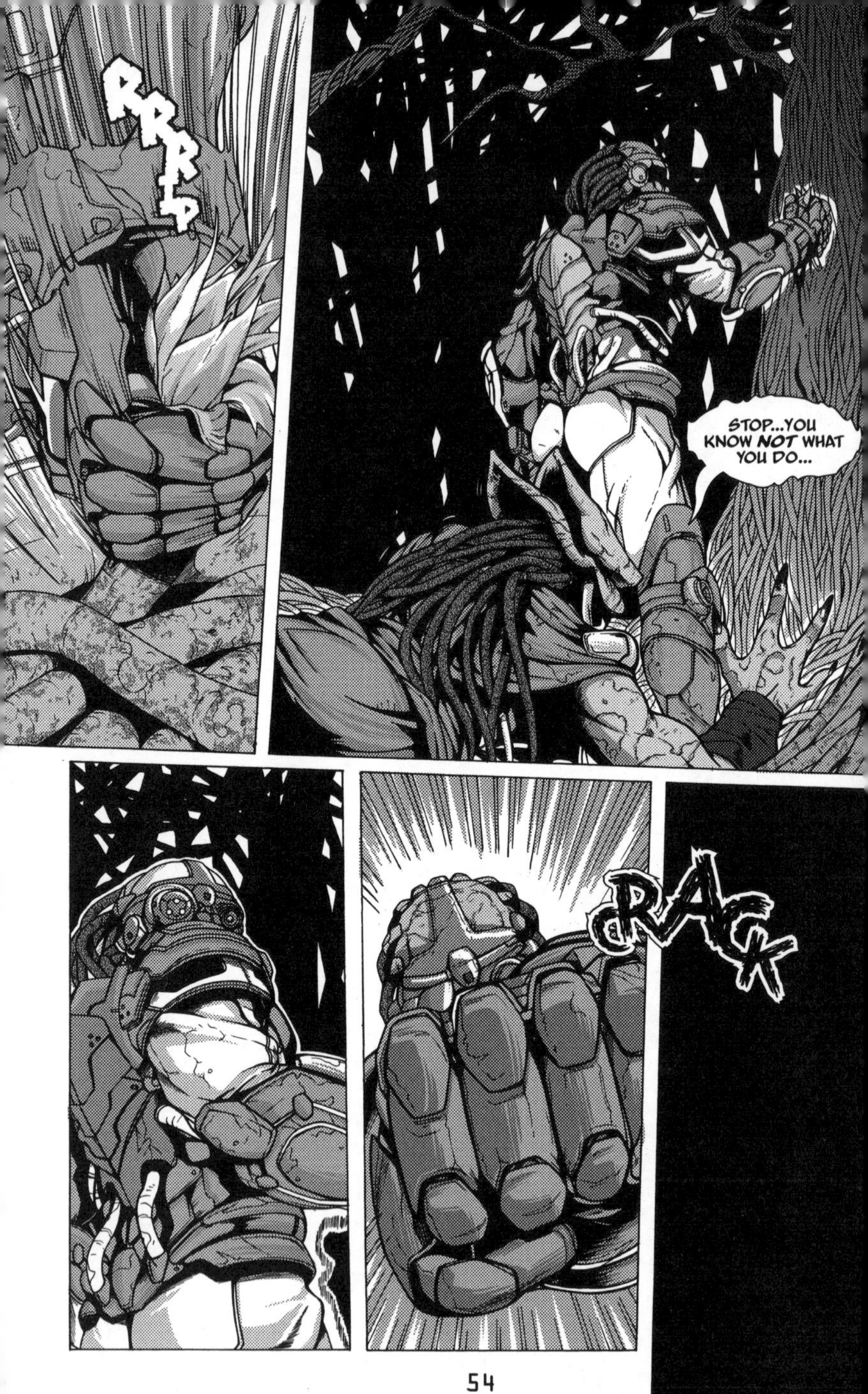
RRRIP
STOP...YOU KNOW *NOT* WHAT YOU DO...
CRACK

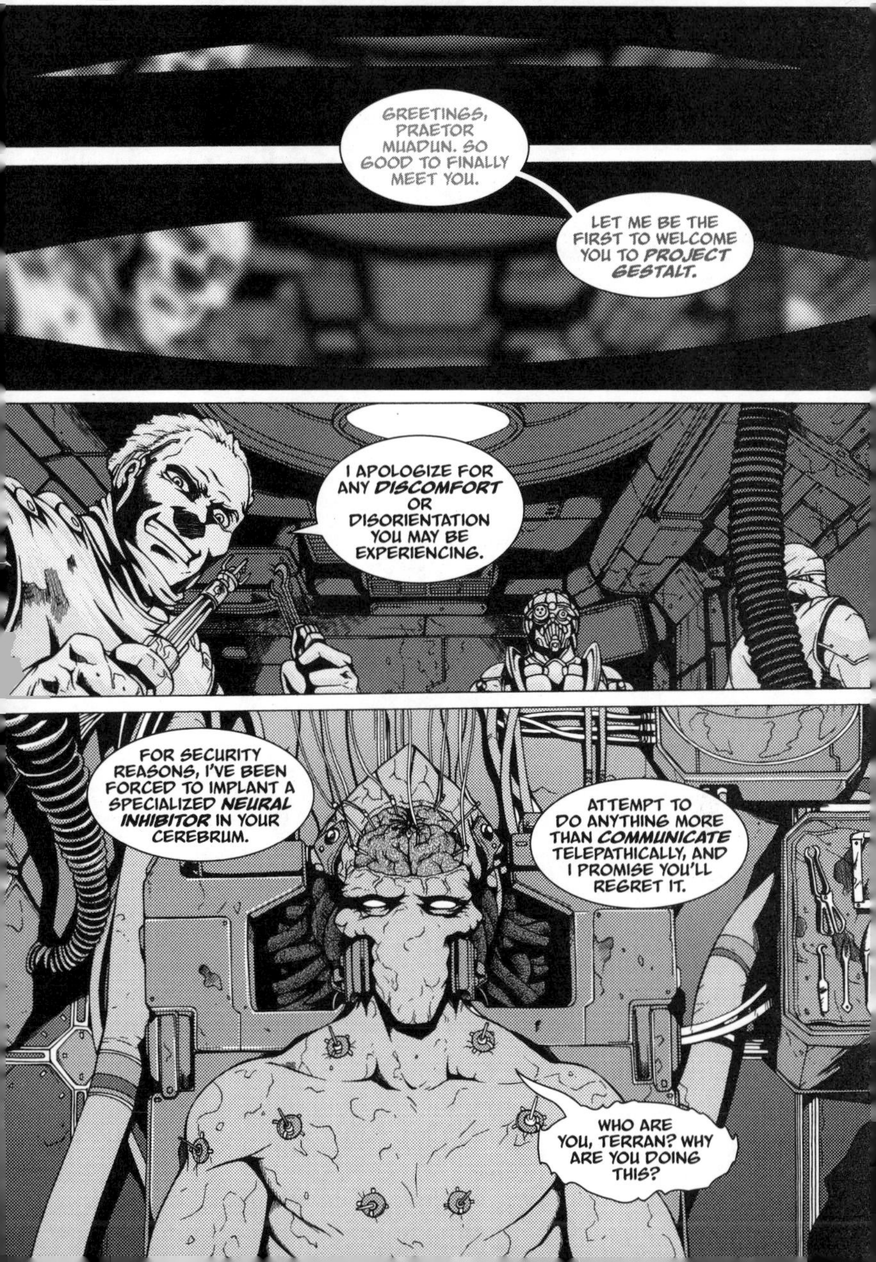
GREETINGS, PRAETOR MUADUN. SO GOOD TO FINALLY MEET YOU.
LET ME BE THE FIRST TO WELCOME YOU TO *PROJECT GESTALT.*
I APOLOGIZE FOR ANY *DISCOMFORT* OR DISORIENTATION YOU MAY BE EXPERIENCING.
FOR SECURITY REASONS, I'VE BEEN FORCED TO IMPLANT A SPECIALIZED *NEURAL INHIBITOR* IN YOUR CEREBRUM.
ATTEMPT TO DO ANYTHING MORE THAN *COMMUNICATE* TELEPATHICALLY, AND I PROMISE YOU'LL REGRET IT.
WHO ARE YOU, TERRAN? WHY ARE YOU DOING THIS?

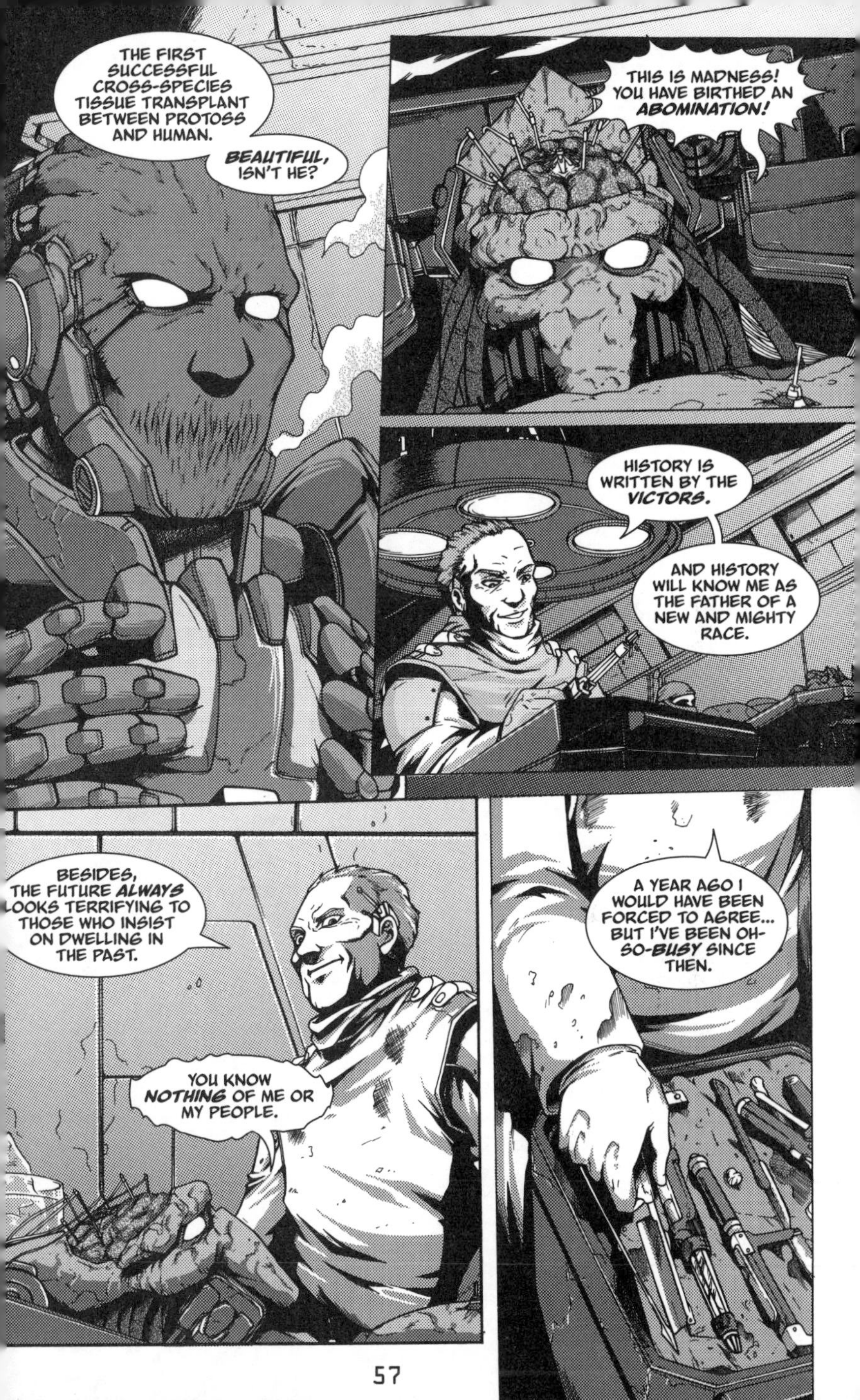
THE FIRST SUCCESSFUL CROSS-SPECIES TISSUE TRANSPLANT BETWEEN PROTOSS AND HUMAN.
BEAUTIFUL, ISN'T HE?
THIS IS MADNESS! YOU HAVE BIRTHED AN ABOMINATION!
HISTORY IS WRITTEN BY THE VICTORS.
AND HISTORY WILL KNOW ME AS THE FATHER OF A NEW AND MIGHTY RACE.
BESIDES, THE FUTURE ALWAYS LOOKS TERRIFYING TO THOSE WHO INSIST ON DWELLING IN THE PAST.
YOU KNOW NOTHING OF ME OR MY PEOPLE.
A YEAR AGO I WOULD HAVE BEEN FORCED TO AGREE... BUT I'VE BEEN OH-SO-BUSY SINCE THEN.

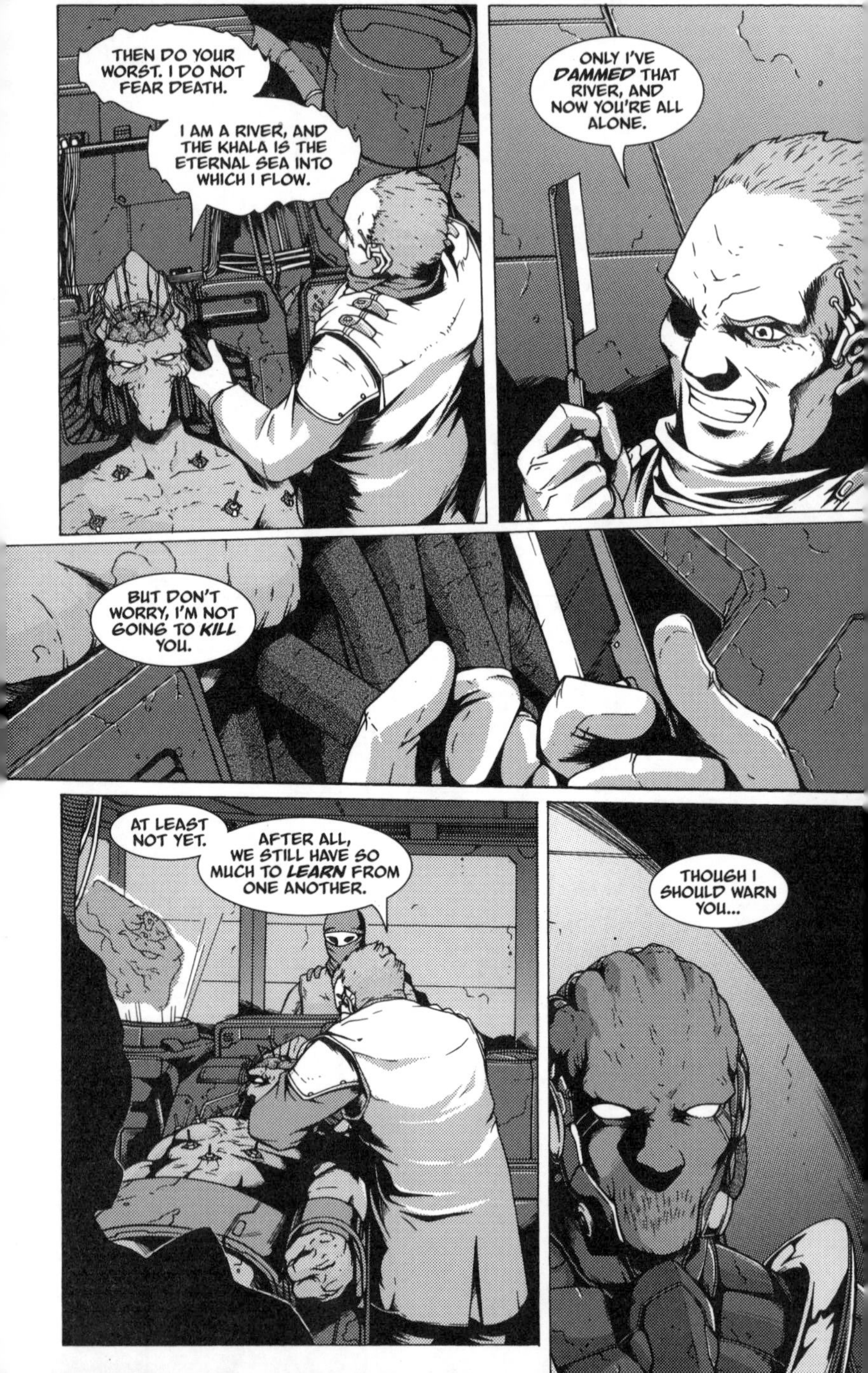
THEN DO YOUR WORST. I DO NOT FEAR DEATH.
I AM A RIVER, AND THE KHALA IS THE ETERNAL SEA INTO WHICH I FLOW.
ONLY I'VE *DAMMED* THAT RIVER, AND NOW YOU'RE ALL ALONE.
BUT DON'T WORRY, I'M NOT GOING TO *KILL* YOU.
AT LEAST NOT YET.
AFTER ALL, WE STILL HAVE SO MUCH TO *LEARN* FROM ONE ANOTHER.
THOUGH I SHOULD WARN YOU...

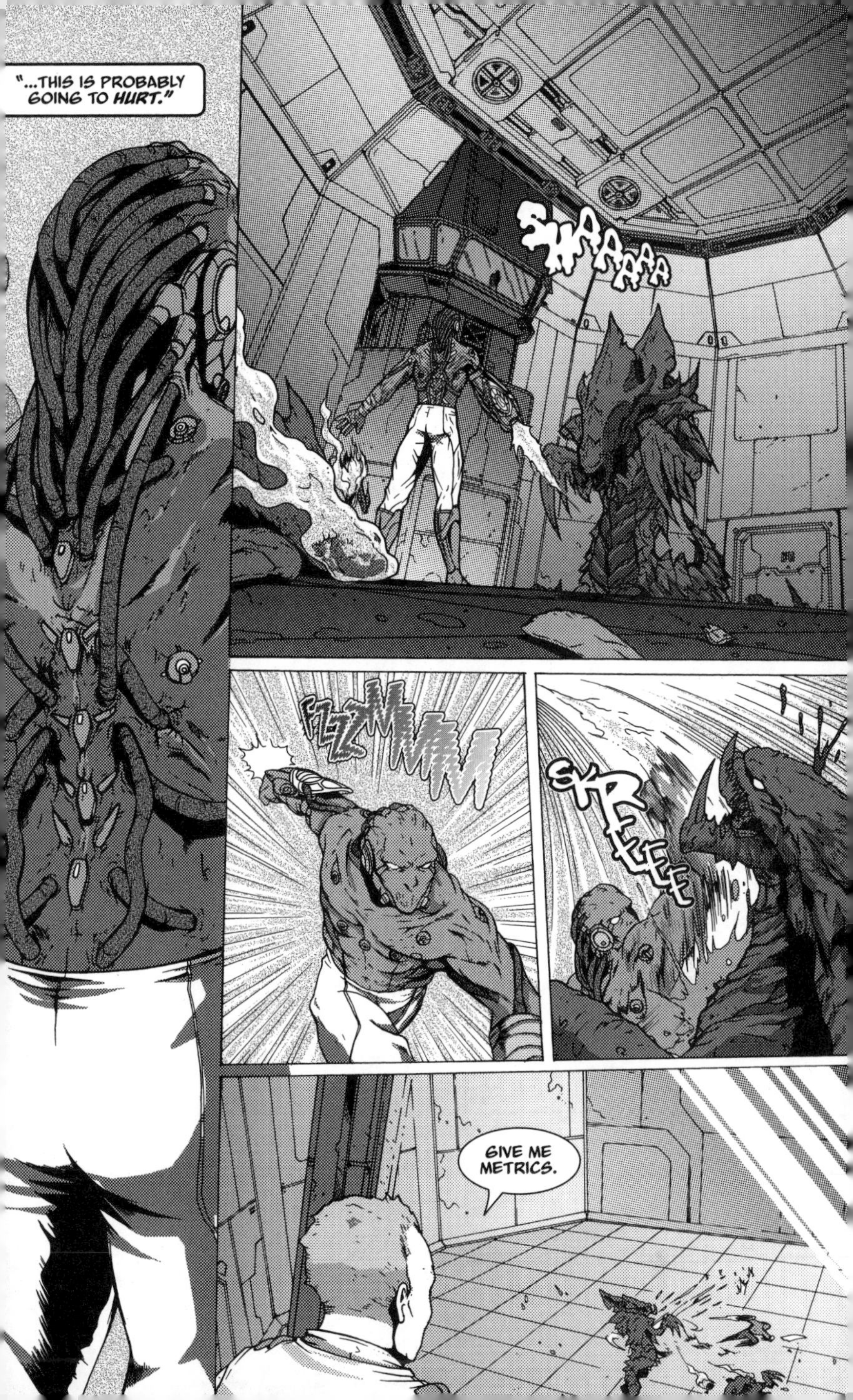
"...THIS IS PROBABLY GOING TO *HURT.*"
SHAAAAA
FZZZMMMM
SKREEEE
GIVE ME METRICS.

"RESEARCH LOG: 04.06.2503.

"AFTER OVER A YEAR OF INTENSIVE RESEARCH AND A SUBSTANTIAL INVESTMENT-- THE PSI-SCREENS *ALONE* COST MORE THAN THE ENTIRE GROSS PLANETARY PRODUCT OF TYRADOR IX--PROJECT GESTALT NEARS COMPLETION.

"DUE TO THE RECENT ACQUISITION OF *TEMPLAR-GRADE* PROTOSS GENETIC MATERIAL, THE ENHANCED GHOST PROTOTYPE, DESIGNATED GESTALT ZERO...

"...IS NOW OPERATING AT NEARLY *TWICE* THE COMBAT EFFECTIVENESS OF A STANDARD GHOST UNIT.

"WE WILL SOON BE ADDING PERSONAL PSIONIC *SHIELDS* TO ZERO'S ARSENAL, AND APPROPRIATING THE PROTOSS NEURAL LINK FOR OUR OWN PSI-NETWORK ONCE WE BEGIN MASS PRODUCTION.

SOON THE DOMINION WILL POSSESS AN ARMY OF INVISIBLE, *UNSTOPPABLE* WARRIORS.

HUMANITY'S FINAL *VICTORY* IN THE PSIONIC ARMS RACE IS ASSURED.

"ALL THIS WITHOUT ANY OF THE UNPREDICTABLE *SIDE EFFECTS* OF TERRAZINE ENHANCEMENT. INTENSE NEURAL CONDITIONING AND SURGICALLY IMPLANTED *NEURAL INHIBITORS* WILL ENSURE THE UNIT'S LOYALTIES."

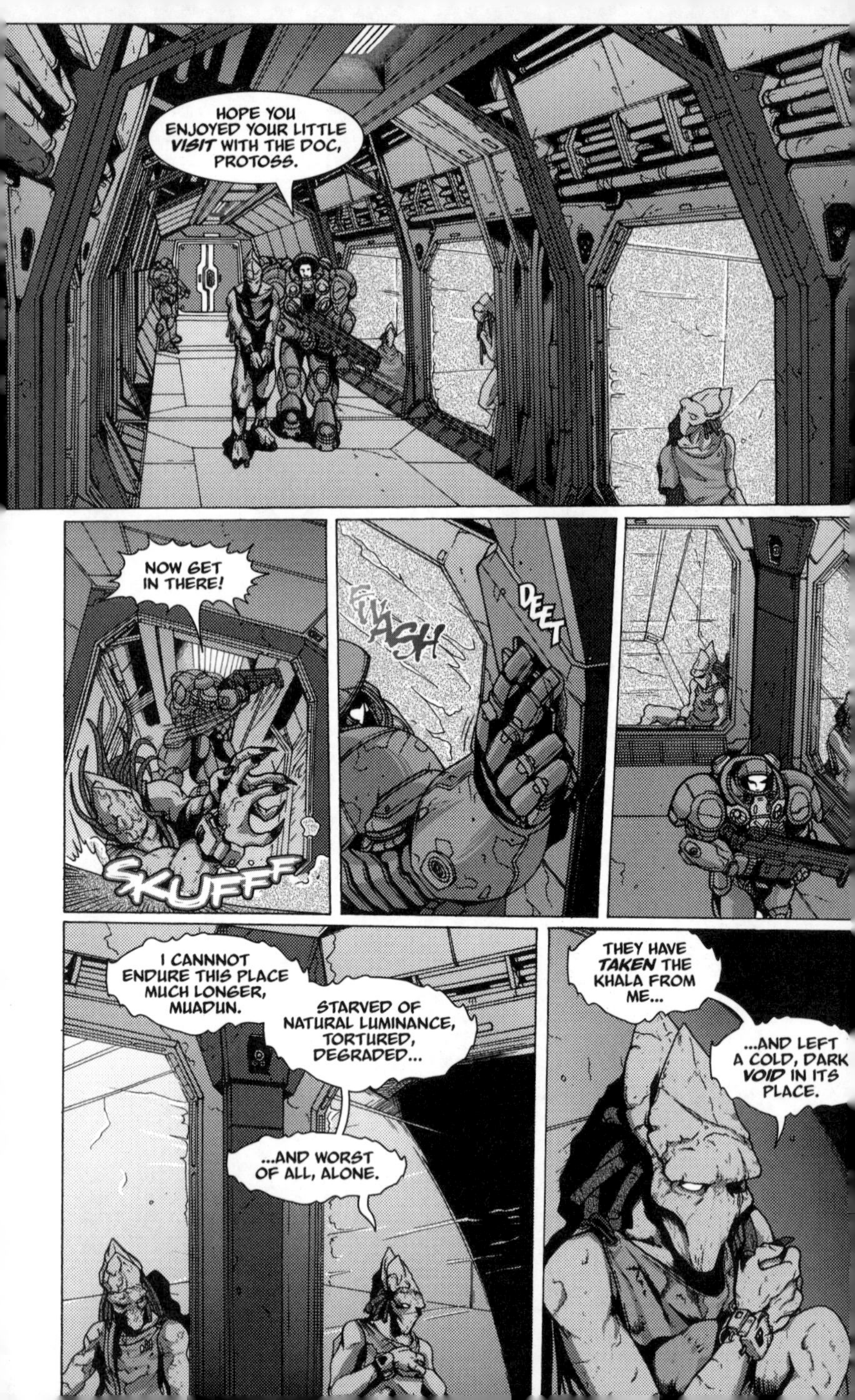
HOPE YOU ENJOYED YOUR LITTLE *VISIT* WITH THE DOC, PROTOSS.
NOW GET IN THERE!
SKUFFF
DEET
I CANNNOT ENDURE THIS PLACE MUCH LONGER, MUADUN.
STARVED OF NATURAL LUMINANCE, TORTURED, DEGRADED...
...AND WORST OF ALL, ALONE.
THEY HAVE *TAKEN* THE KHALA FROM ME...
...AND LEFT A COLD, DARK *VOID* IN ITS PLACE.

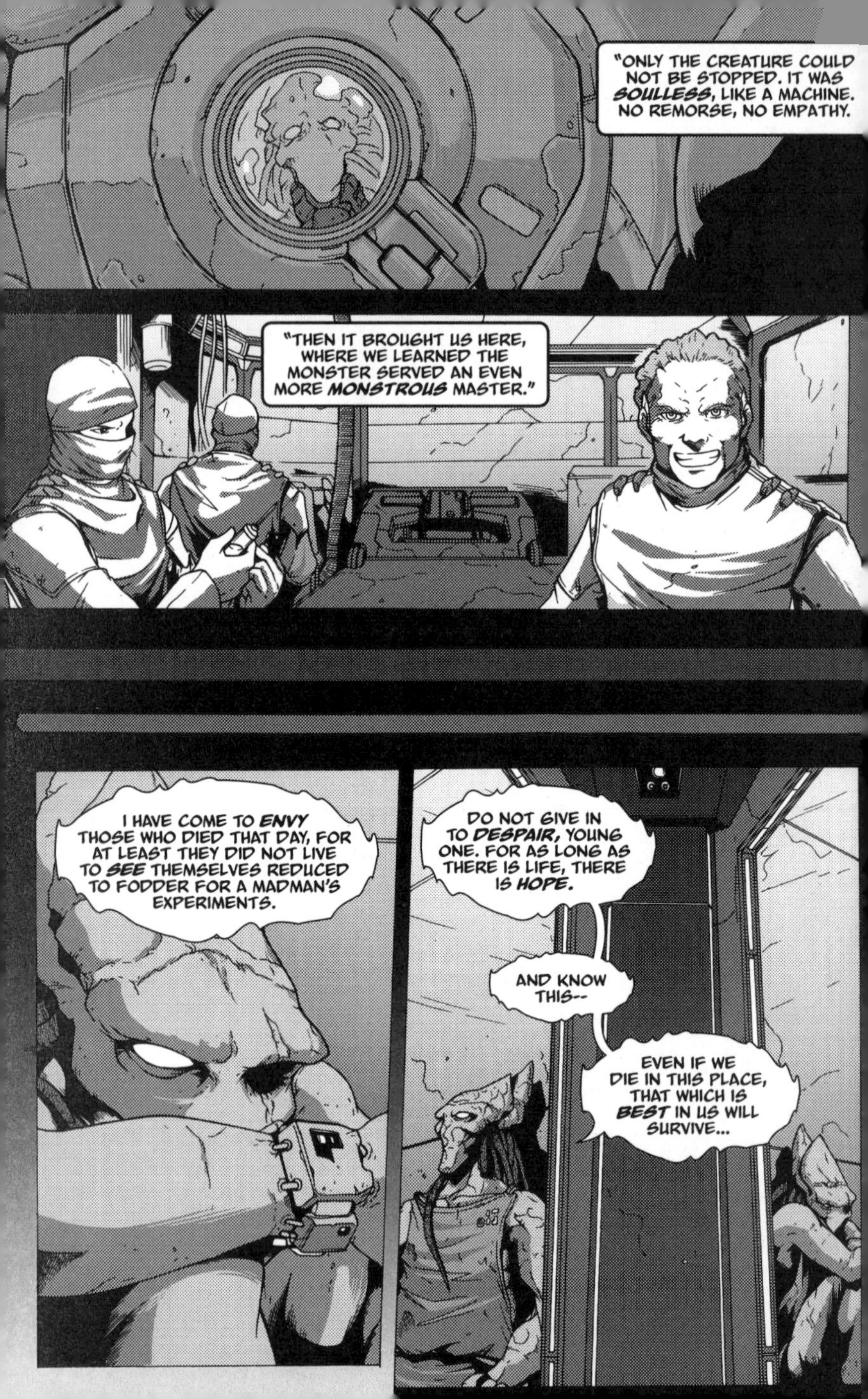
"ONLY THE CREATURE COULD NOT BE STOPPED. IT WAS SOULLESS, LIKE A MACHINE. NO REMORSE, NO EMPATHY.
"THEN IT BROUGHT US HERE, WHERE WE LEARNED THE MONSTER SERVED AN EVEN MORE MONSTROUS MASTER."
I HAVE COME TO ENVY THOSE WHO DIED THAT DAY, FOR AT LEAST THEY DID NOT LIVE TO SEE THEMSELVES REDUCED TO FODDER FOR A MADMAN'S EXPERIMENTS.
DO NOT GIVE IN TO DESPAIR, YOUNG ONE. FOR AS LONG AS THERE IS LIFE, THERE IS HOPE.
AND KNOW THIS--
EVEN IF WE DIE IN THIS PLACE, THAT WHICH IS BEST IN US WILL SURVIVE...

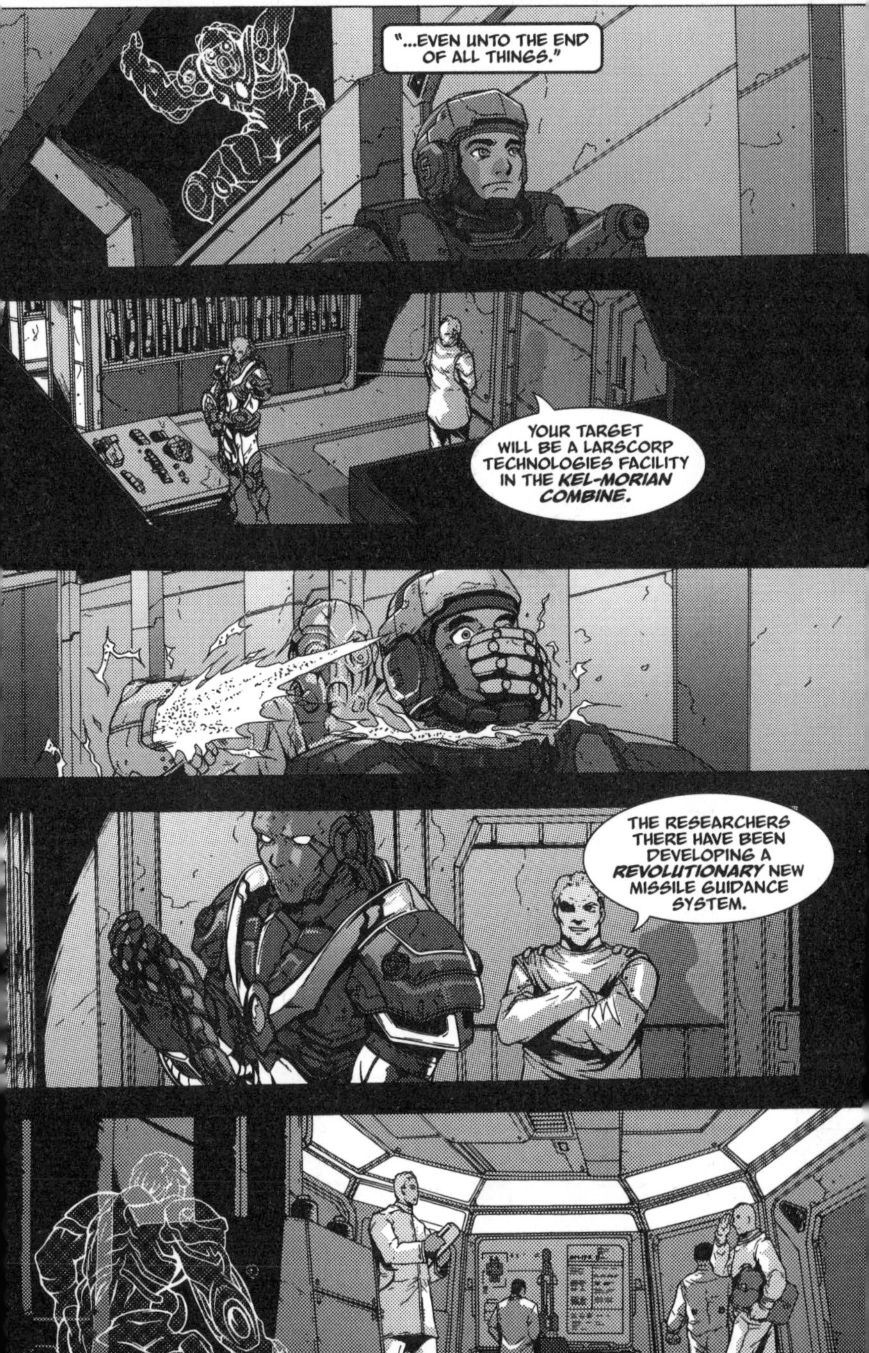
"...EVEN UNTO THE END OF ALL THINGS."
YOUR TARGET WILL BE A LARSCORP TECHNOLOGIES FACILITY IN THE *KEL-MORIAN COMBINE.*
THE RESEARCHERS THERE HAVE BEEN DEVELOPING A *REVOLUTIONARY* NEW MISSILE GUIDANCE SYSTEM.

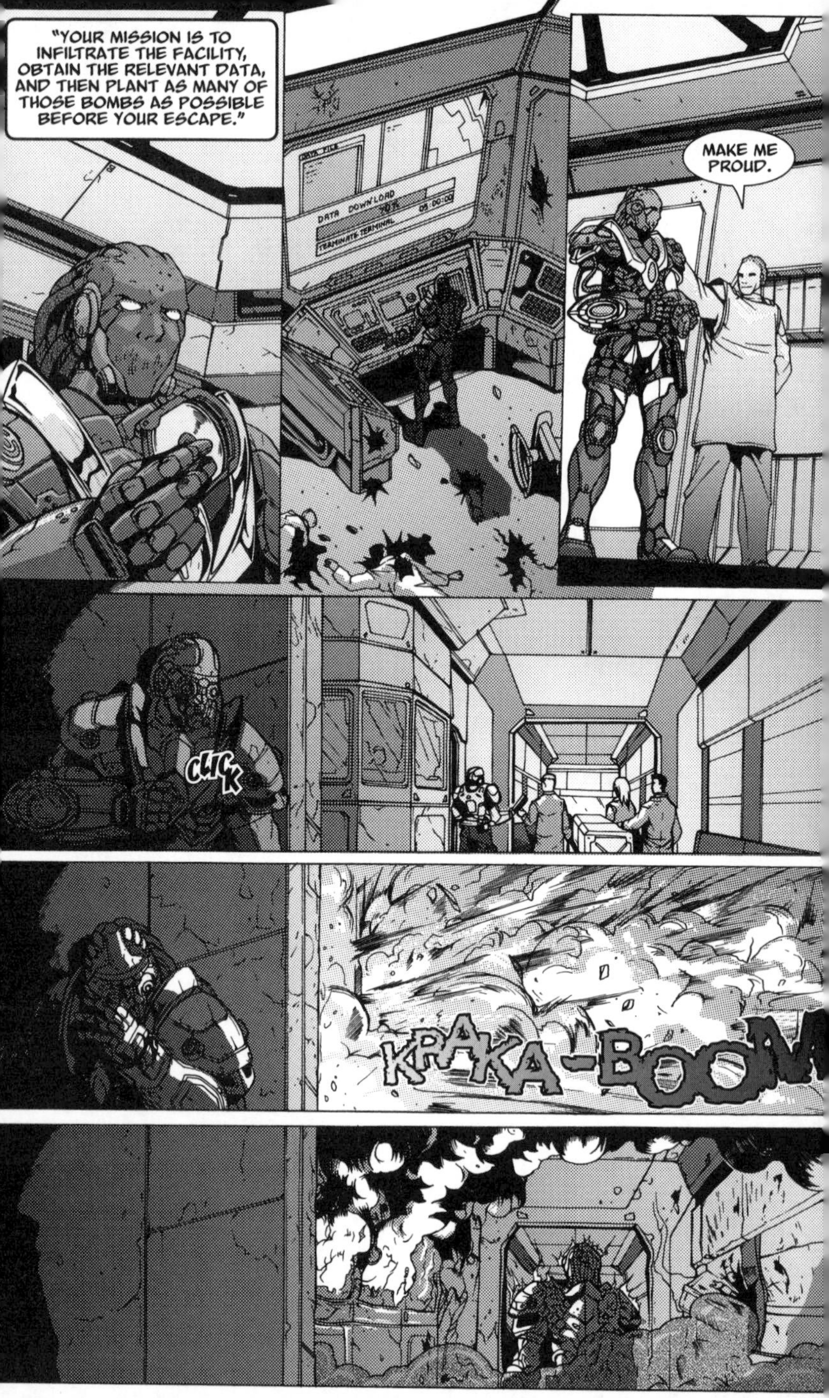
"YOUR MISSION IS TO INFILTRATE THE FACILITY, OBTAIN THE RELEVANT DATA, AND THEN PLANT AS MANY OF THOSE BOMBS AS POSSIBLE BEFORE YOUR ESCAPE."
MAKE ME PROUD.
CLICK
KRAKA-BOOM

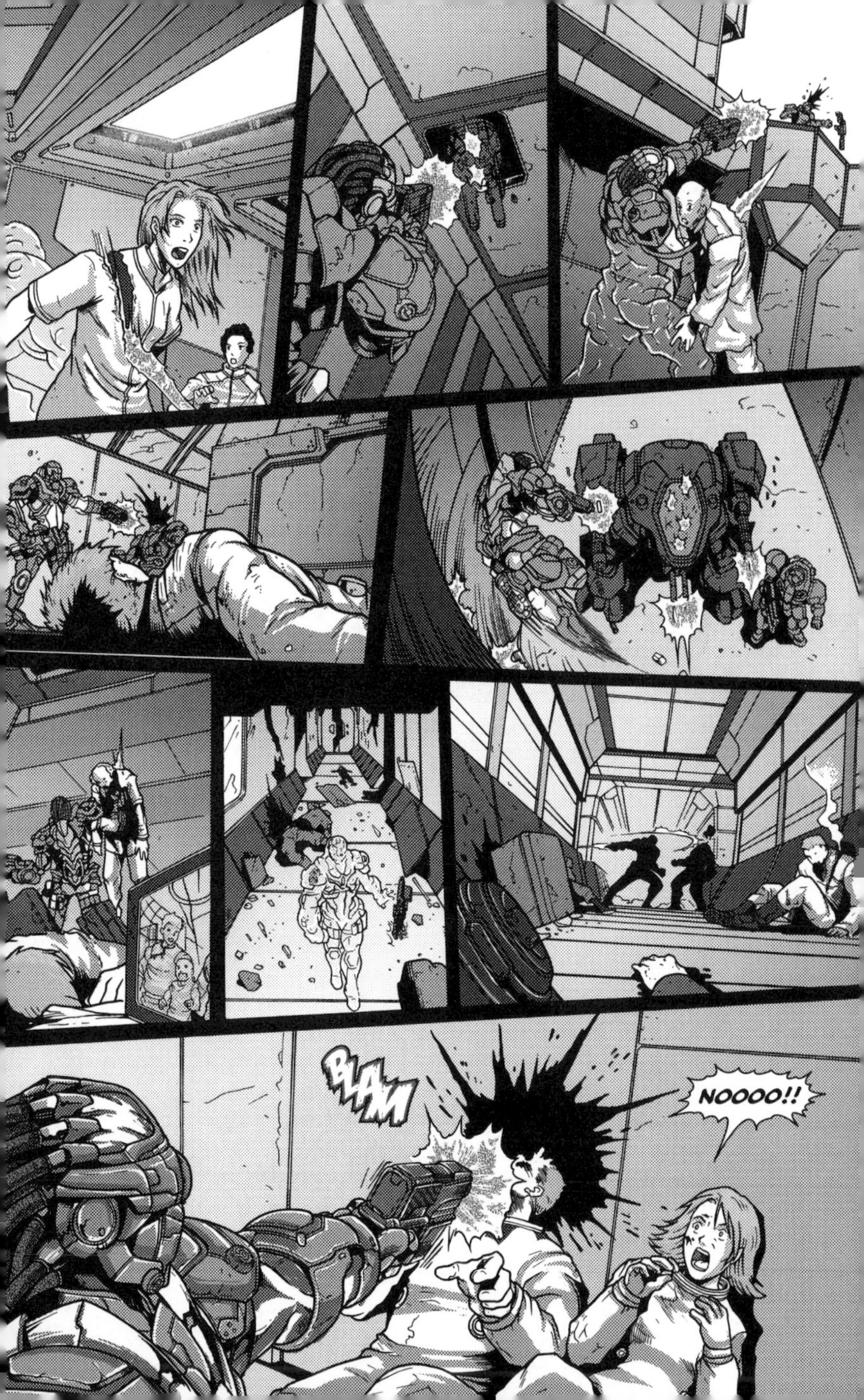
BLAM
NOOOO!!

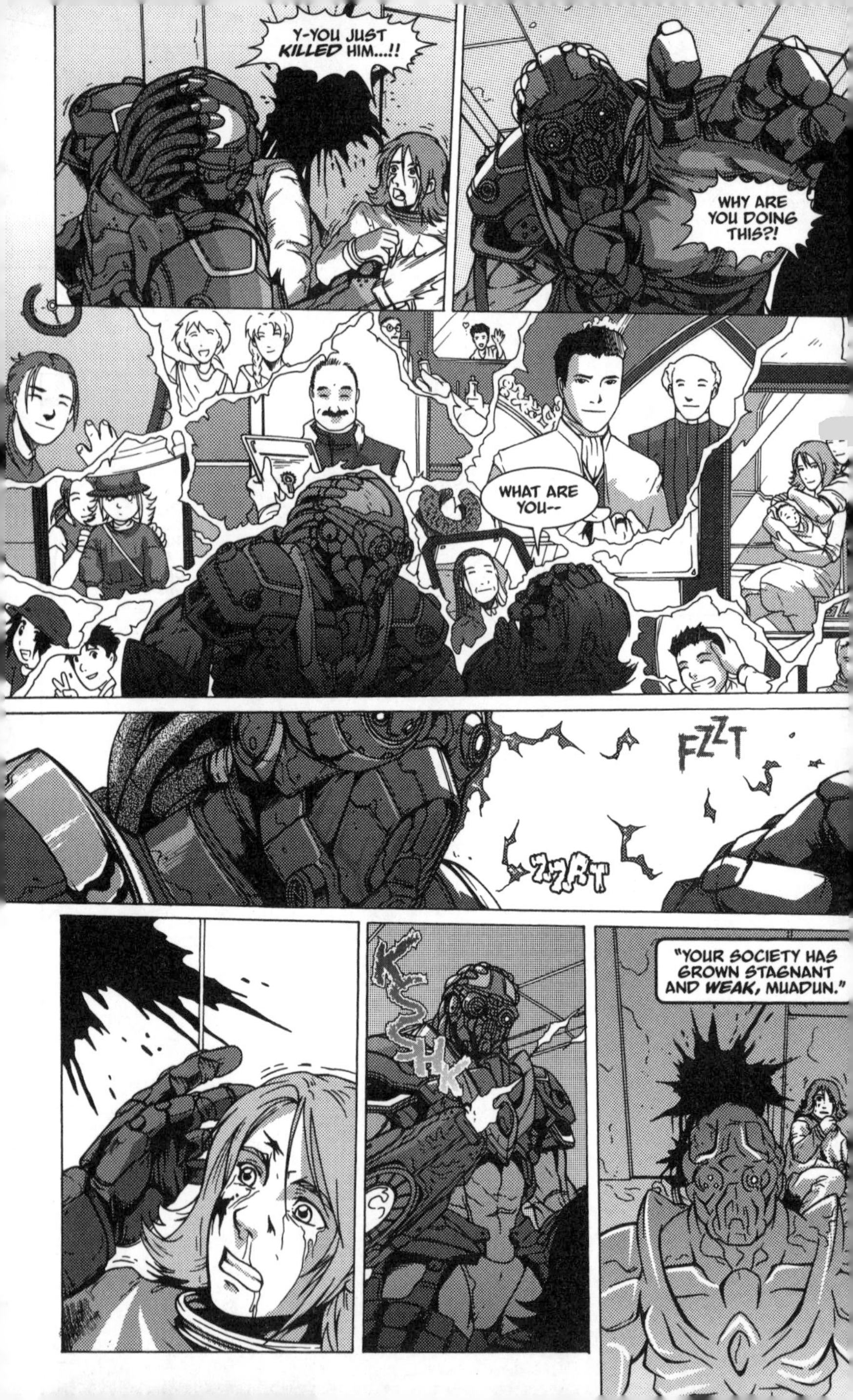
Y-YOU JUST KILLED HIM...!!
WHY ARE YOU DOING THIS?!
WHAT ARE YOU--
FZZT
ZZRT
KSHK
"YOUR SOCIETY HAS GROWN STAGNANT AND WEAK, MUADUN."

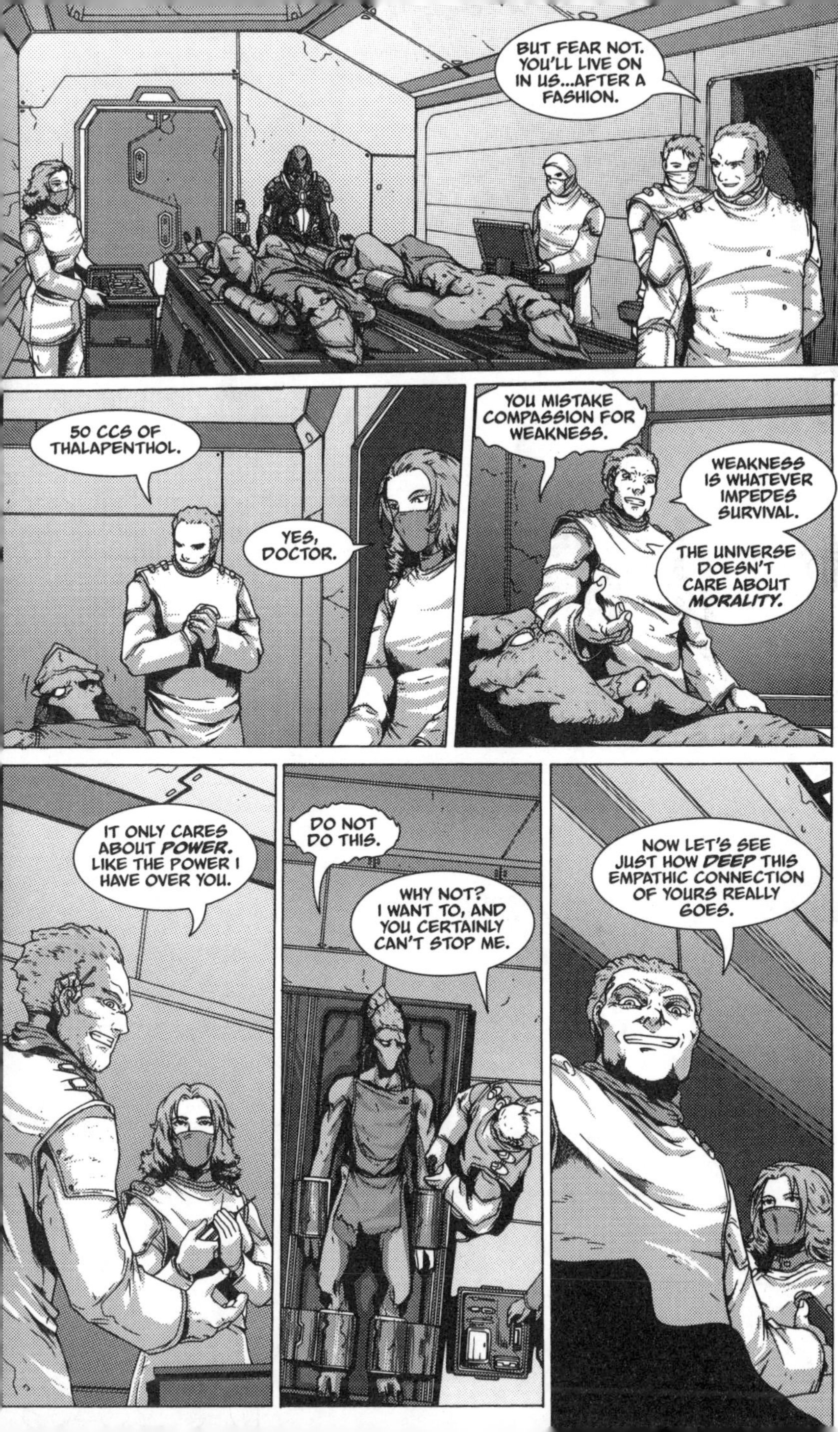
BUT FEAR NOT. YOU'LL LIVE ON IN US...AFTER A FASHION.
50 CCS OF THALAPENTHOL.
YES, DOCTOR.
YOU MISTAKE COMPASSION FOR WEAKNESS.
WEAKNESS IS WHATEVER IMPEDES SURVIVAL.
THE UNIVERSE DOESN'T CARE ABOUT *MORALITY*.
IT ONLY CARES ABOUT *POWER*. LIKE THE POWER I HAVE OVER YOU.
DO NOT DO THIS.
WHY NOT? I WANT TO, AND YOU CERTAINLY CAN'T STOP ME.
NOW LET'S SEE JUST HOW *DEEP* THIS EMPATHIC CONNECTION OF YOURS REALLY GOES.

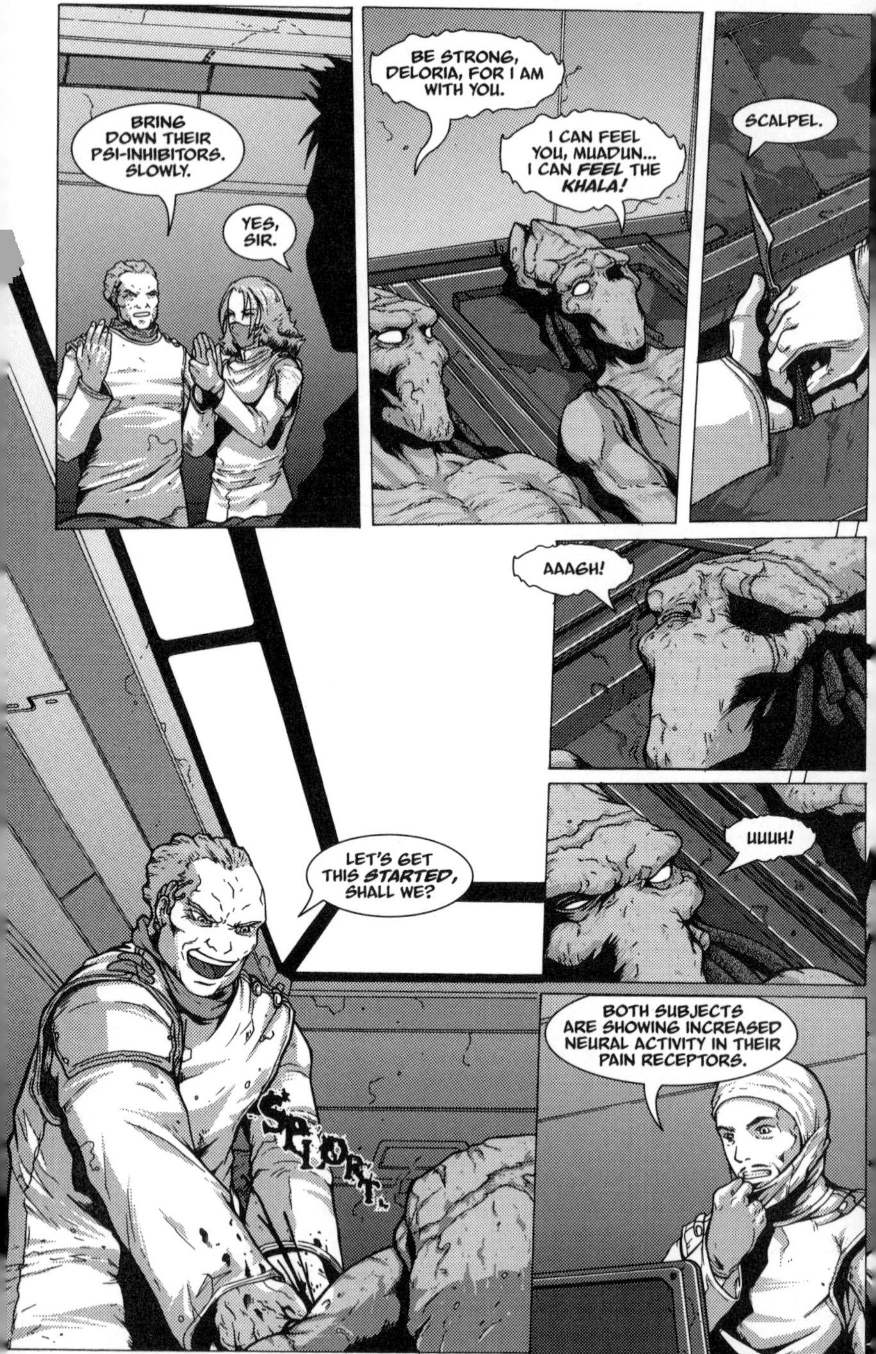
BRING DOWN THEIR PSI-INHIBITORS. SLOWLY.
YES, SIR.
BE STRONG, DELORIA, FOR I AM WITH YOU.
I CAN FEEL YOU, MUADUN... I CAN FEEL THE KHALA!
SCALPEL.
AAAGH!
LET'S GET THIS STARTED, SHALL WE?
UUUH!
BOTH SUBJECTS ARE SHOWING INCREASED NEURAL ACTIVITY IN THEIR PAIN RECEPTORS.

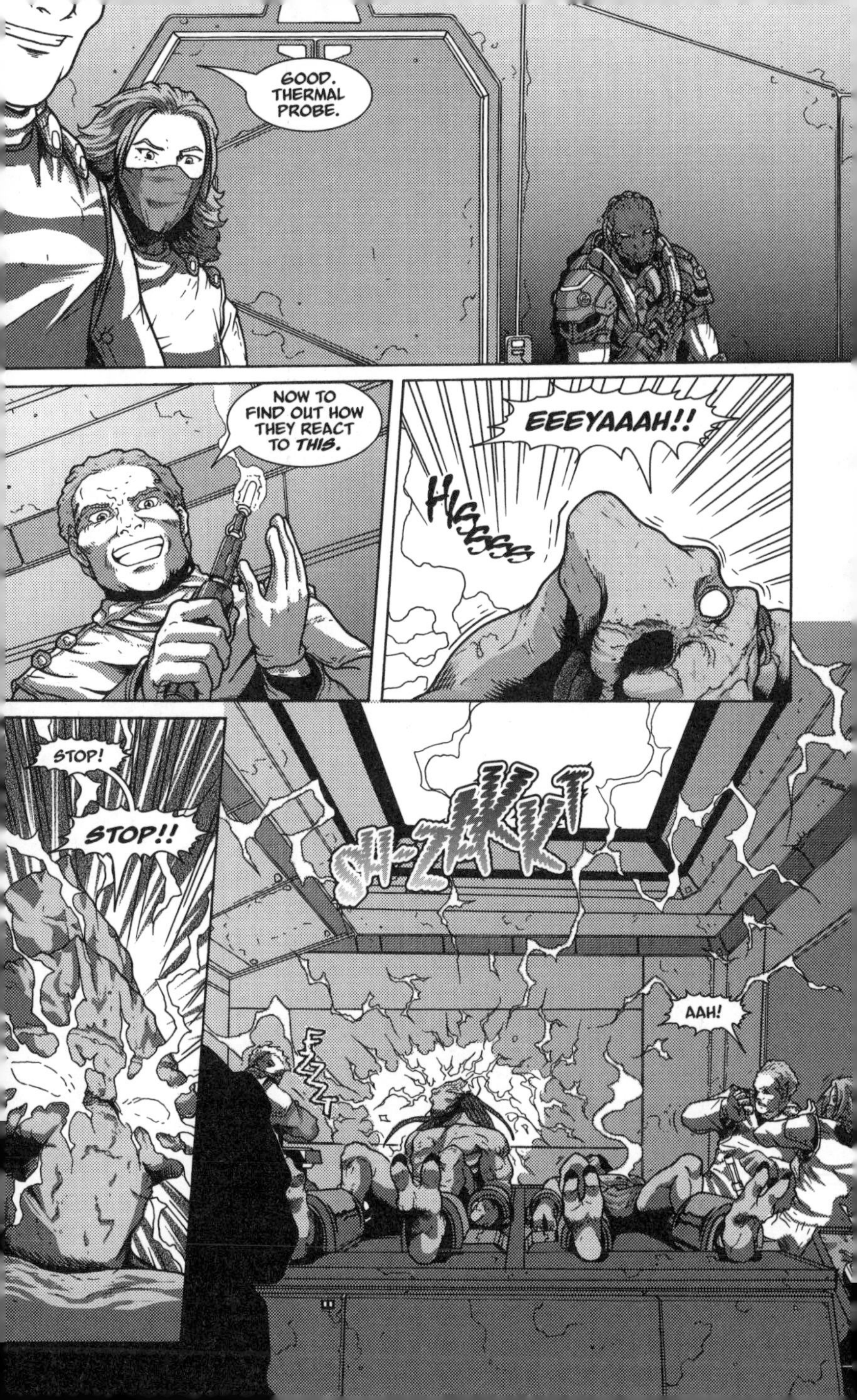
GOOD. THERMAL PROBE.
NOW TO FIND OUT HOW THEY REACT TO THIS.
EEEYAAAH!!
HISSSSS
STOP!
STOP!!
SH-ZAKKT
FZZZT
AAH!

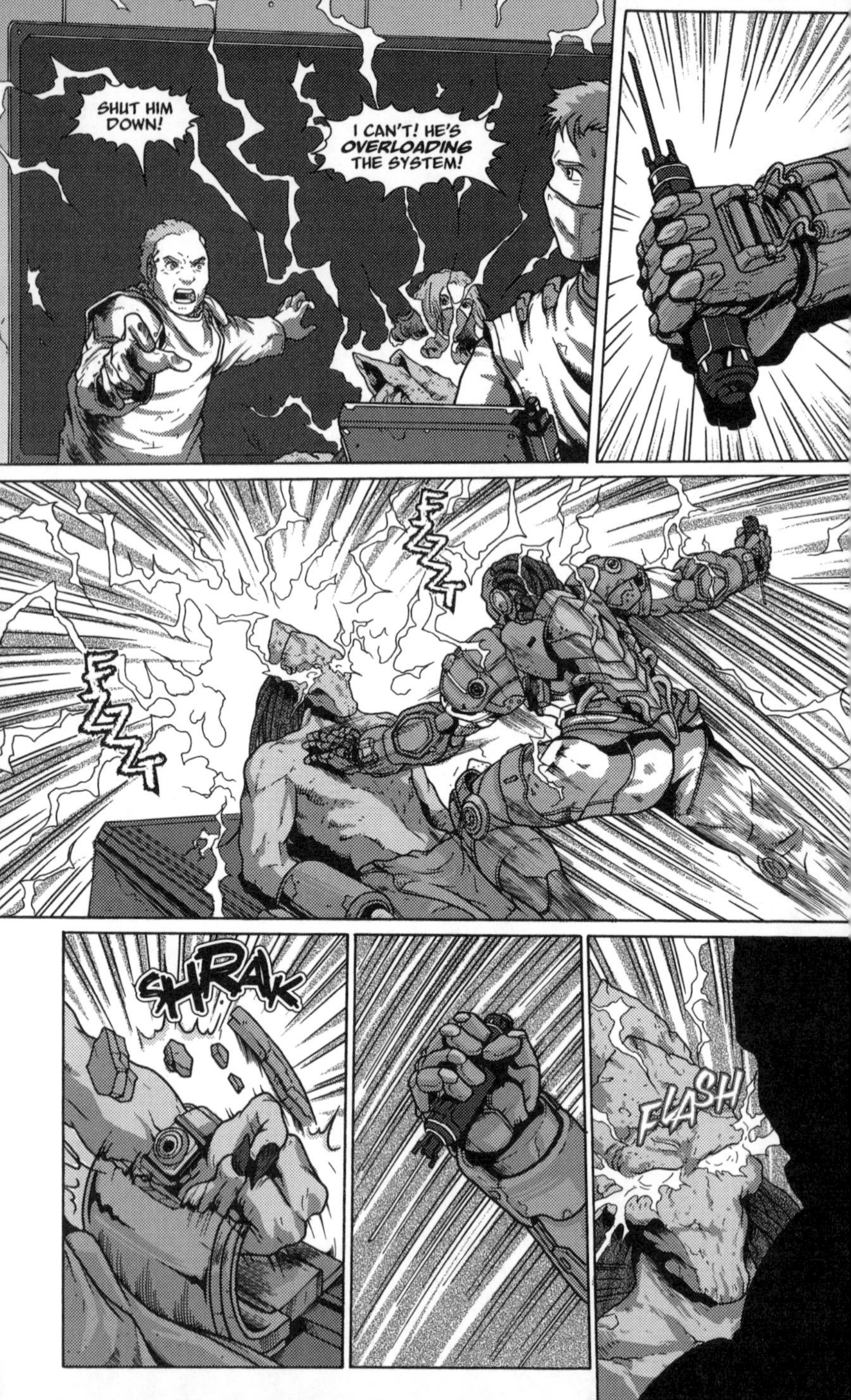
SHUT HIM DOWN!
I CAN'T! HE'S OVERLOADING THE SYSTEM!
FZZZT
FZZZT
SHRAK
FLASH

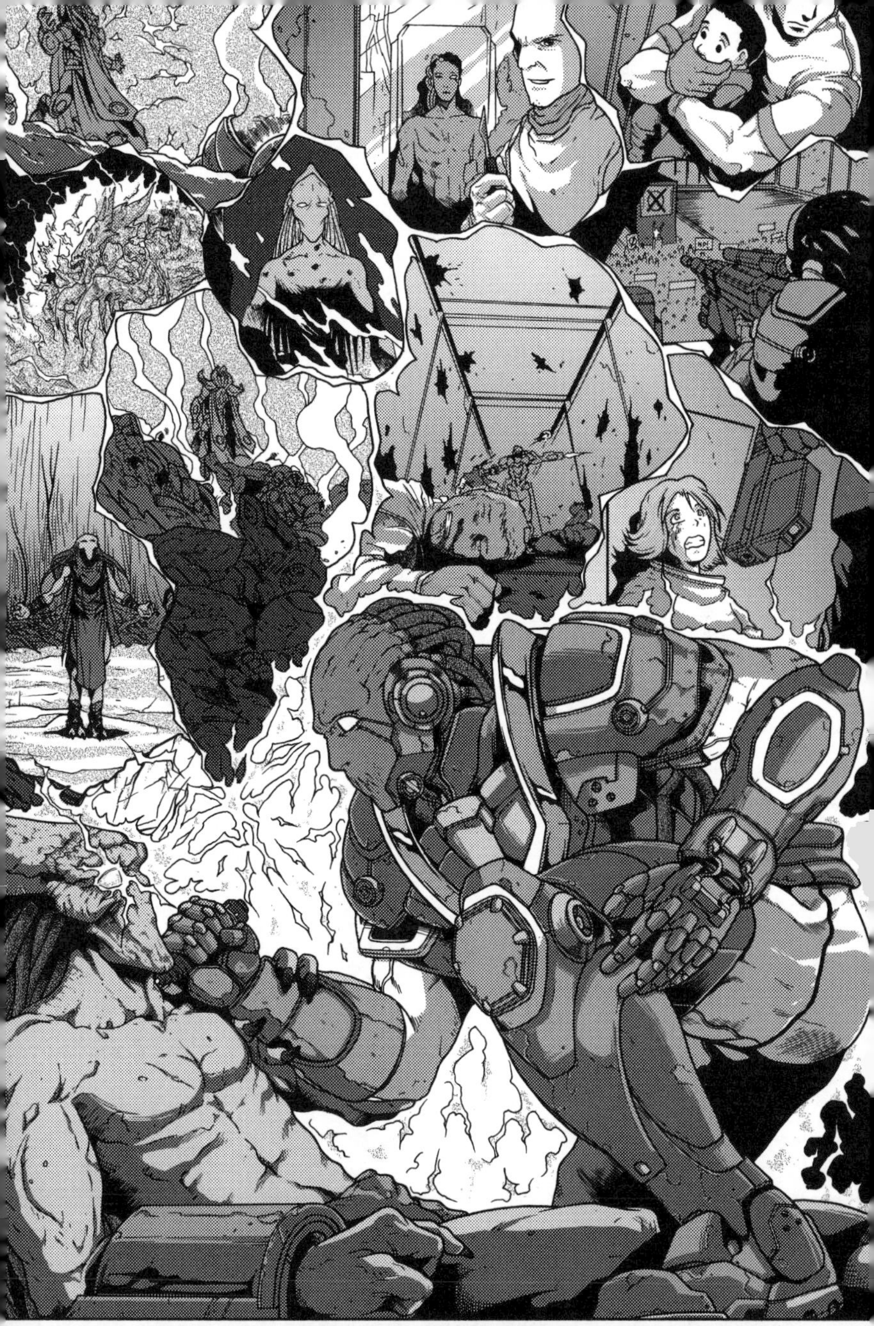

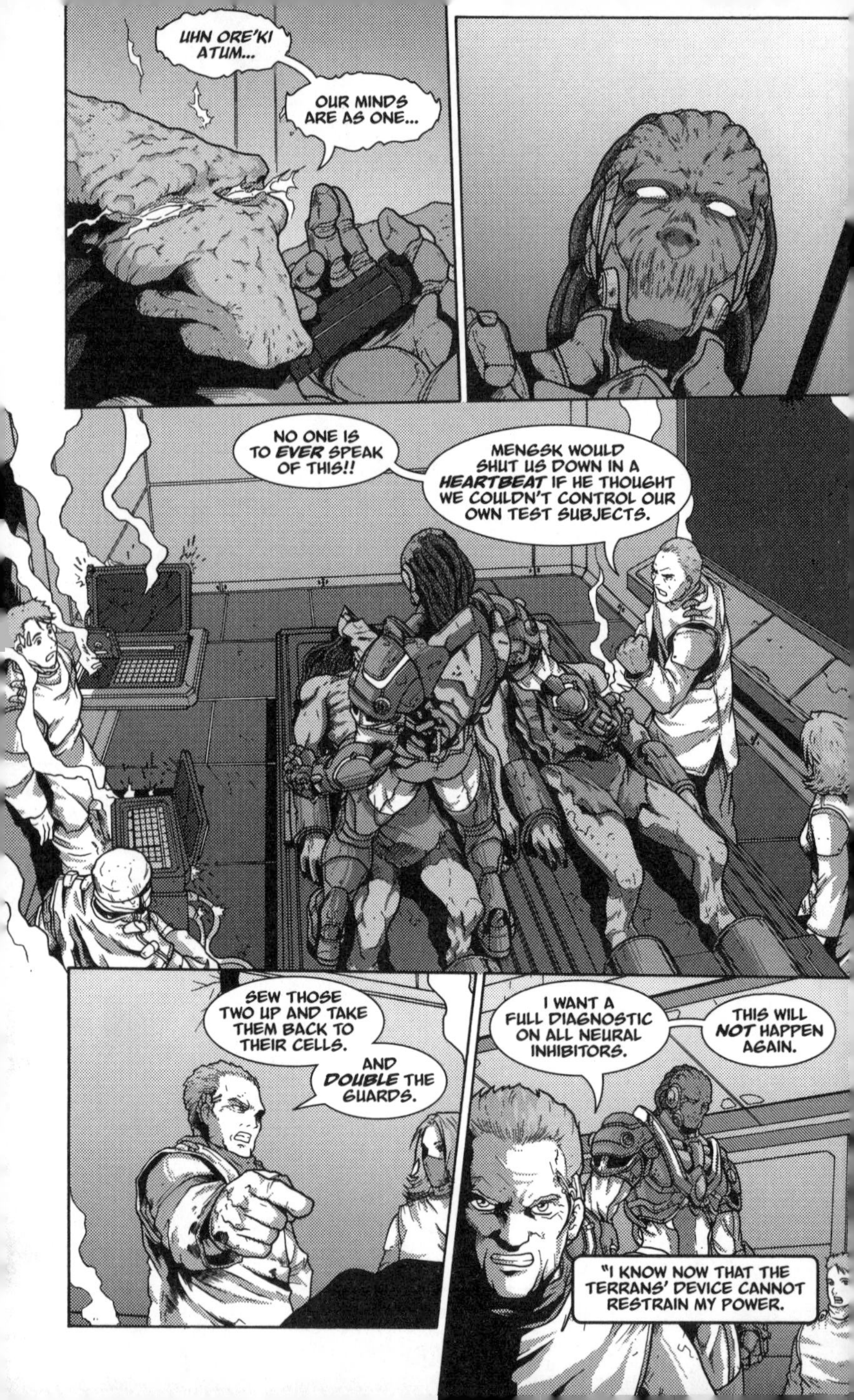
UHN ORE'KI ATUM...
OUR MINDS ARE AS ONE...
NO ONE IS TO EVER SPEAK OF THIS!!
MENGSK WOULD SHUT US DOWN IN A HEARTBEAT IF HE THOUGHT WE COULDN'T CONTROL OUR OWN TEST SUBJECTS.
SEW THOSE TWO UP AND TAKE THEM BACK TO THEIR CELLS.
AND DOUBLE THE GUARDS.
I WANT A FULL DIAGNOSTIC ON ALL NEURAL INHIBITORS.
THIS WILL NOT HAPPEN AGAIN.
"I KNOW NOW THAT THE TERRANS' DEVICE CANNOT RESTRAIN MY POWER.

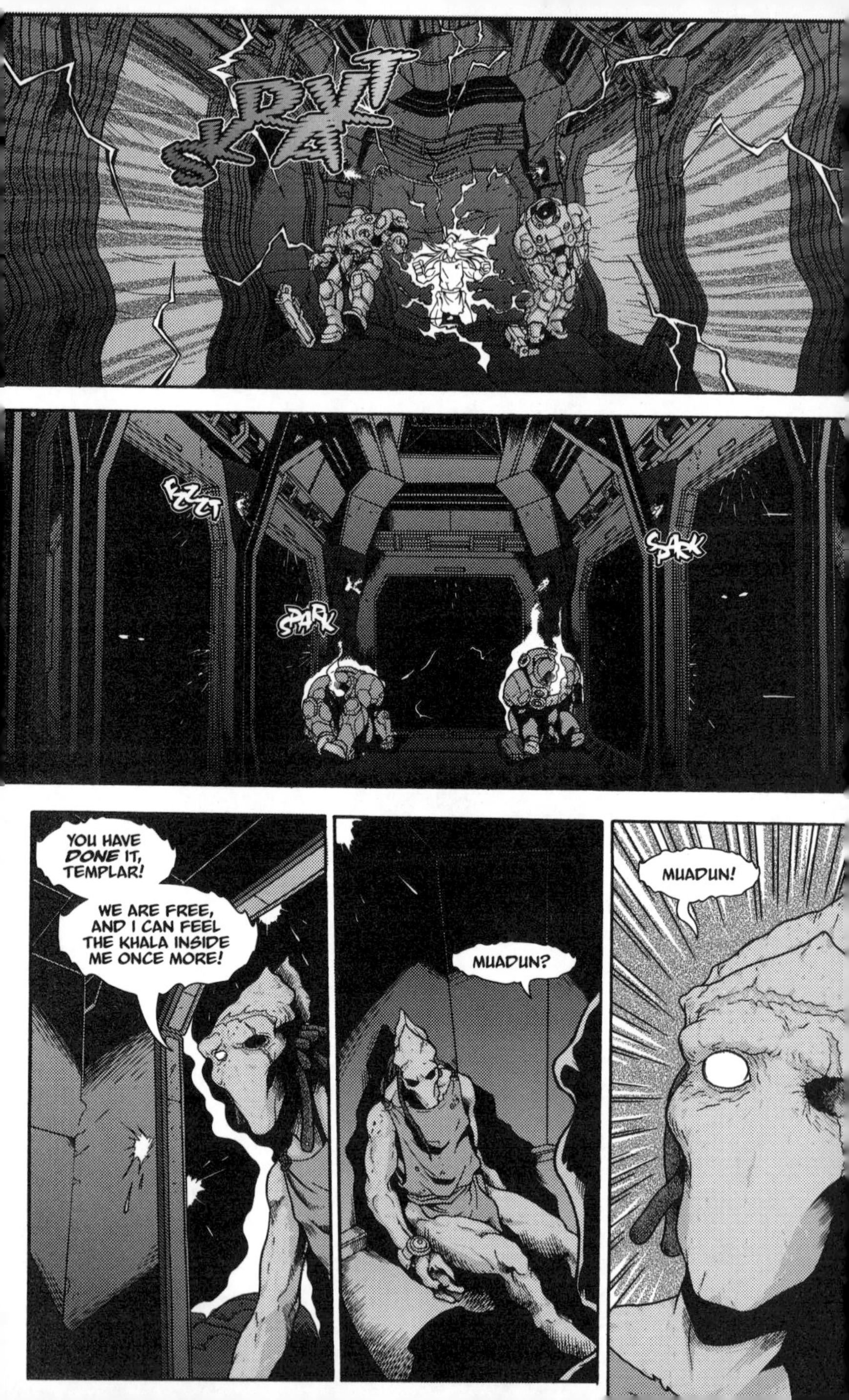
KRAK
KRAK
FZZZT
SPARK
SPARK
YOU HAVE *DONE* IT, TEMPLAR!
WE ARE FREE, AND I CAN FEEL THE KHALA INSIDE ME ONCE MORE!
MUADUN?
MUADUN!

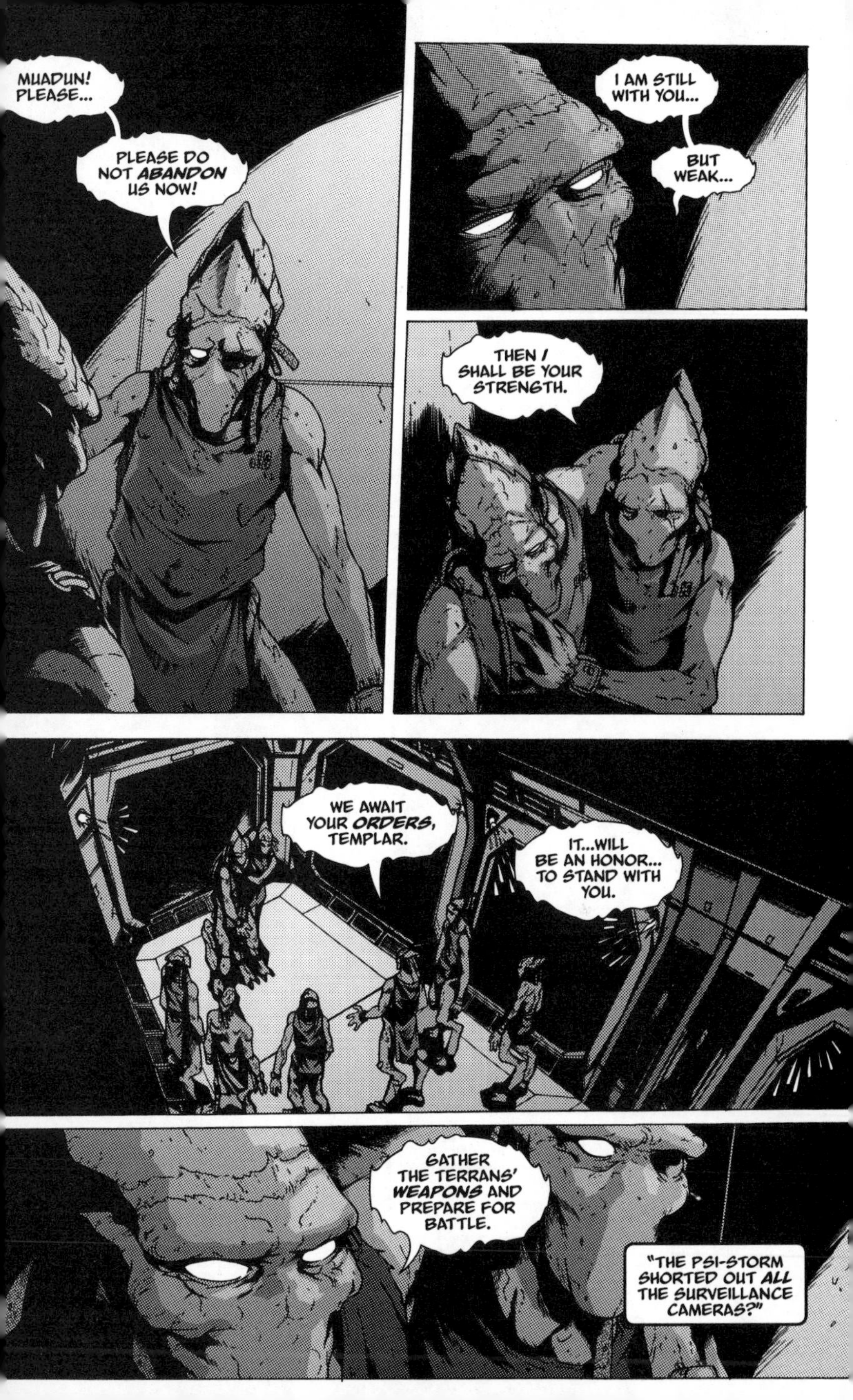

MUADUN! PLEASE...
PLEASE DO NOT ABANDON US NOW!
I AM STILL WITH YOU...
BUT WEAK...
THEN I SHALL BE YOUR STRENGTH.
WE AWAIT YOUR ORDERS, TEMPLAR.
IT...WILL BE AN HONOR... TO STAND WITH YOU.
GATHER THE TERRANS' WEAPONS AND PREPARE FOR BATTLE.
"THE PSI-STORM SHORTED OUT ALL THE SURVEILLANCE CAMERAS?"

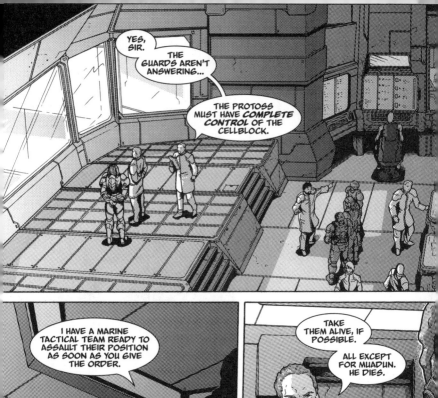

YES, SIR.

THE GUARDS AREN'T ANSWERING...

THE PROTOSS MUST HAVE *COMPLETE CONTROL* OF THE CELLBLOCK.

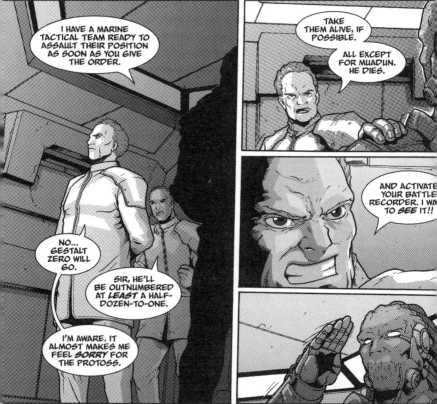

I HAVE A MARINE TACTICAL TEAM READY TO ASSAULT THEIR POSITION AS SOON AS YOU GIVE THE ORDER.

TAKE THEM ALIVE, IF POSSIBLE.

ALL EXCEPT FOR MUADUN. HE DIES.

AND ACTIVATE YOUR BATTLE RECORDER. I WA TO *SEE* IT!!

NO... GESTALT ZERO WILL GO.

SIR, HE'LL BE OUTNUMBERED AT *LEAST* A HALF-DOZEN-TO-ONE.

I'M AWARE. IT ALMOST MAKES ME FEEL *SORRY* FOR THE PROTOSS.

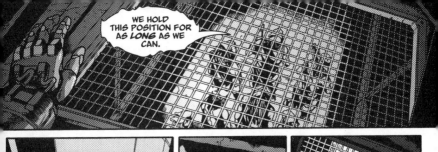

WE HOLD THIS POSITION FOR AS *LONG* AS WE CAN.

BE READY. THE ATTACK MAY COME FROM ANYTIME, *ANYWHERE--*

WAIT...

HE IS *HERE.*

VRRRT

BLAM

BLAM

BLAM

VRRRT

UHN!

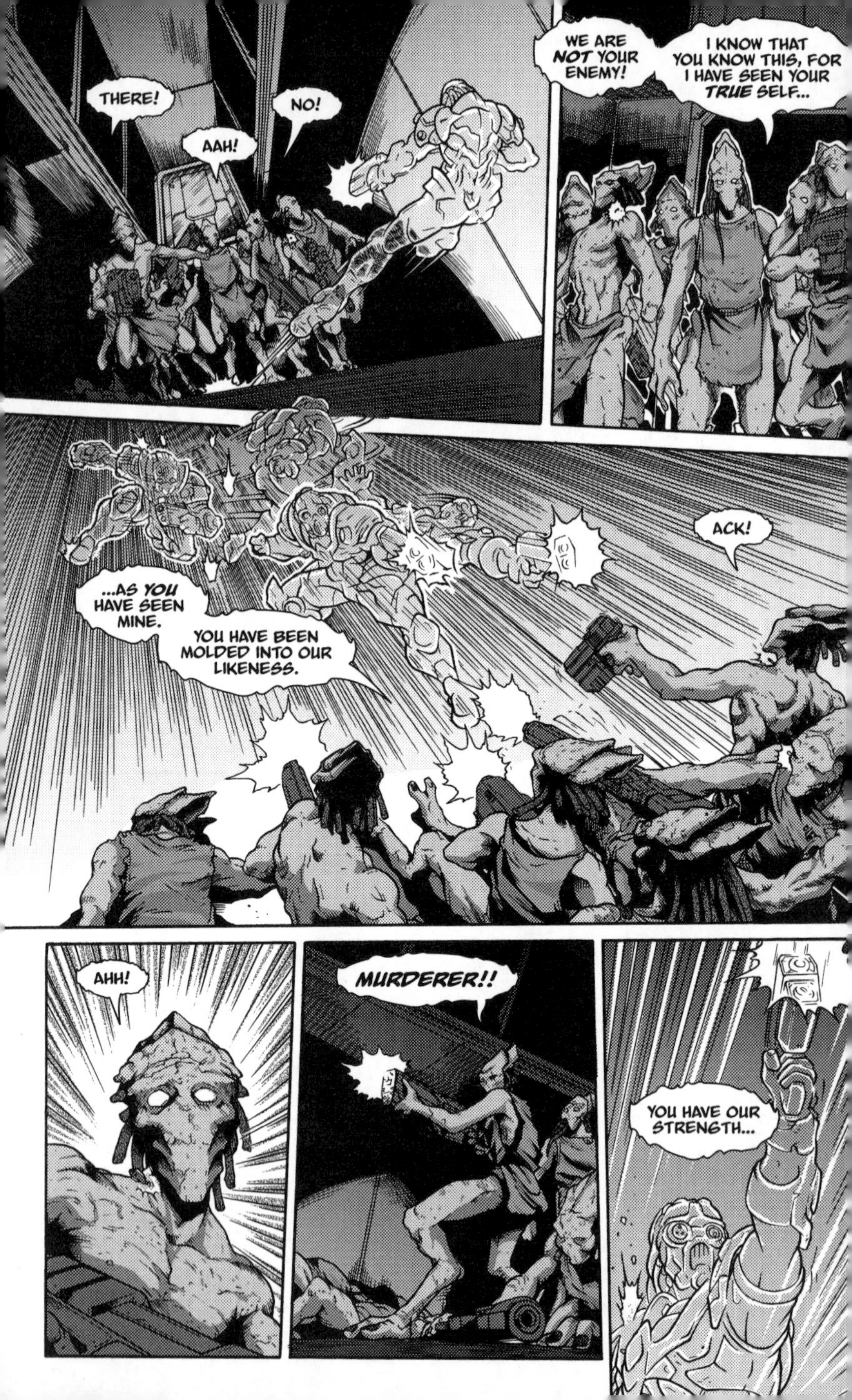

THERE!
AAH!
NO!
WE ARE NOT YOUR ENEMY!
I KNOW THAT YOU KNOW THIS, FOR I HAVE SEEN YOUR TRUE SELF...
...AS YOU HAVE SEEN MINE.
YOU HAVE BEEN MOLDED INTO OUR LIKENESS.
ACK!
AHH!
MURDERER!!
YOU HAVE OUR STRENGTH...

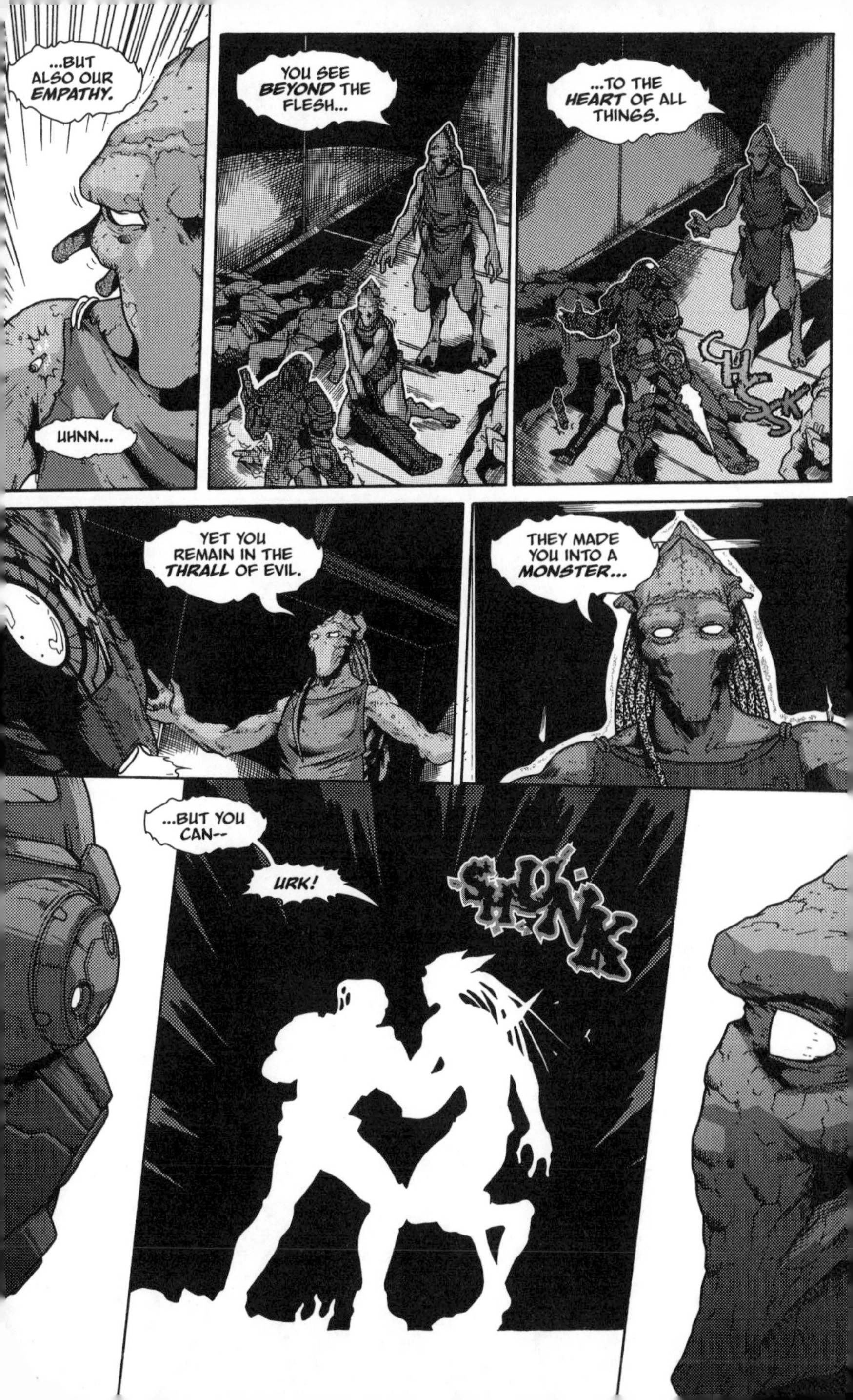
...BUT ALSO OUR EMPATHY.
UHNN...
YOU SEE BEYOND THE FLESH...
...TO THE HEART OF ALL THINGS.
YET YOU REMAIN IN THE THRALL OF EVIL.
THEY MADE YOU INTO A MONSTER...
...BUT YOU CAN--
URK!

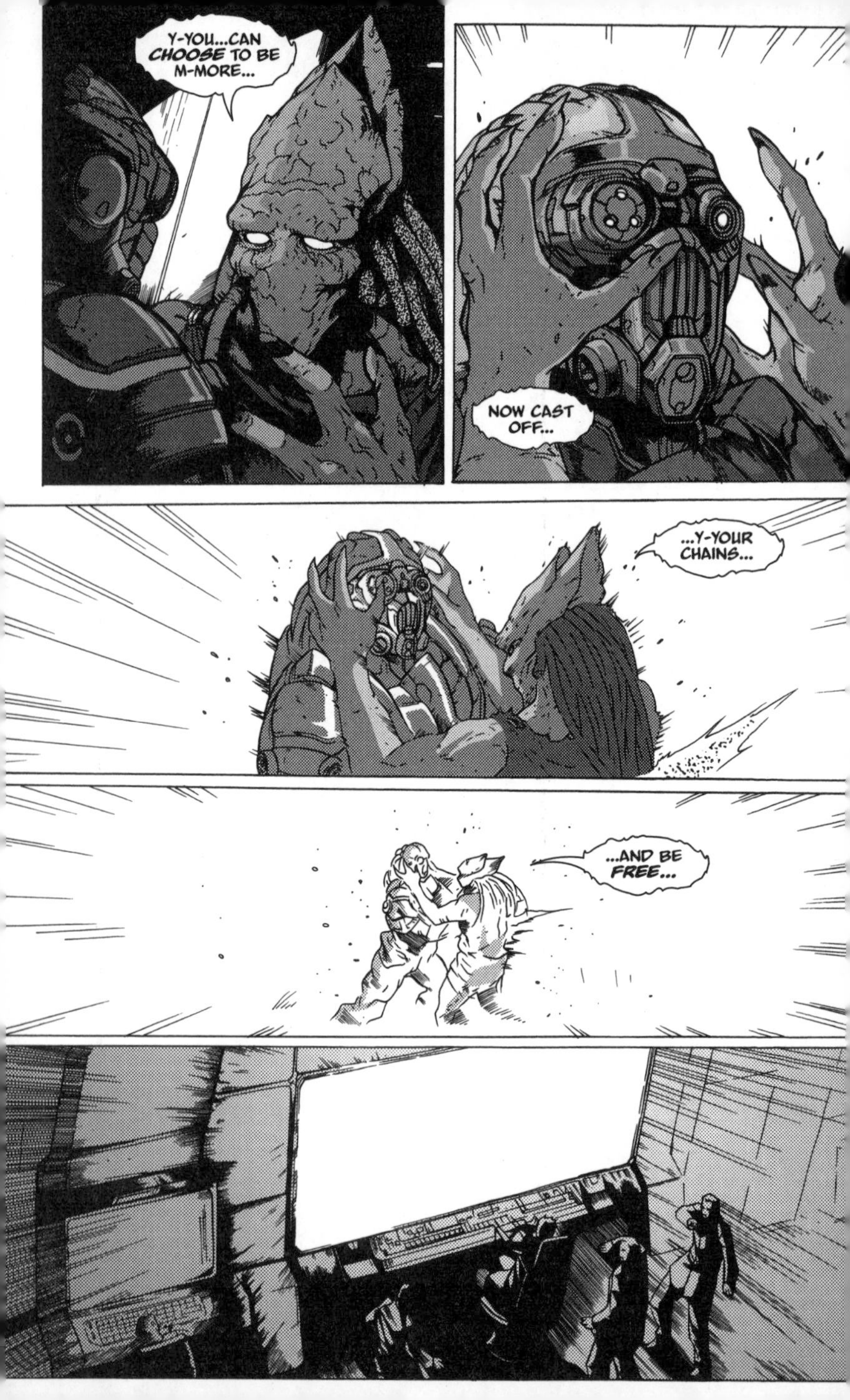
Y-YOU...CAN CHOOSE TO BE M-MORE...
NOW CAST OFF...
...Y-YOUR CHAINS...
...AND BE FREE...

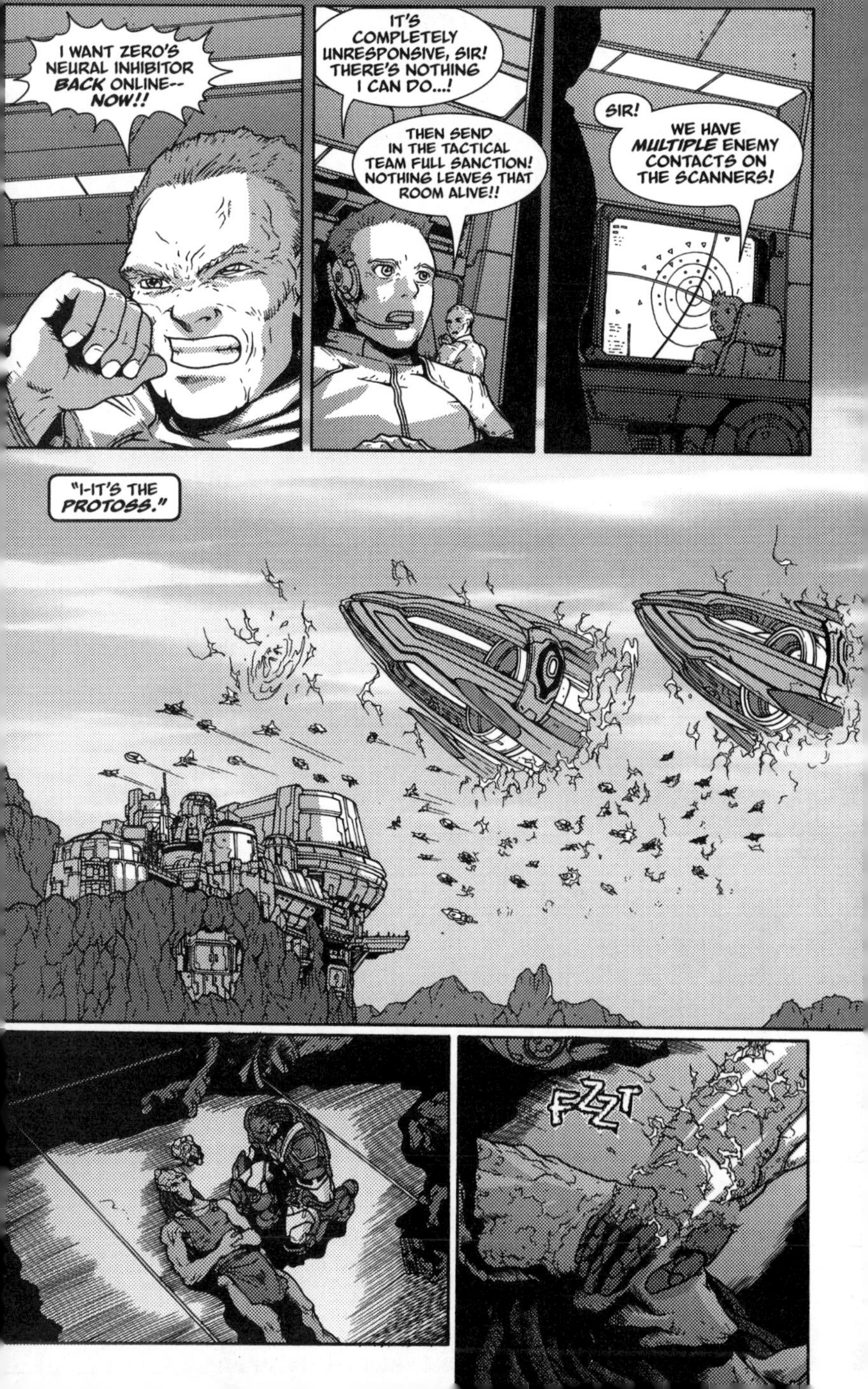
I WANT ZERO'S NEURAL INHIBITOR BACK ONLINE--NOW!!
IT'S COMPLETELY UNRESPONSIVE, SIR! THERE'S NOTHING I CAN DO...!
THEN SEND IN THE TACTICAL TEAM FULL SANCTION! NOTHING LEAVES THAT ROOM ALIVE!!
SIR!
WE HAVE MULTIPLE ENEMY CONTACTS ON THE SCANNERS!
"I-IT'S THE PROTOSS."
FZZT

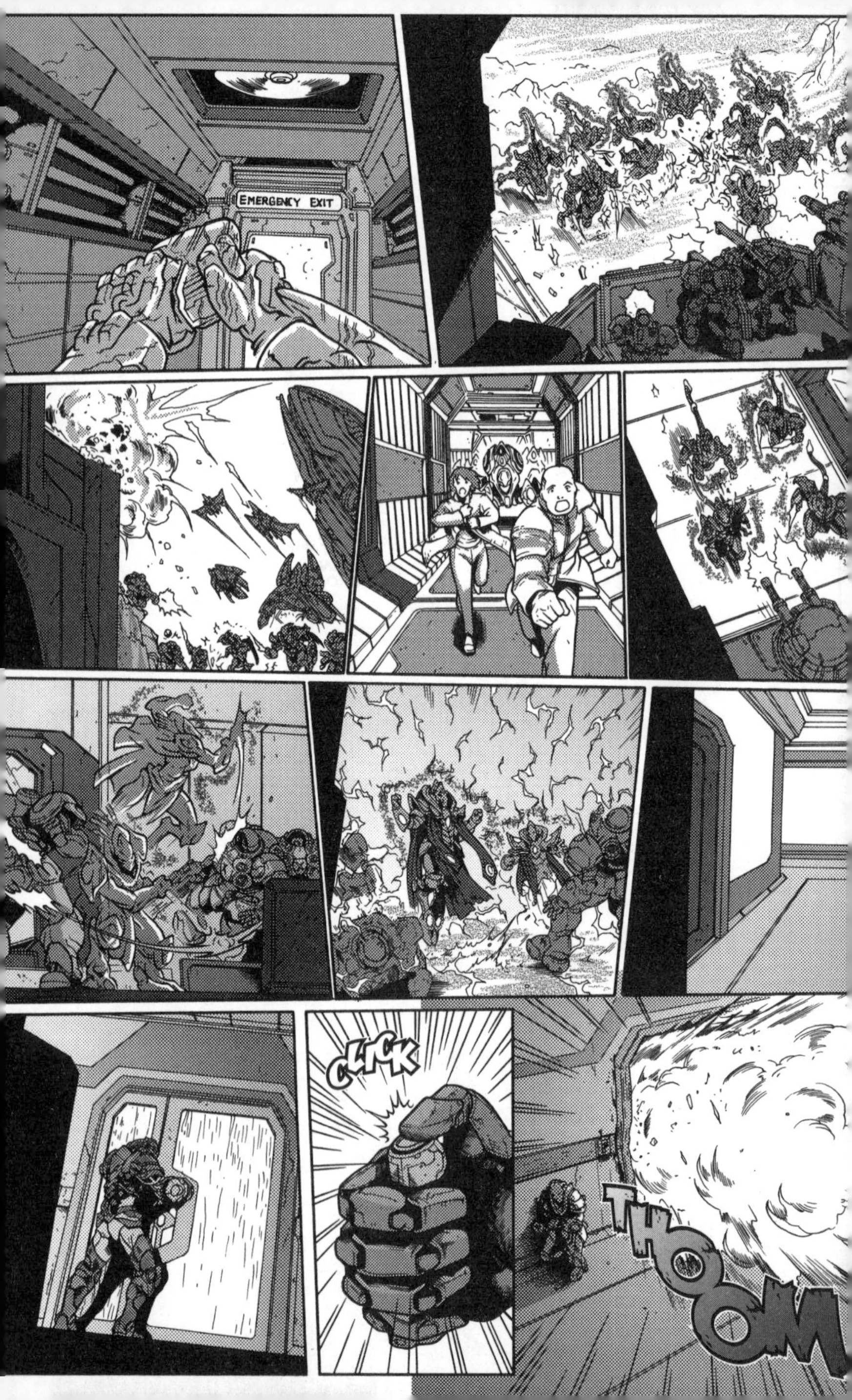
EMERGENCY EXIT
CLICK
THOOM

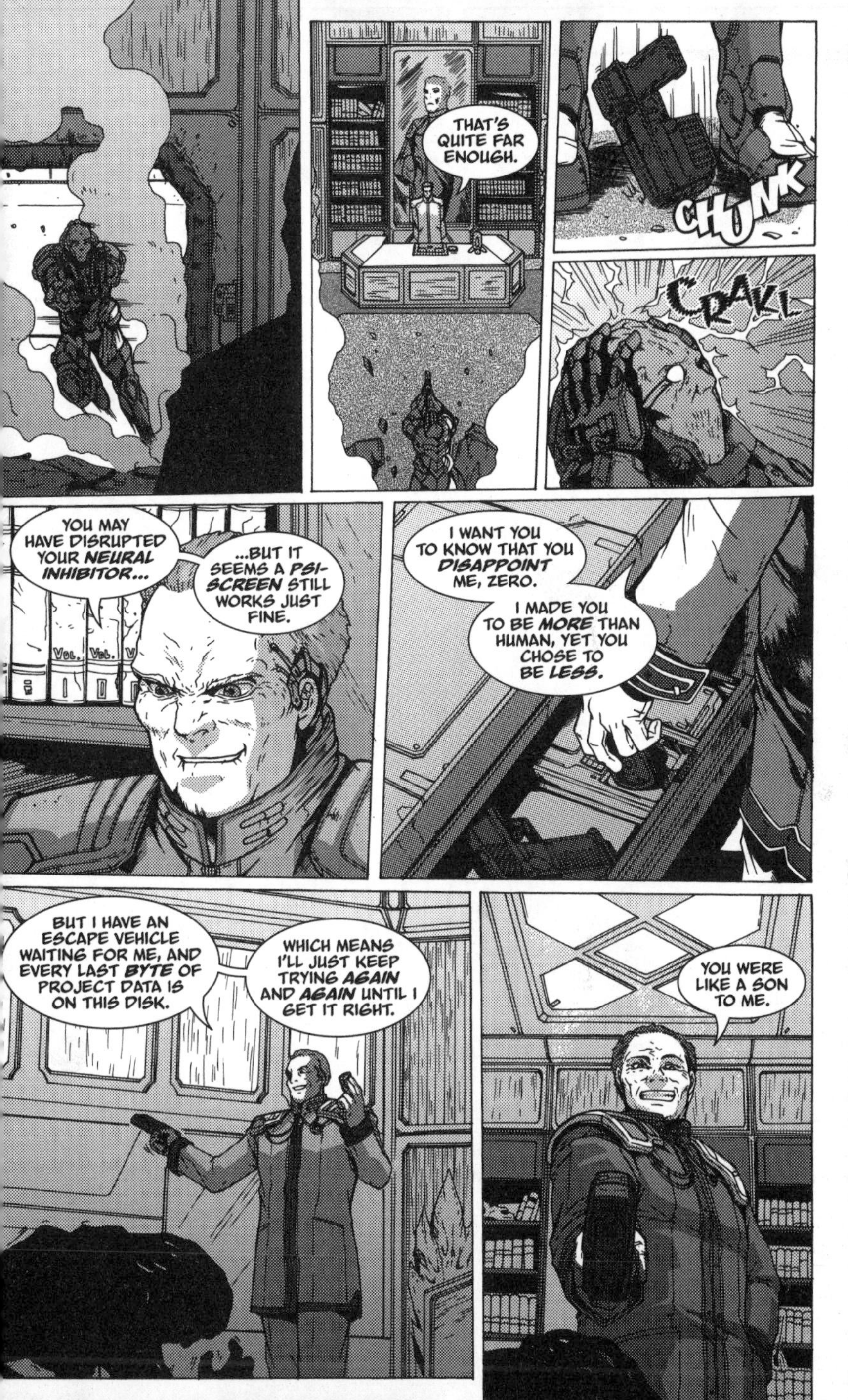
THAT'S QUITE FAR ENOUGH.
CHUNK
CRAKL
YOU MAY HAVE DISRUPTED YOUR NEURAL INHIBITOR...
...BUT IT SEEMS A PSI-SCREEN STILL WORKS JUST FINE.
I WANT YOU TO KNOW THAT YOU DISAPPOINT ME, ZERO.
I MADE YOU TO BE MORE THAN HUMAN, YET YOU CHOSE TO BE LESS.
BUT I HAVE AN ESCAPE VEHICLE WAITING FOR ME, AND EVERY LAST BYTE OF PROJECT DATA IS ON THIS DISK.
WHICH MEANS I'LL JUST KEEP TRYING AGAIN AND AGAIN UNTIL I GET IT RIGHT.
YOU WERE LIKE A SON TO ME.

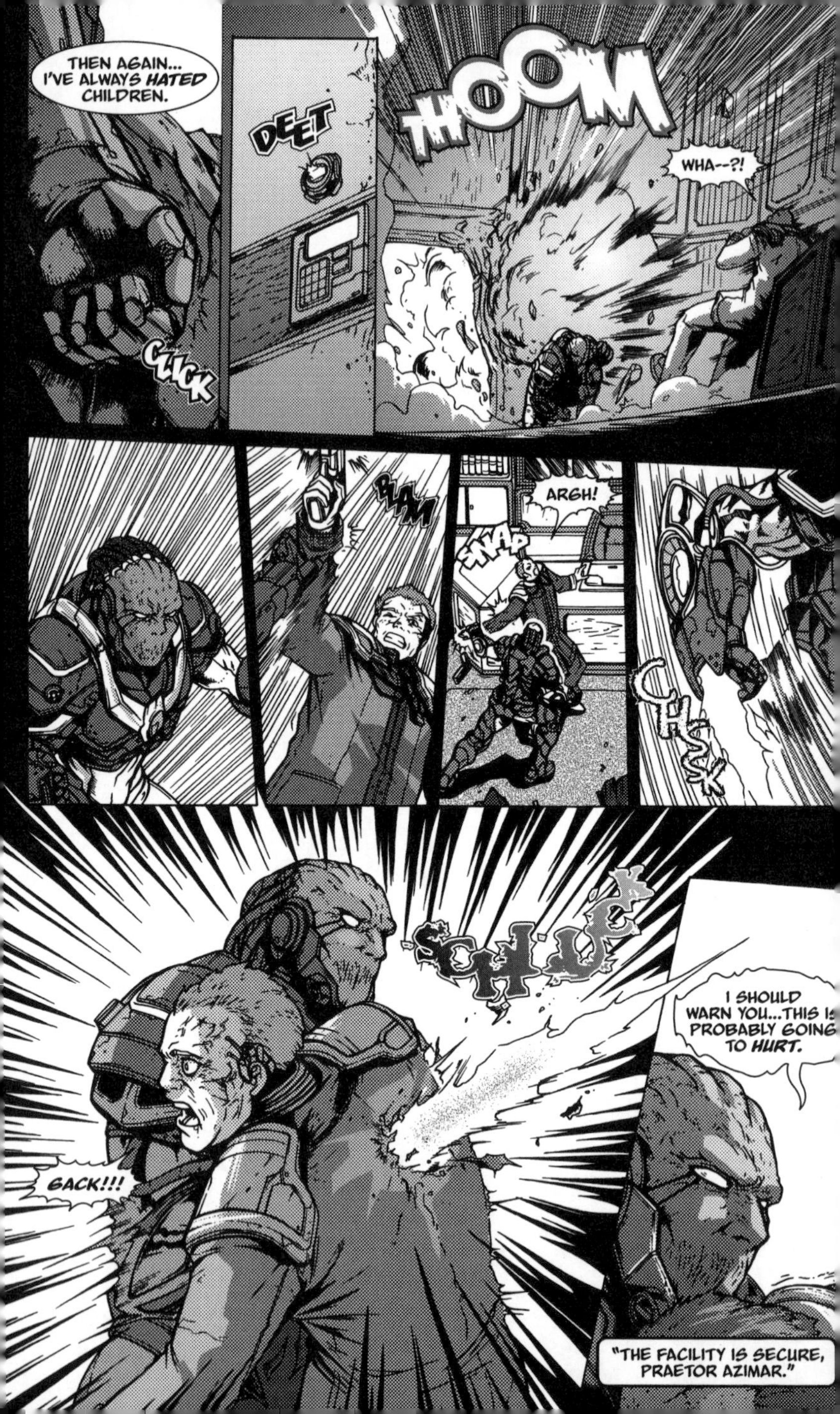
THEN AGAIN... I'VE ALWAYS HATED CHILDREN.
CLICK
DEET
THOOOM
WHA--?!
BLAM
ARGH!
SNAP
CHSK
SCHLUCK
I SHOULD WARN YOU...THIS IS PROBABLY GOING TO HURT.
GACK!!!
"THE FACILITY IS SECURE, PRAETOR AZIMAR."

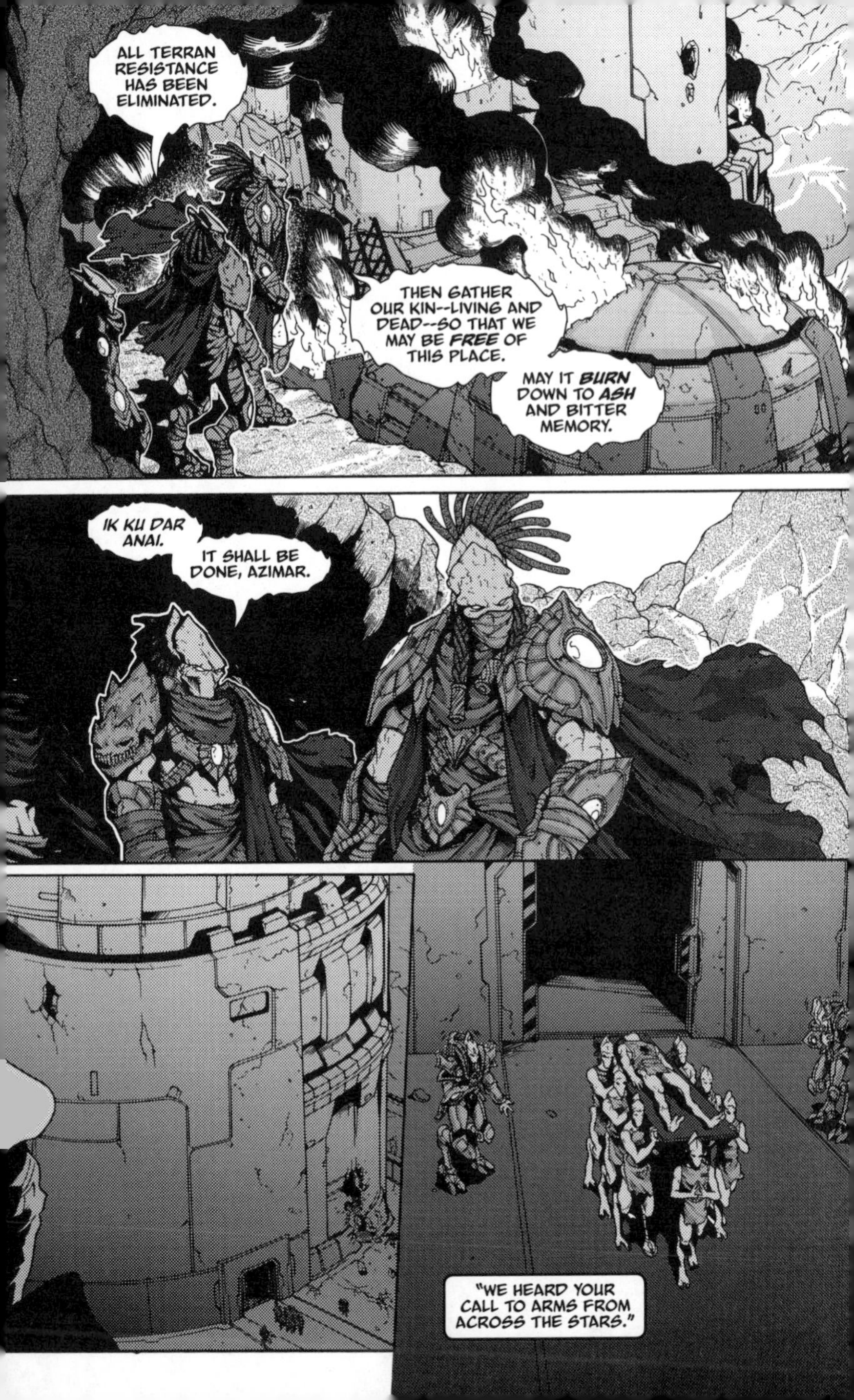
ALL TERRAN RESISTANCE HAS BEEN ELIMINATED.
THEN GATHER OUR KIN--LIVING AND DEAD--SO THAT WE MAY BE *FREE* OF THIS PLACE.
MAY IT *BURN* DOWN TO *ASH* AND BITTER MEMORY.
IK KU DAR ANAI.
IT SHALL BE DONE, AZIMAR.
"WE HEARD YOUR CALL TO ARMS FROM ACROSS THE STARS."

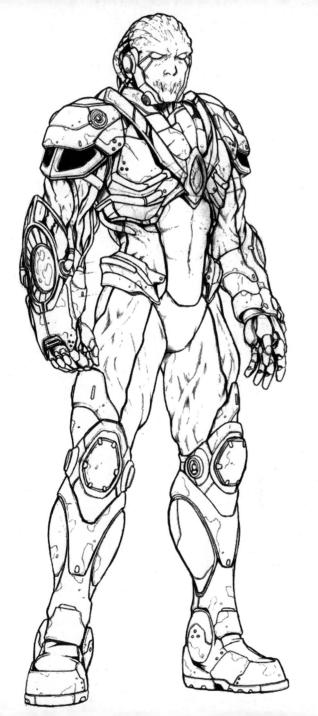

STARCRAFT

FRONTLINE
VOLUME 3

LAST CALL

Written by Grace Randolph

Art by Seung-hui Kye

Letterer: Michael Paolilli

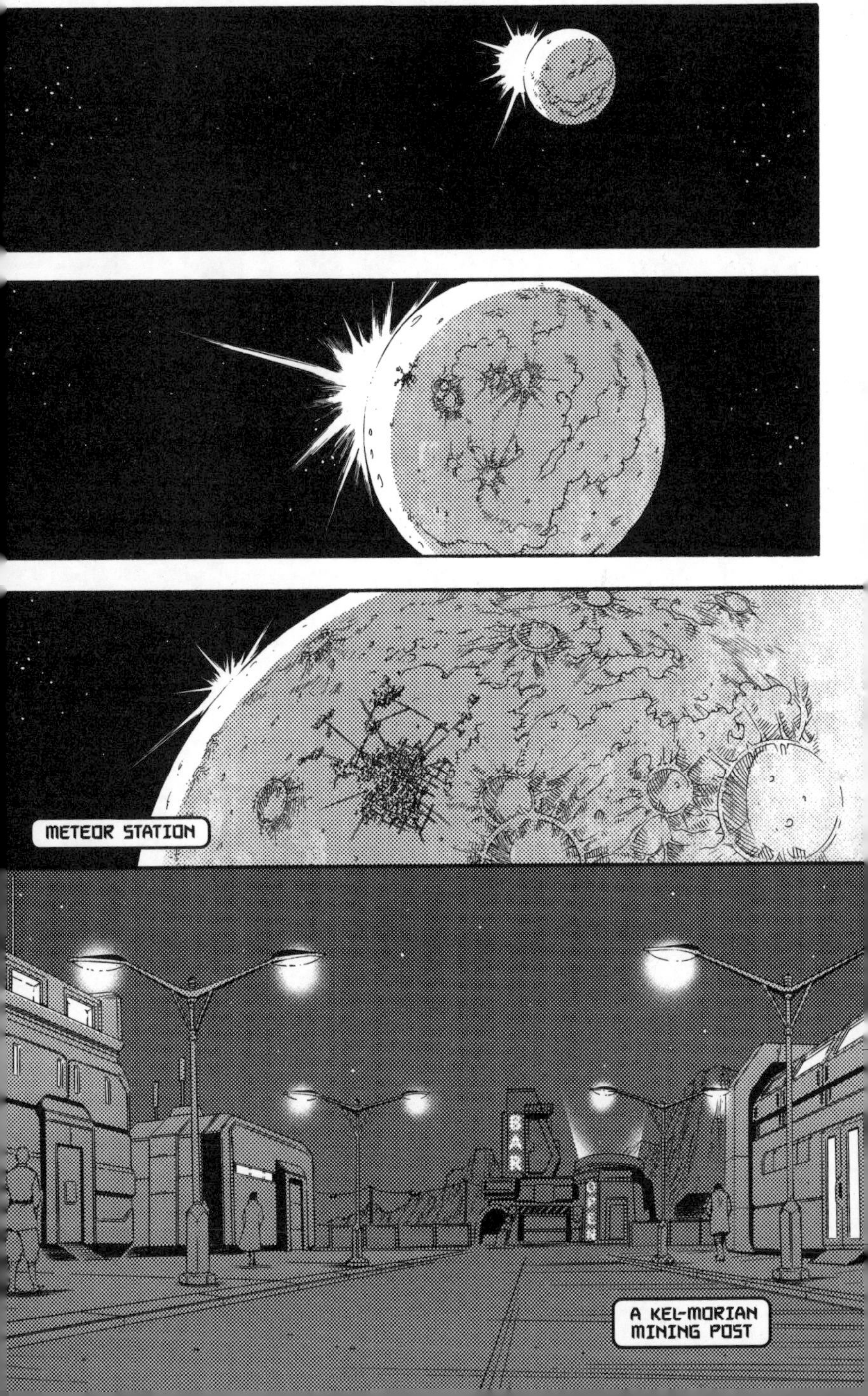
METEOR STATION
BAR
A KEL-MORIAN MINING POST

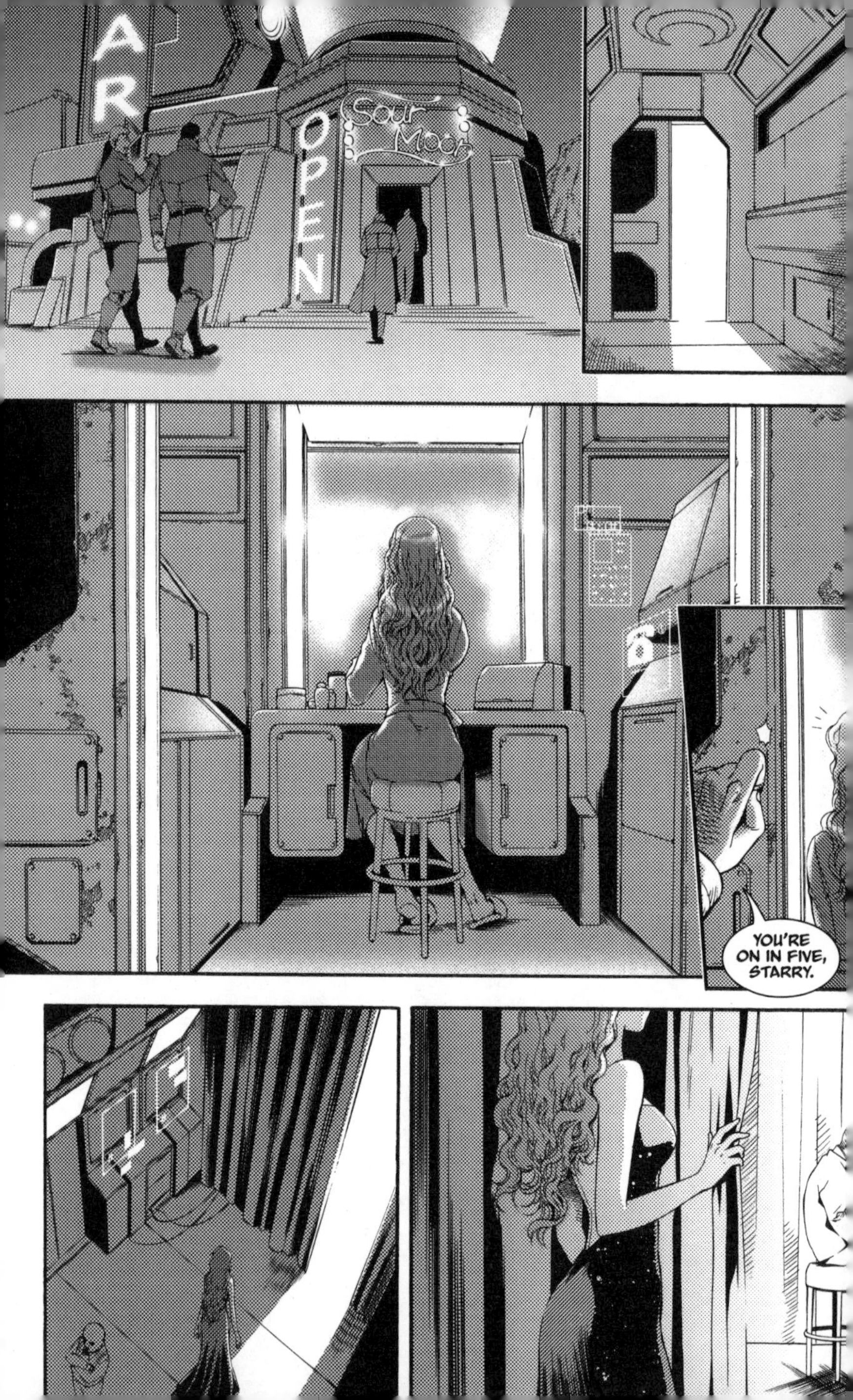
AR
Sour Moon
OPEN
YOU'RE ON IN FIVE, STARRY.

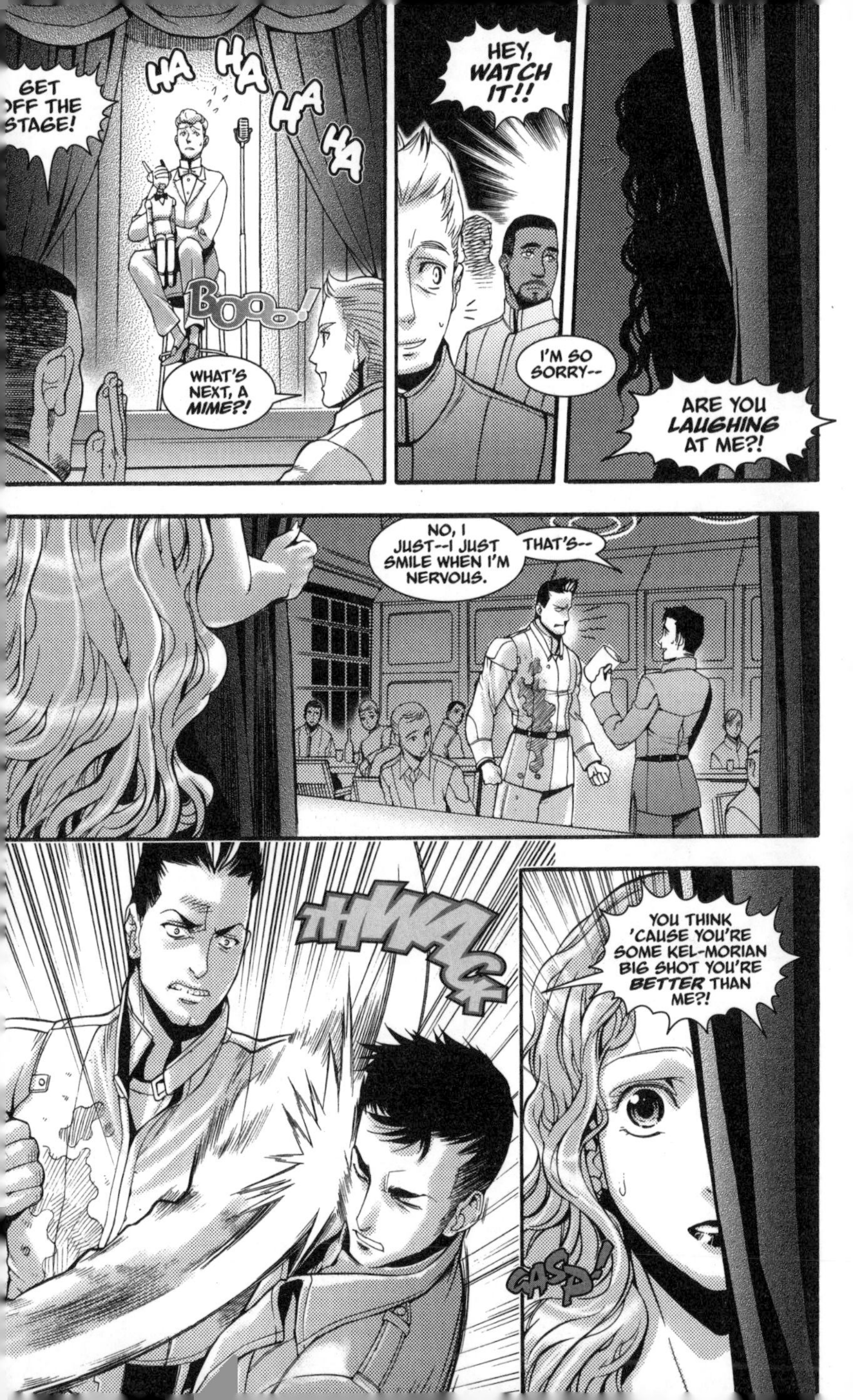
GET OFF THE STAGE!
HA HA HA HA
BOOO!
WHAT'S NEXT, A MIME?!
HEY, WATCH IT!!
I'M SO SORRY--
ARE YOU LAUGHING AT ME?!
NO, I JUST--I JUST SMILE WHEN I'M NERVOUS.
THAT'S--
THWACK
YOU THINK 'CAUSE YOU'RE SOME KEL-MORIAN BIG SHOT YOU'RE BETTER THAN ME?!
GASP!

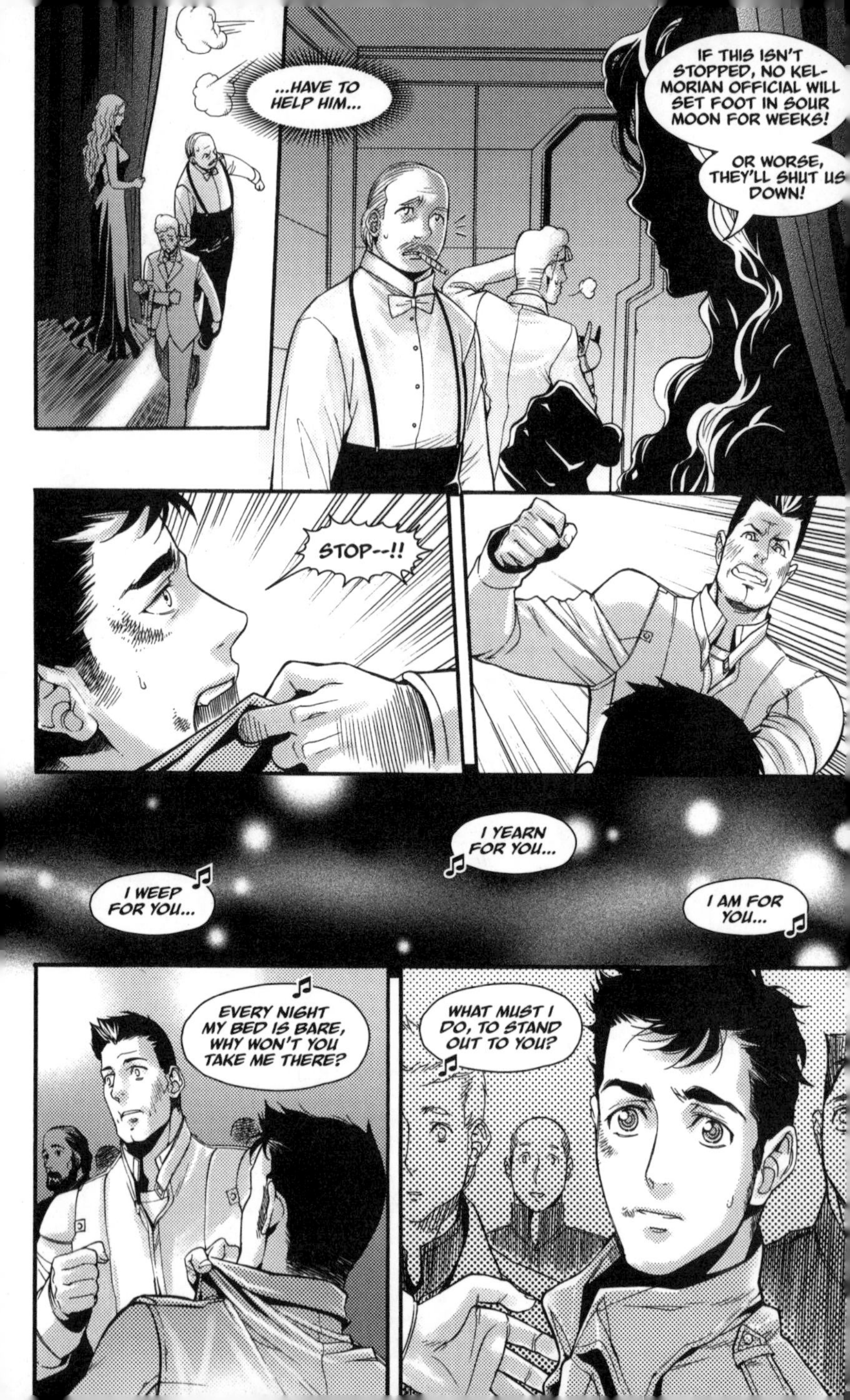
...HAVE TO HELP HIM...
IF THIS ISN'T STOPPED, NO KEL-MORIAN OFFICIAL WILL SET FOOT IN SOUR MOON FOR WEEKS!
OR WORSE, THEY'LL SHUT US DOWN!
STOP--!!
I WEEP FOR YOU...
I YEARN FOR YOU...
I AM FOR YOU...
EVERY NIGHT MY BED IS BARE, WHY WON'T YOU TAKE ME THERE?
WHAT MUST I DO, TO STAND OUT TO YOU?

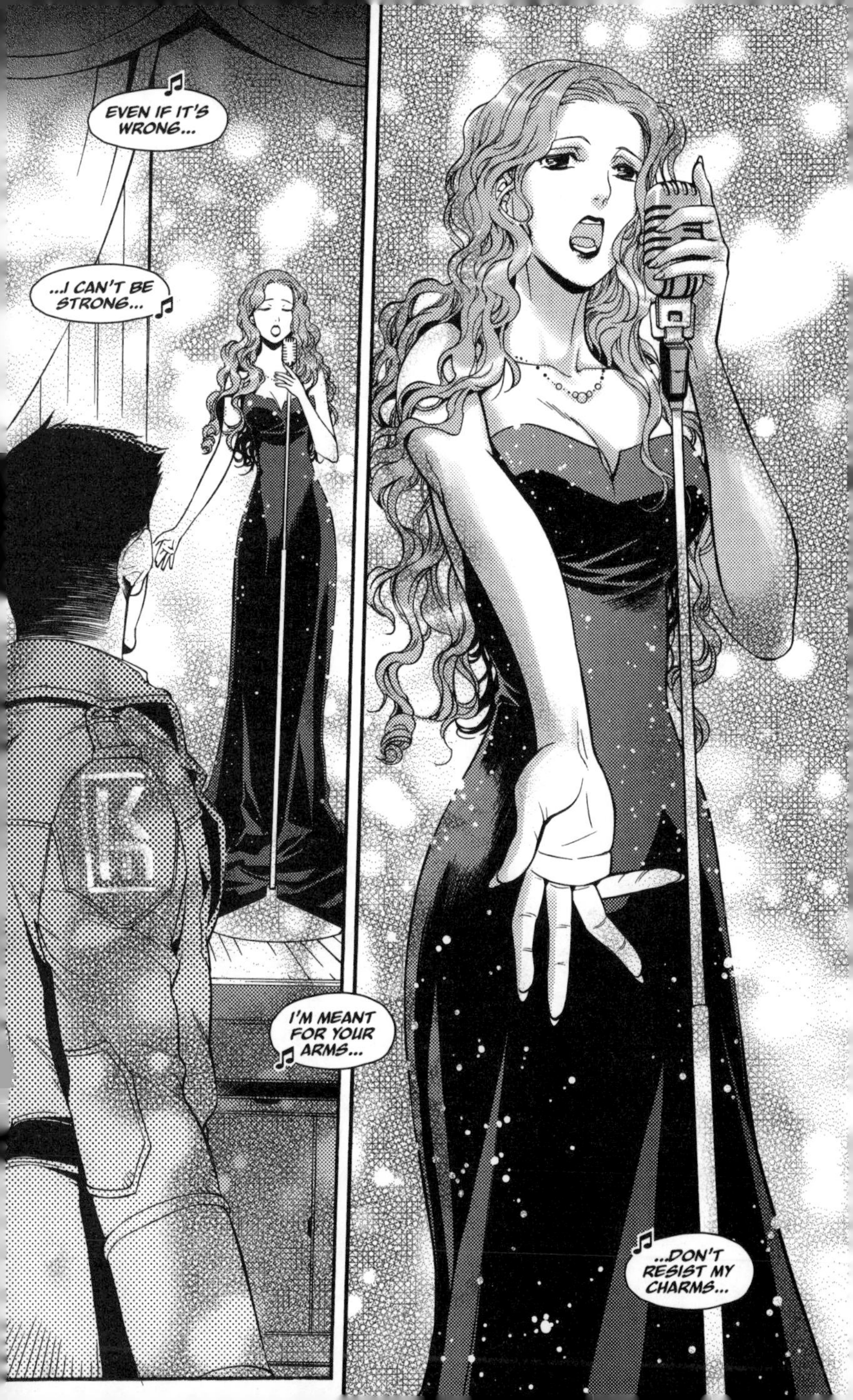
EVEN IF IT'S WRONG...
...I CAN'T BE STRONG...
I'M MEANT FOR YOUR ARMS...
...DON'T RESIST MY CHARMS...

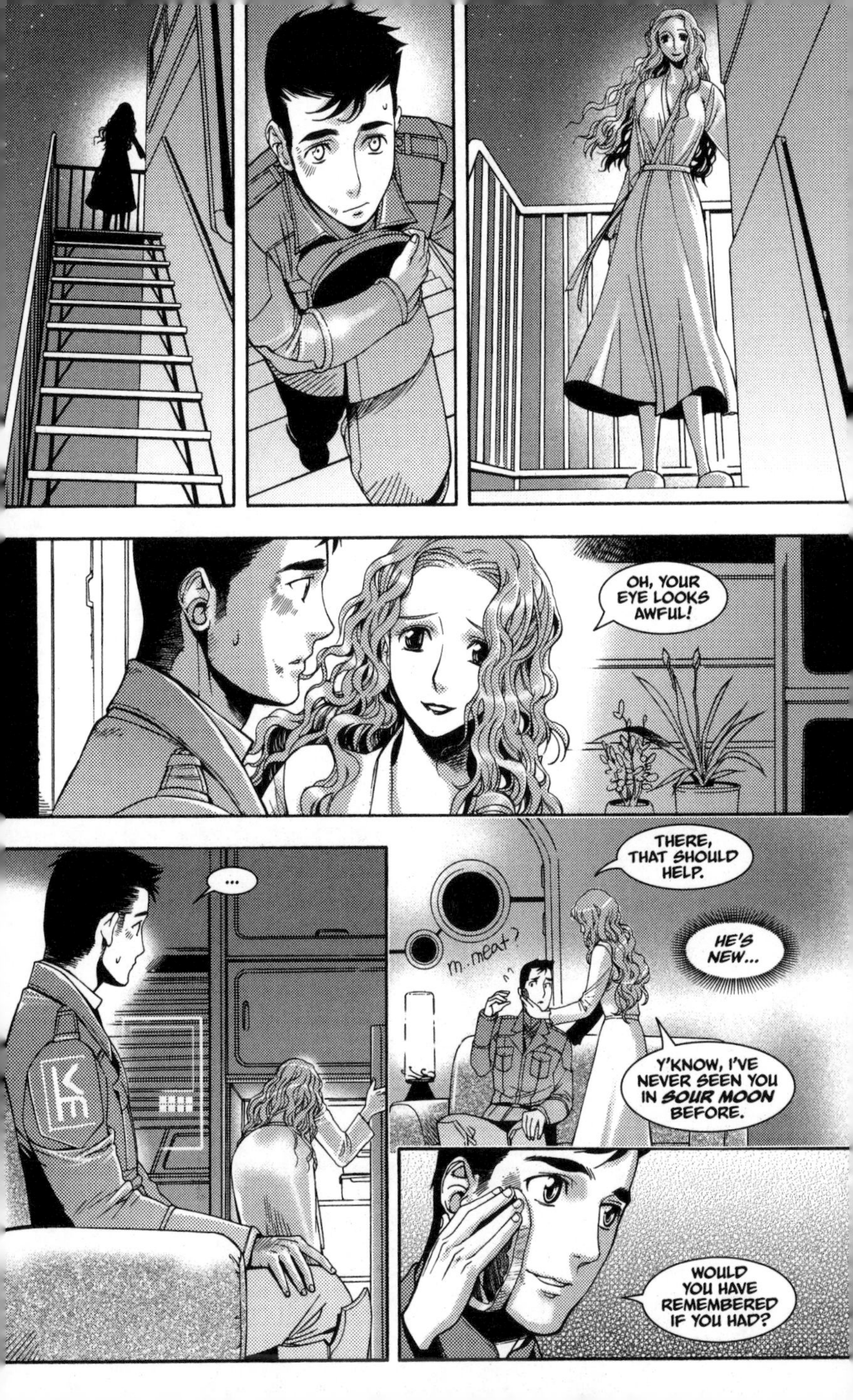
OH, YOUR EYE LOOKS AWFUL!
...
THERE, THAT SHOULD HELP.
HE'S NEW...
m..meat?
Y'KNOW, I'VE NEVER SEEN YOU IN SOUR MOON BEFORE.
WOULD YOU HAVE REMEMBERED IF YOU HAD?

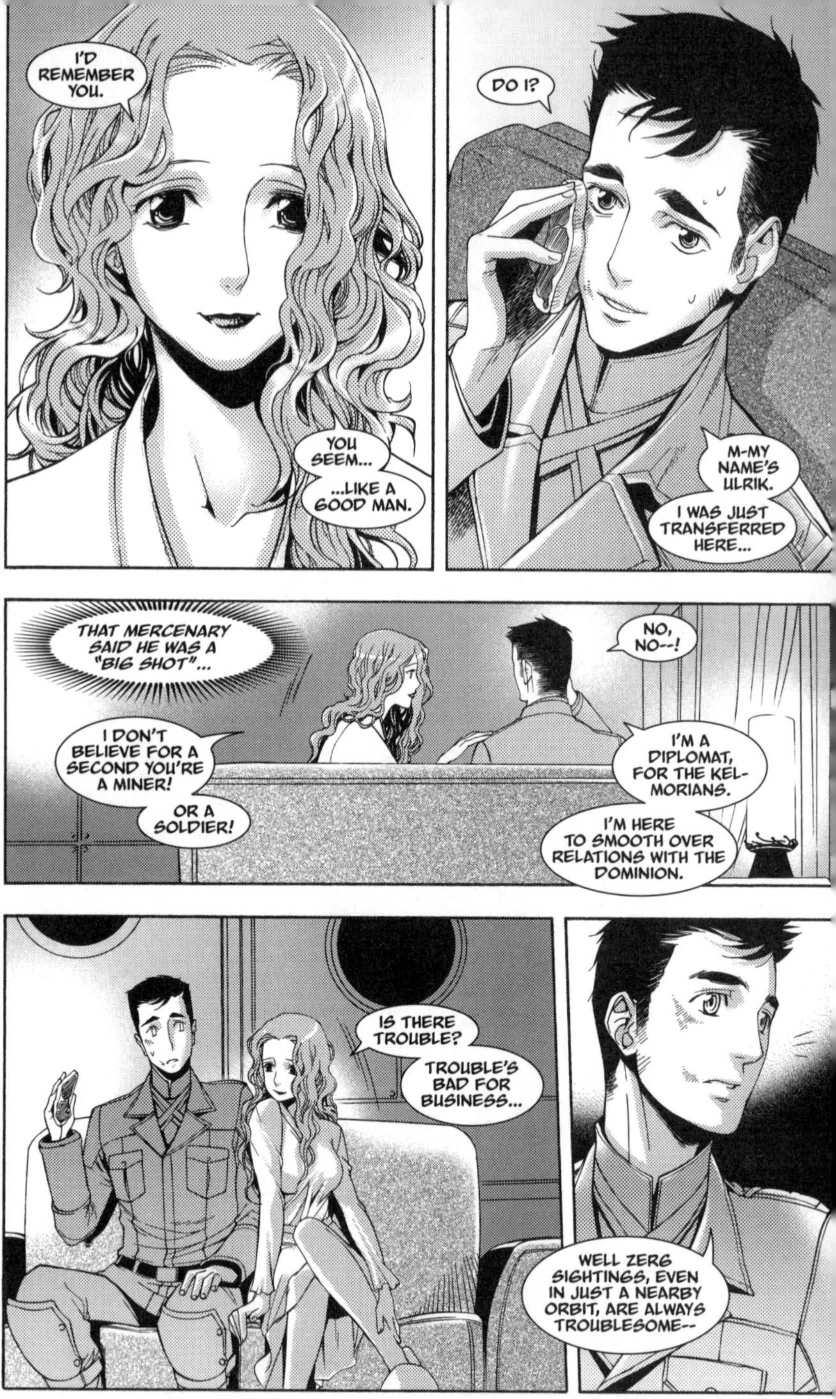
I'D REMEMBER YOU.
DO I?
YOU SEEM...
...LIKE A GOOD MAN.
M-MY NAME'S ULRIK.
I WAS JUST TRANSFERRED HERE...
THAT MERCENARY SAID HE WAS A "BIG SHOT"...
I DON'T BELIEVE FOR A SECOND YOU'RE A MINER!
OR A SOLDIER!
NO, NO--!
I'M A DIPLOMAT, FOR THE KEL-MORIANS.
I'M HERE TO SMOOTH OVER RELATIONS WITH THE DOMINION.
IS THERE TROUBLE?
TROUBLE'S BAD FOR BUSINESS...
WELL ZERG SIGHTINGS, EVEN IN JUST A NEARBY ORBIT, ARE ALWAYS TROUBLESOME--

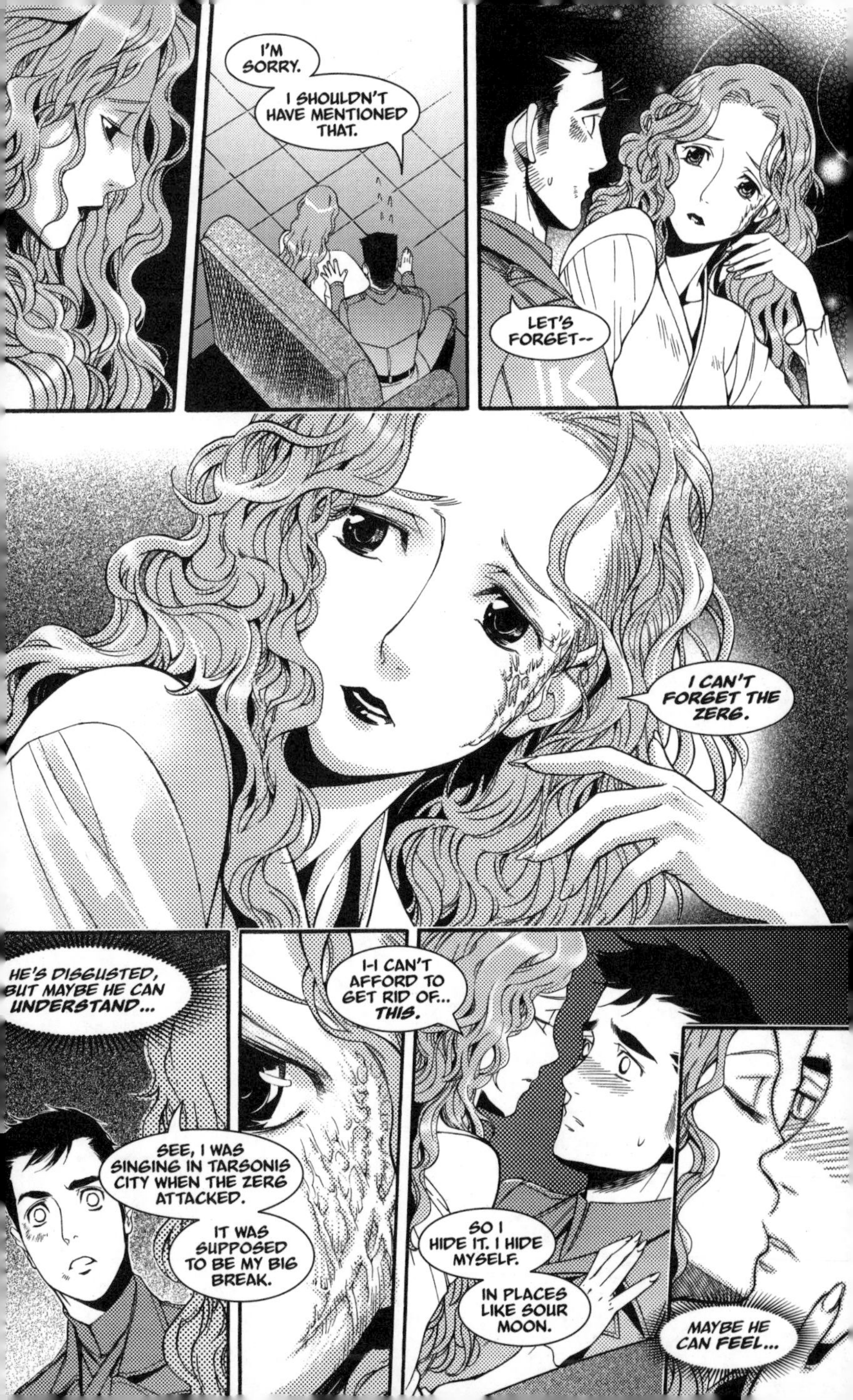
I'M SORRY.
I SHOULDN'T HAVE MENTIONED THAT.
LET'S FORGET--
I CAN'T FORGET THE ZERG.
HE'S DISGUSTED, BUT MAYBE HE CAN UNDERSTAND...
I-I CAN'T AFFORD TO GET RID OF... THIS.
SEE, I WAS SINGING IN TARSONIS CITY WHEN THE ZERG ATTACKED.
IT WAS SUPPOSED TO BE MY BIG BREAK.
SO I HIDE IT. I HIDE MYSELF.
IN PLACES LIKE SOUR MOON.
MAYBE HE CAN FEEL...

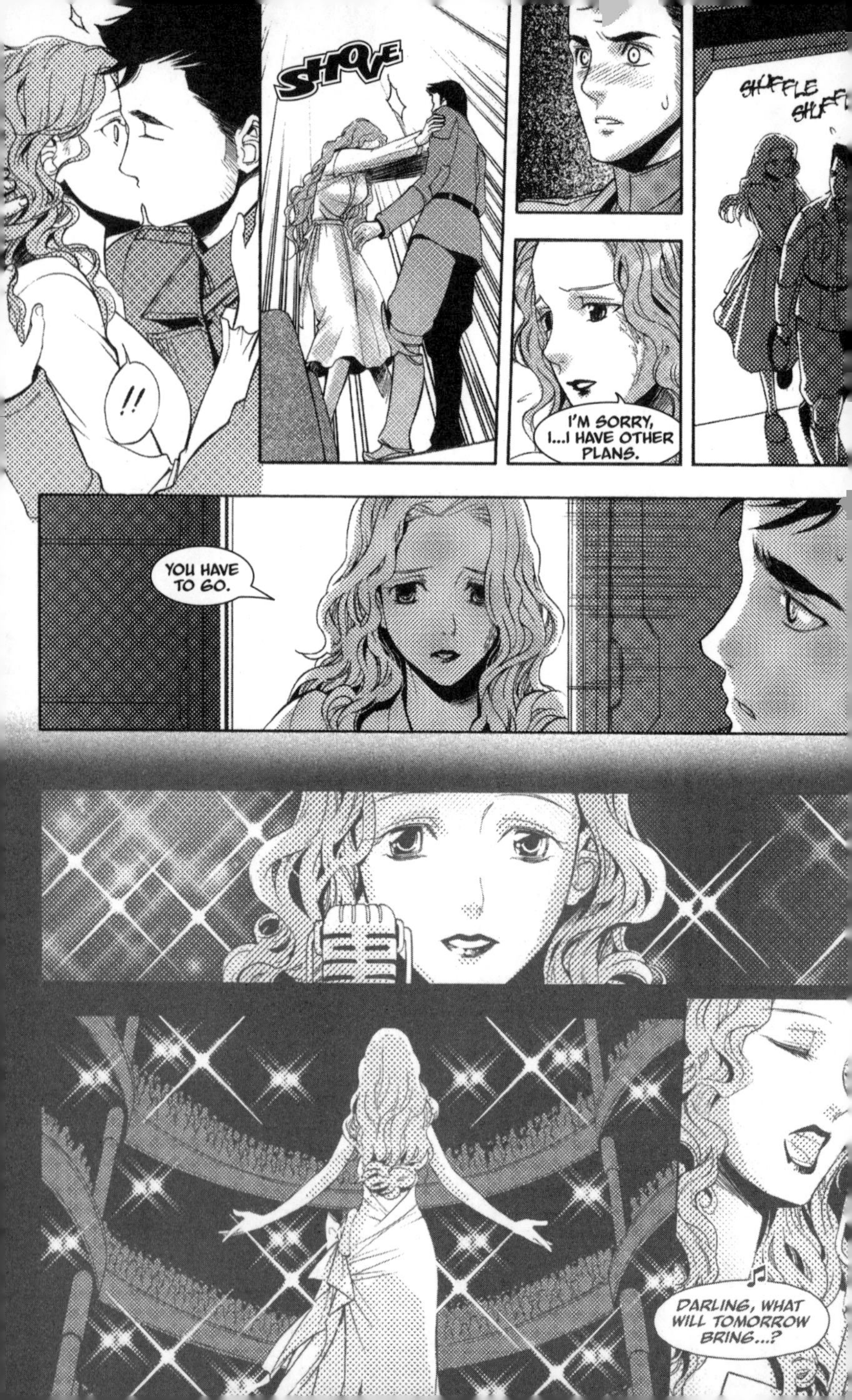
!!
SHOVE
I'M SORRY, I...I HAVE OTHER PLANS.
SHUFFLE SHUFF
YOU HAVE TO GO.
DARLING, WHAT WILL TOMORROW BRING...?

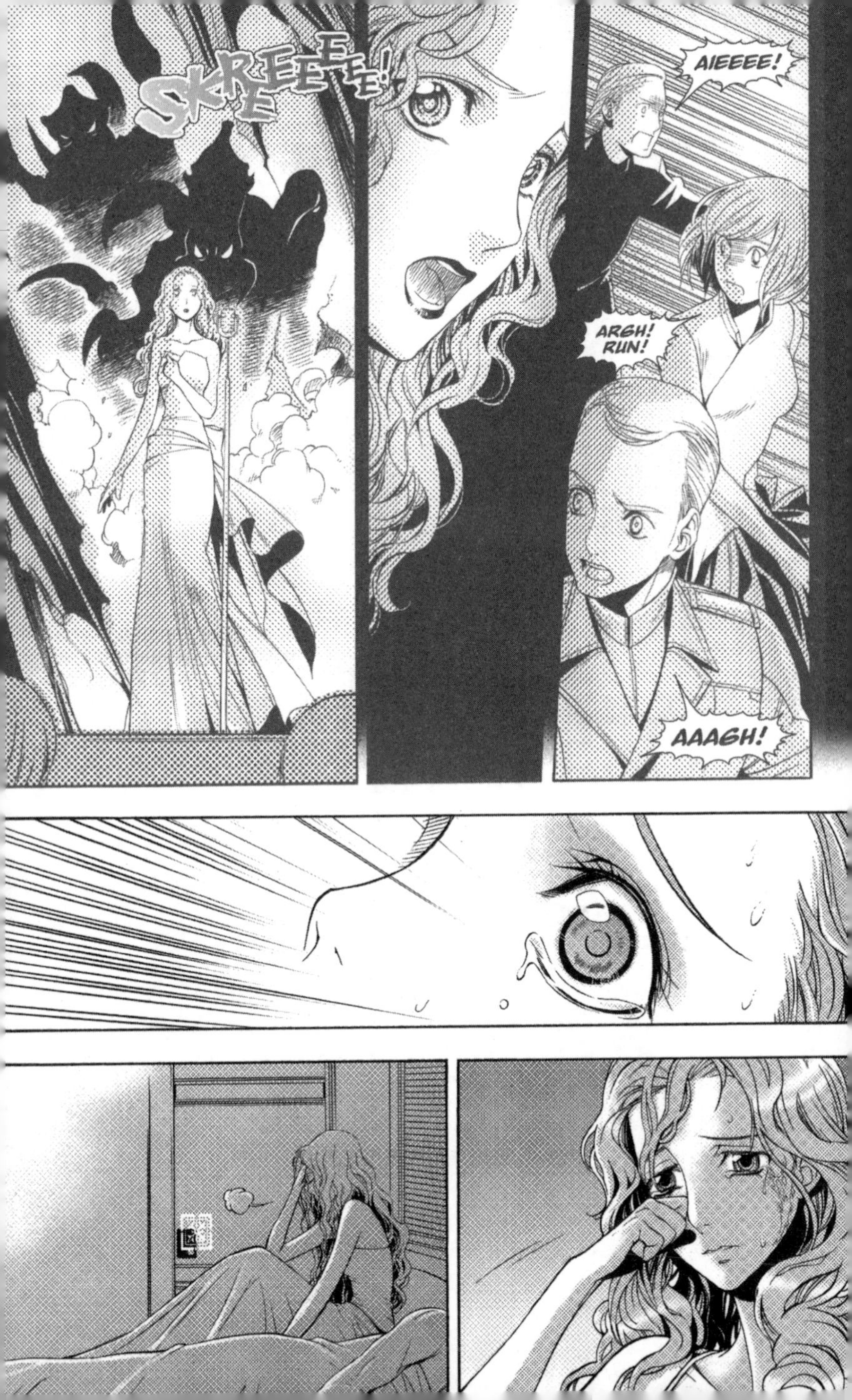
SKREEEEEE!
AIEEEE!
ARGH! RUN!
AAAGH!

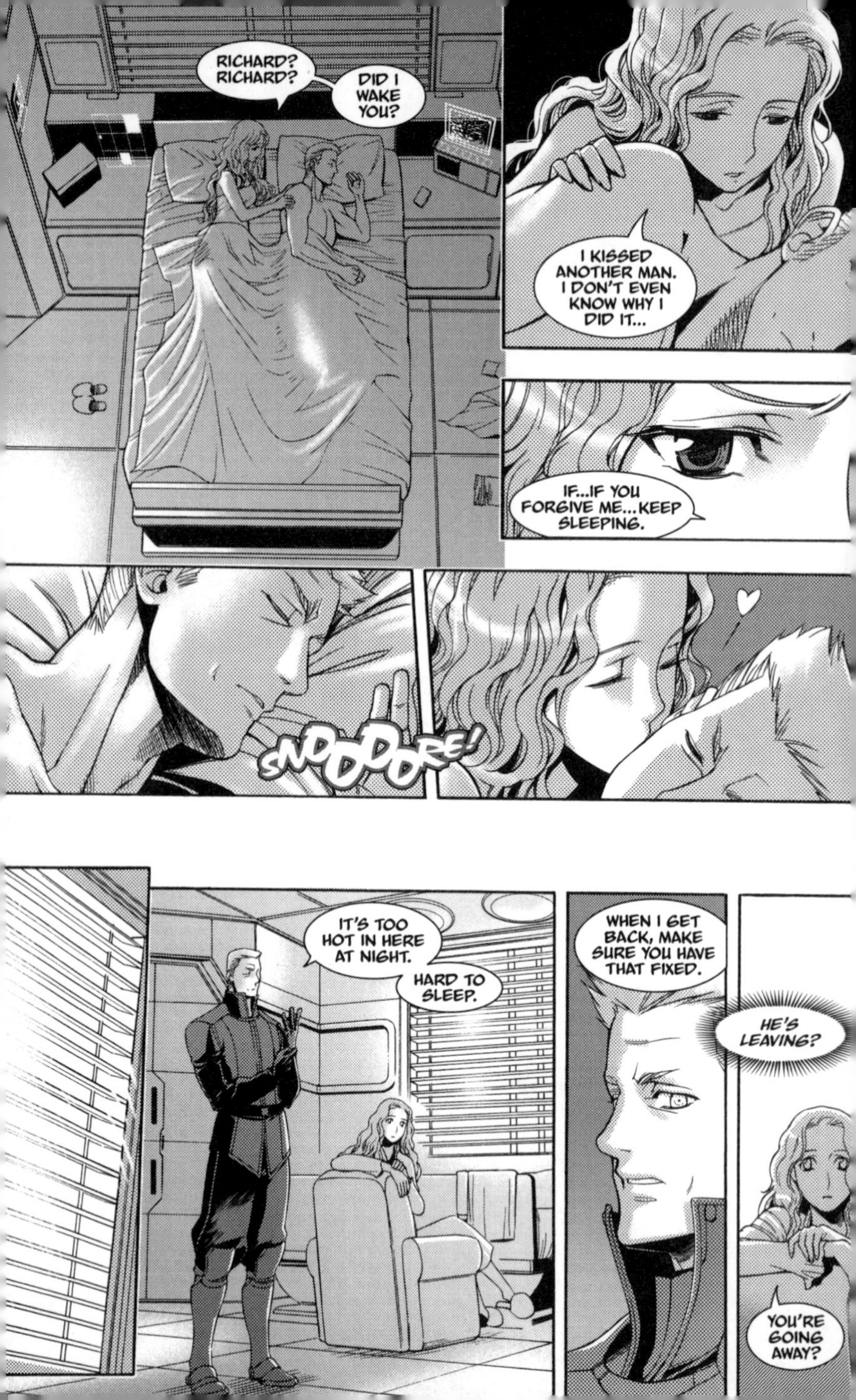

RICHARD? RICHARD?
DID I WAKE YOU?
I KISSED ANOTHER MAN. I DON'T EVEN KNOW WHY I DID IT...
IF...IF YOU FORGIVE ME...KEEP SLEEPING.
SNOOOORE!
IT'S TOO HOT IN HERE AT NIGHT.
HARD TO SLEEP.
WHEN I GET BACK, MAKE SURE YOU HAVE THAT FIXED.
HE'S LEAVING?
YOU'RE GOING AWAY?

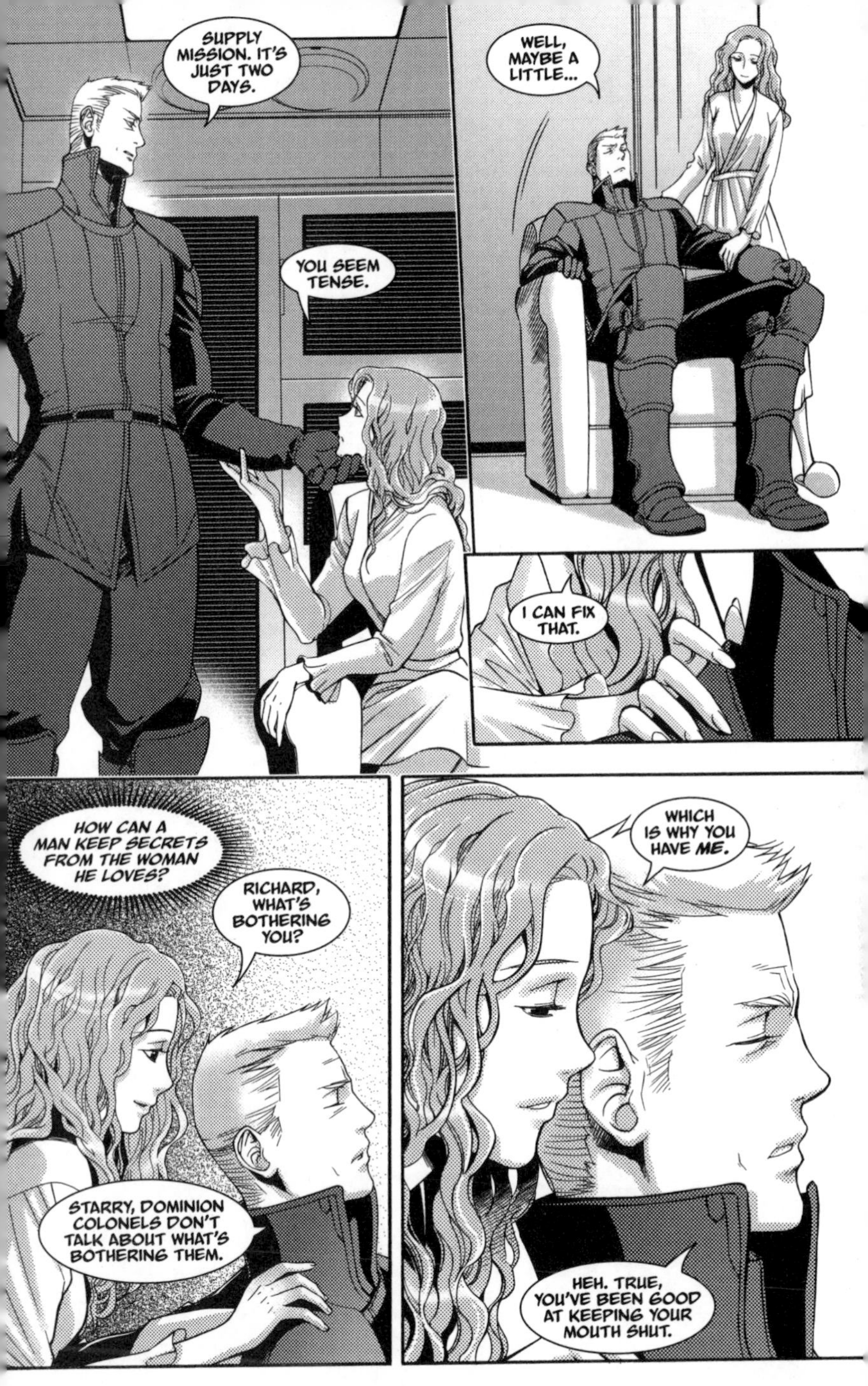
SUPPLY MISSION. IT'S JUST TWO DAYS.
YOU SEEM TENSE.
WELL, MAYBE A LITTLE...
I CAN FIX THAT.
HOW CAN A MAN KEEP SECRETS FROM THE WOMAN HE LOVES?
RICHARD, WHAT'S BOTHERING YOU?
STARRY, DOMINION COLONELS DON'T TALK ABOUT WHAT'S BOTHERING THEM.
WHICH IS WHY YOU HAVE *ME*.
HEH. TRUE, YOU'VE BEEN GOOD AT KEEPING YOUR MOUTH SHUT.

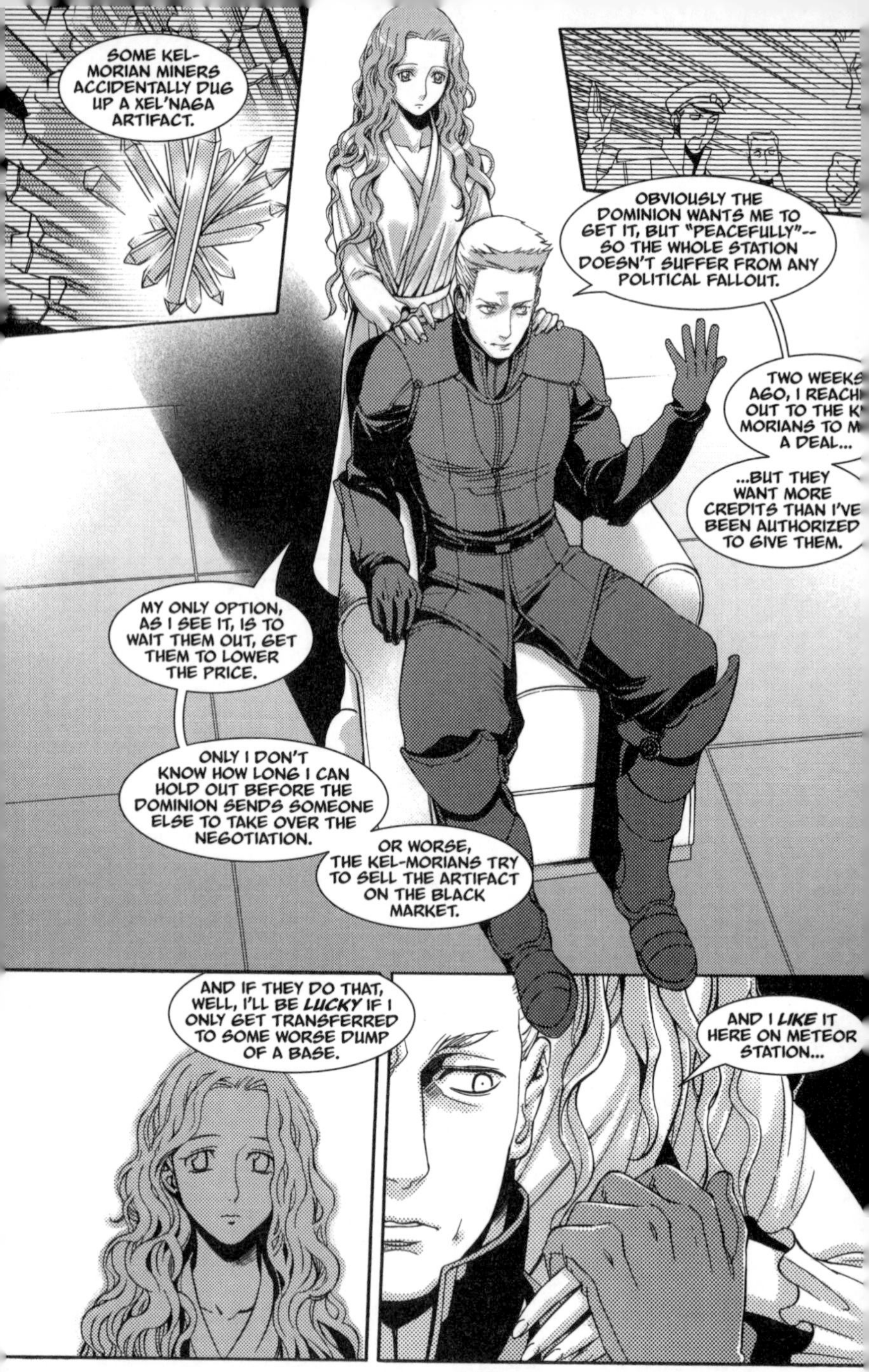
SOME KEL-MORIAN MINERS ACCIDENTALLY DUG UP A XEL'NAGA ARTIFACT.
OBVIOUSLY THE DOMINION WANTS ME TO GET IT, BUT "PEACEFULLY"--SO THE WHOLE STATION DOESN'T SUFFER FROM ANY POLITICAL FALLOUT.
TWO WEEKS AGO, I REACH OUT TO THE K MORIANS TO M A DEAL...
...BUT THEY WANT MORE CREDITS THAN I'VE BEEN AUTHORIZED TO GIVE THEM.
MY ONLY OPTION, AS I SEE IT, IS TO WAIT THEM OUT, GET THEM TO LOWER THE PRICE.
ONLY I DON'T KNOW HOW LONG I CAN HOLD OUT BEFORE THE DOMINION SENDS SOMEONE ELSE TO TAKE OVER THE NEGOTIATION.
OR WORSE, THE KEL-MORIANS TRY TO SELL THE ARTIFACT ON THE BLACK MARKET.
AND IF THEY DO THAT, WELL, I'LL BE *LUCKY* IF I ONLY GET TRANSFERRED TO SOME WORSE DUMP OF A BASE.
AND I *LIKE* IT HERE ON METEOR STATION...

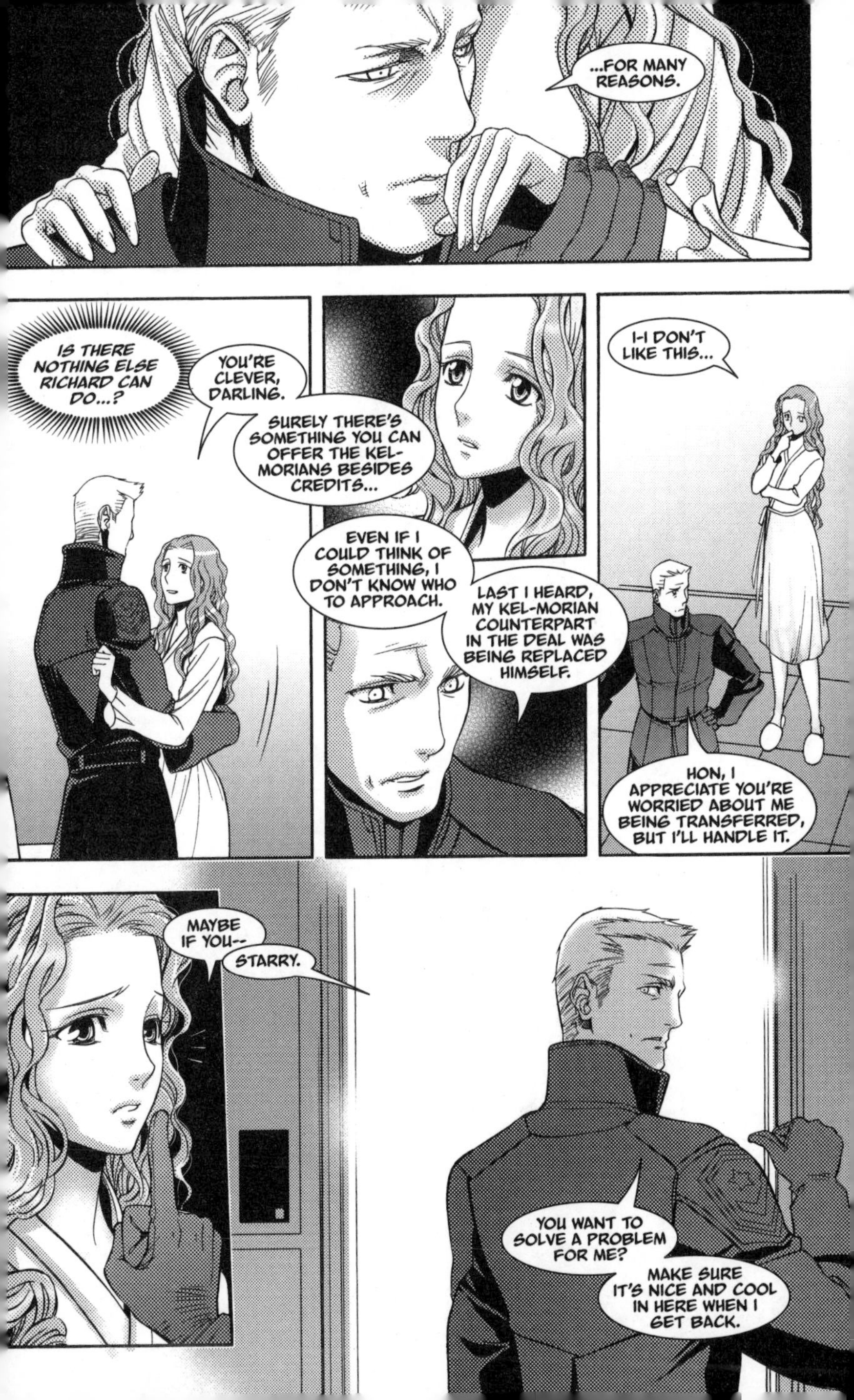
...FOR MANY REASONS.
IS THERE NOTHING ELSE RICHARD CAN DO...?
YOU'RE CLEVER, DARLING.
SURELY THERE'S SOMETHING YOU CAN OFFER THE KEL-MORIANS BESIDES CREDITS...
EVEN IF I COULD THINK OF SOMETHING, I DON'T KNOW WHO TO APPROACH.
LAST I HEARD, MY KEL-MORIAN COUNTERPART IN THE DEAL WAS BEING REPLACED HIMSELF.
I-I DON'T LIKE THIS...
HON, I APPRECIATE YOU'RE WORRIED ABOUT ME BEING TRANSFERRED, BUT I'LL HANDLE IT.
MAYBE IF YOU--
STARRY.
YOU WANT TO SOLVE A PROBLEM FOR ME?
MAKE SURE IT'S NICE AND COOL IN HERE WHEN I GET BACK.

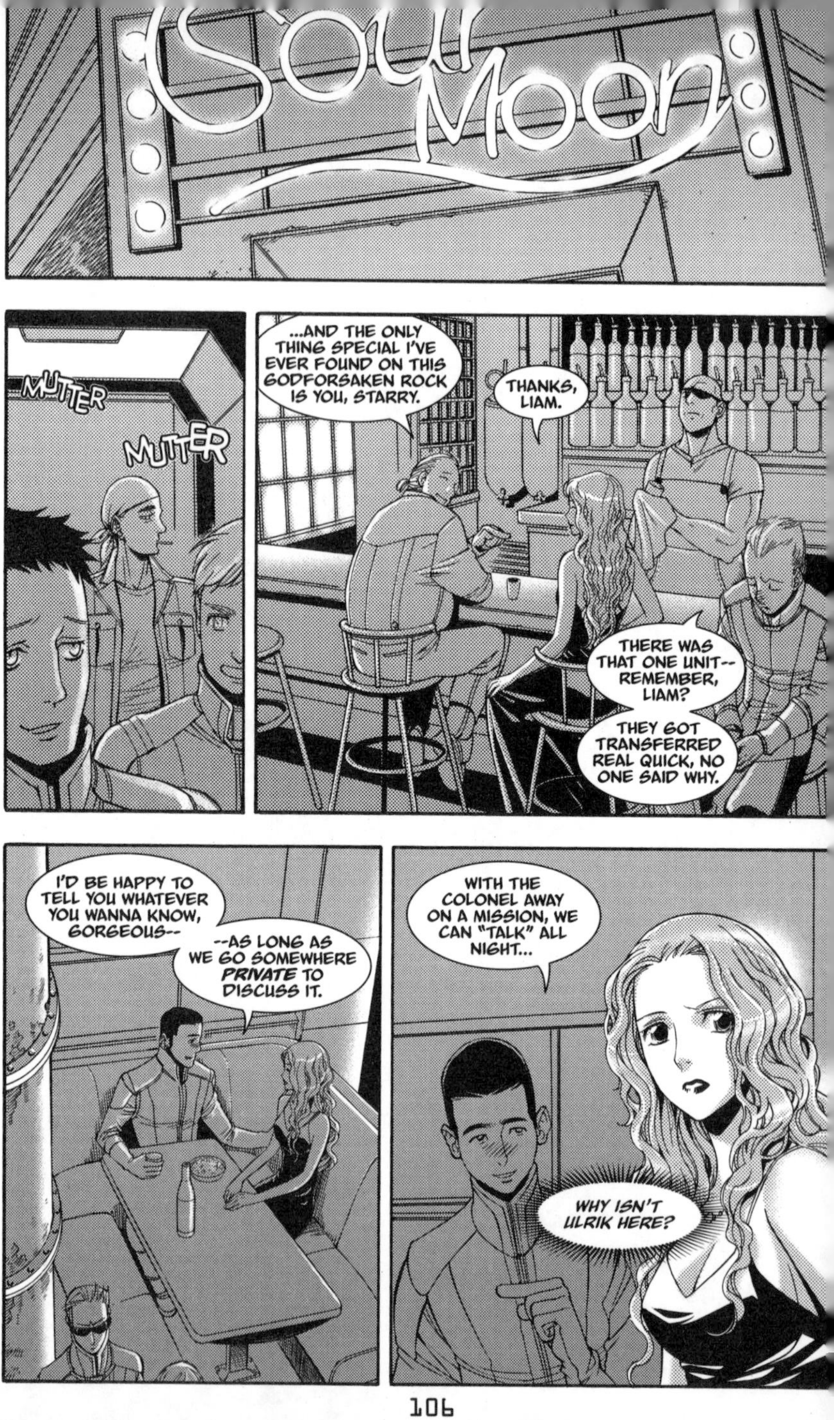
Soul Moon
MUTTER
MUTTER
...AND THE ONLY THING SPECIAL I'VE EVER FOUND ON THIS GODFORSAKEN ROCK IS YOU, STARRY.
THANKS, LIAM.
THERE WAS THAT ONE UNIT--REMEMBER, LIAM?
THEY GOT TRANSFERRED REAL QUICK, NO ONE SAID WHY.
I'D BE HAPPY TO TELL YOU WHATEVER YOU WANNA KNOW, GORGEOUS--
--AS LONG AS WE GO SOMEWHERE PRIVATE TO DISCUSS IT.
WITH THE COLONEL AWAY ON A MISSION, WE CAN "TALK" ALL NIGHT...
WHY ISN'T ULRIK HERE?

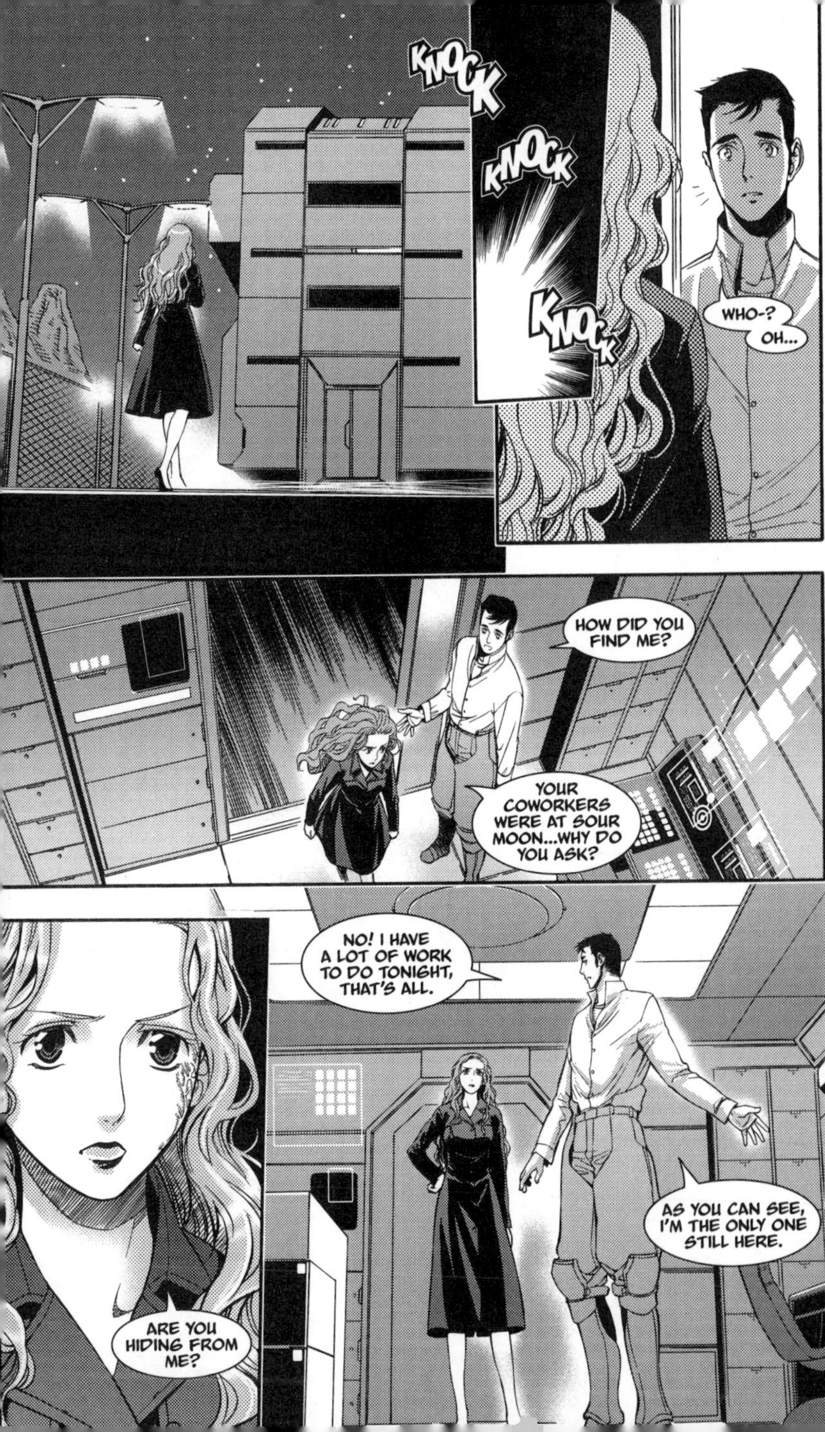

KNOCK
KNOCK
KNOCK
WHO-? OH...
HOW DID YOU FIND ME?
YOUR COWORKERS WERE AT SOUR MOON...WHY DO YOU ASK?
ARE YOU HIDING FROM ME?
NO! I HAVE A LOT OF WORK TO DO TONIGHT, THAT'S ALL.
AS YOU CAN SEE, I'M THE ONLY ONE STILL HERE.

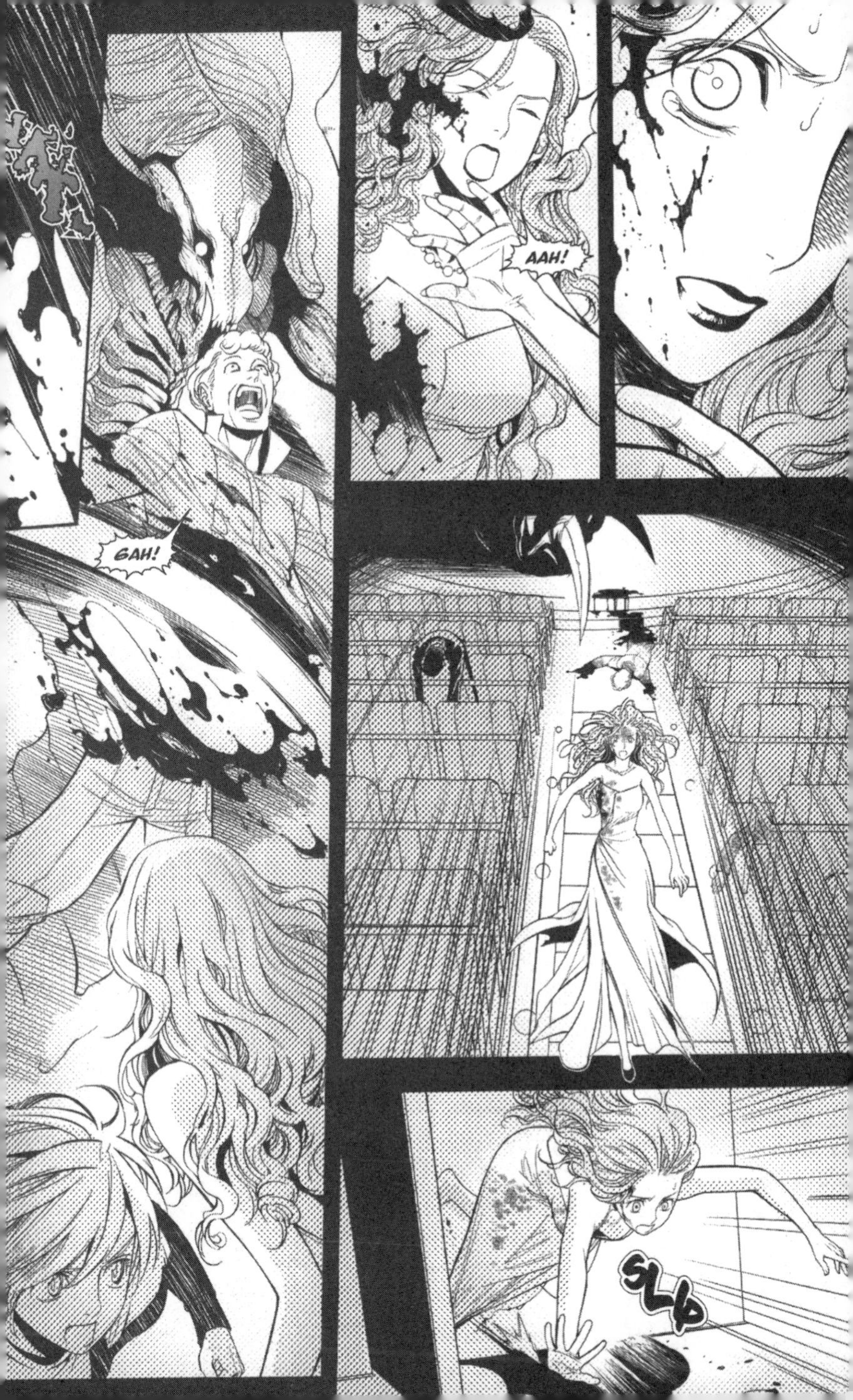
AAH!
GAH!
SLIP

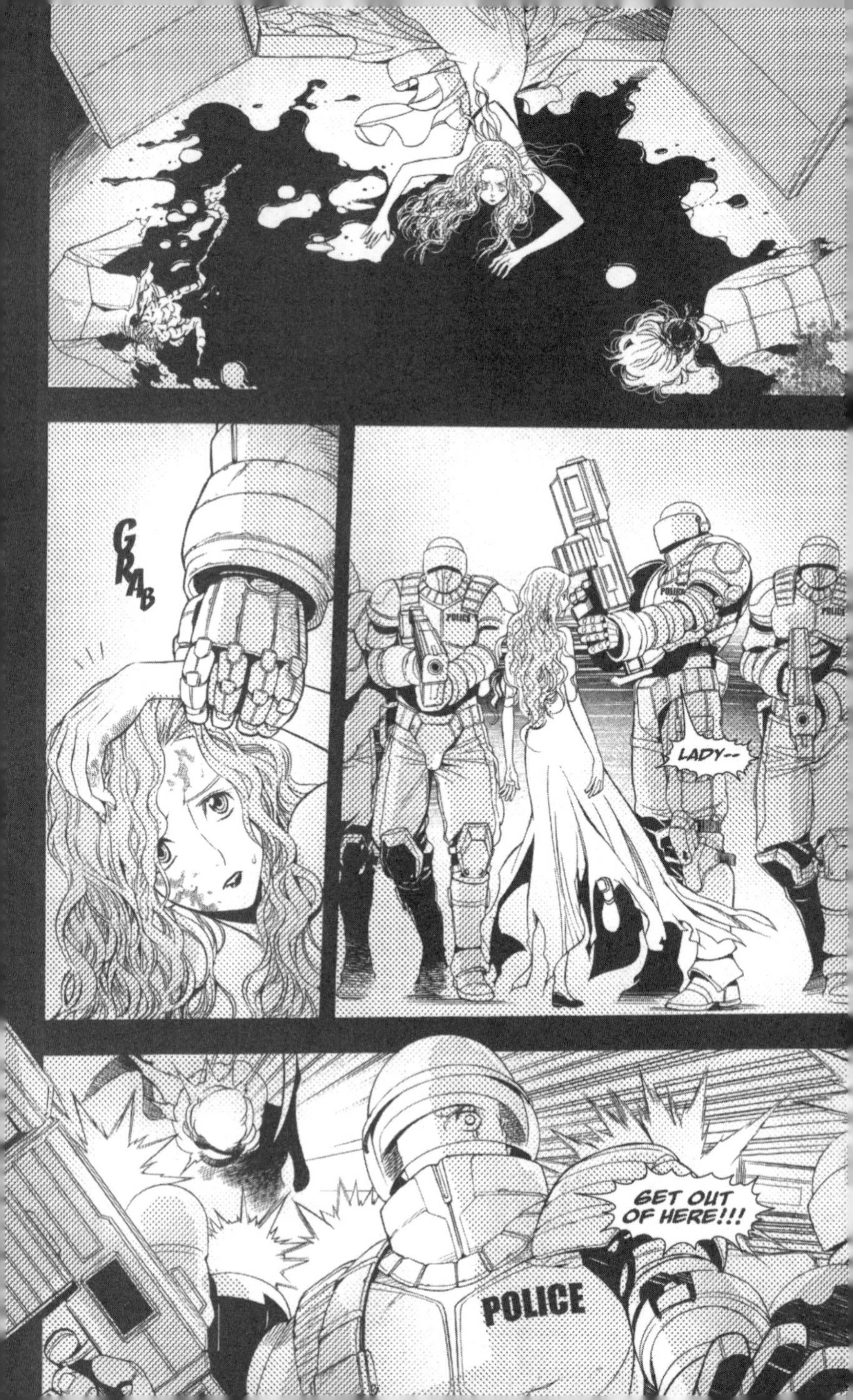
GRAB
POLICE
POLICE
POLICE
LADY--
GET OUT OF HERE!!!
POLICE

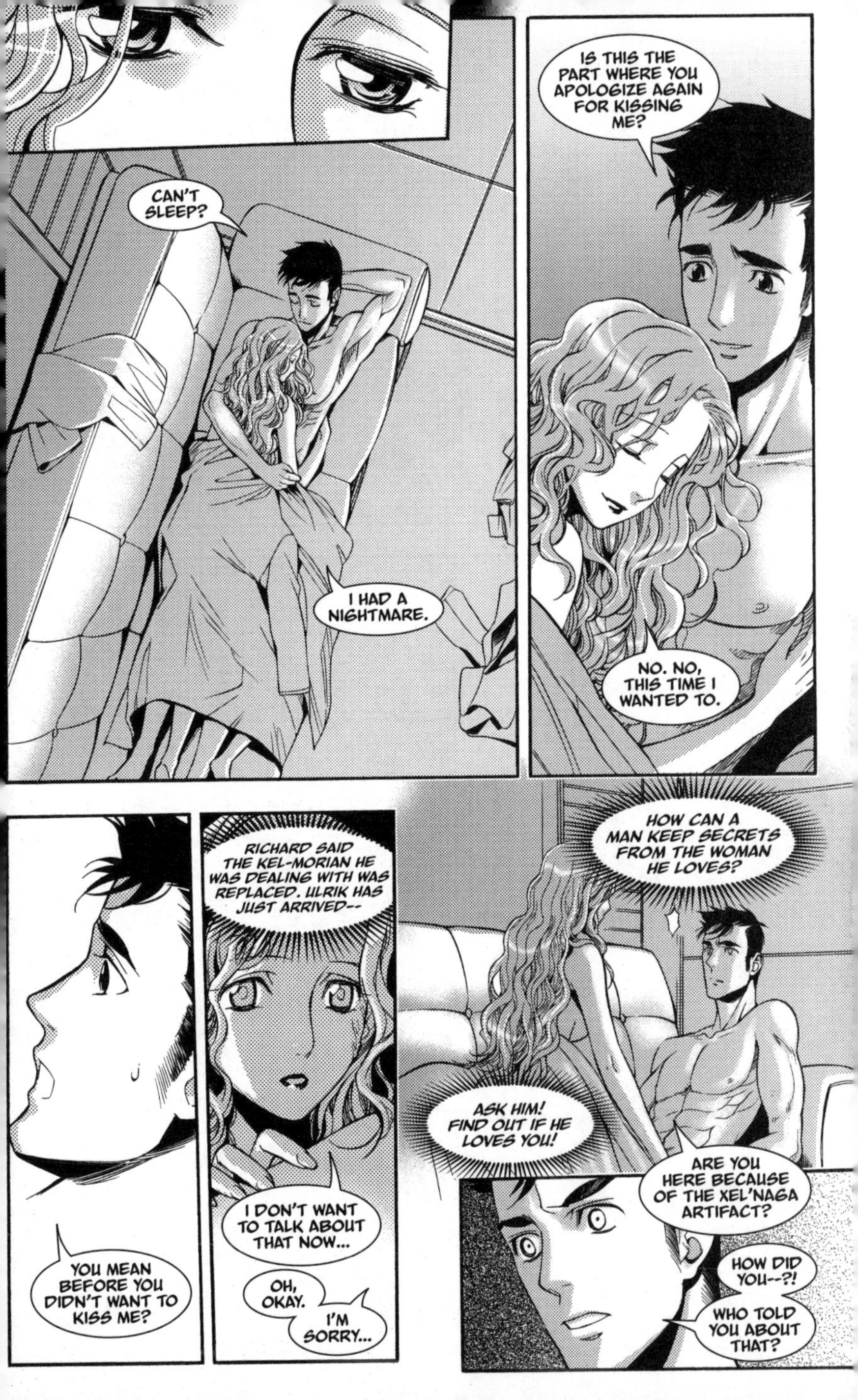
IS THIS THE PART WHERE YOU APOLOGIZE AGAIN FOR KISSING ME?
CAN'T SLEEP?
I HAD A NIGHTMARE.
NO. NO, THIS TIME I WANTED TO.
YOU MEAN BEFORE YOU DIDN'T WANT TO KISS ME?
RICHARD SAID THE KEL-MORIAN HE WAS DEALING WITH WAS REPLACED. ULRIK HAS JUST ARRIVED--
I DON'T WANT TO TALK ABOUT THAT NOW...
OH, OKAY.
I'M SORRY...
HOW CAN A MAN KEEP SECRETS FROM THE WOMAN HE LOVES?
ASK HIM! FIND OUT IF HE LOVES YOU!
ARE YOU HERE BECAUSE OF THE XEL'NAGA ARTIFACT?
HOW DID YOU--?!
WHO TOLD YOU ABOUT THAT?

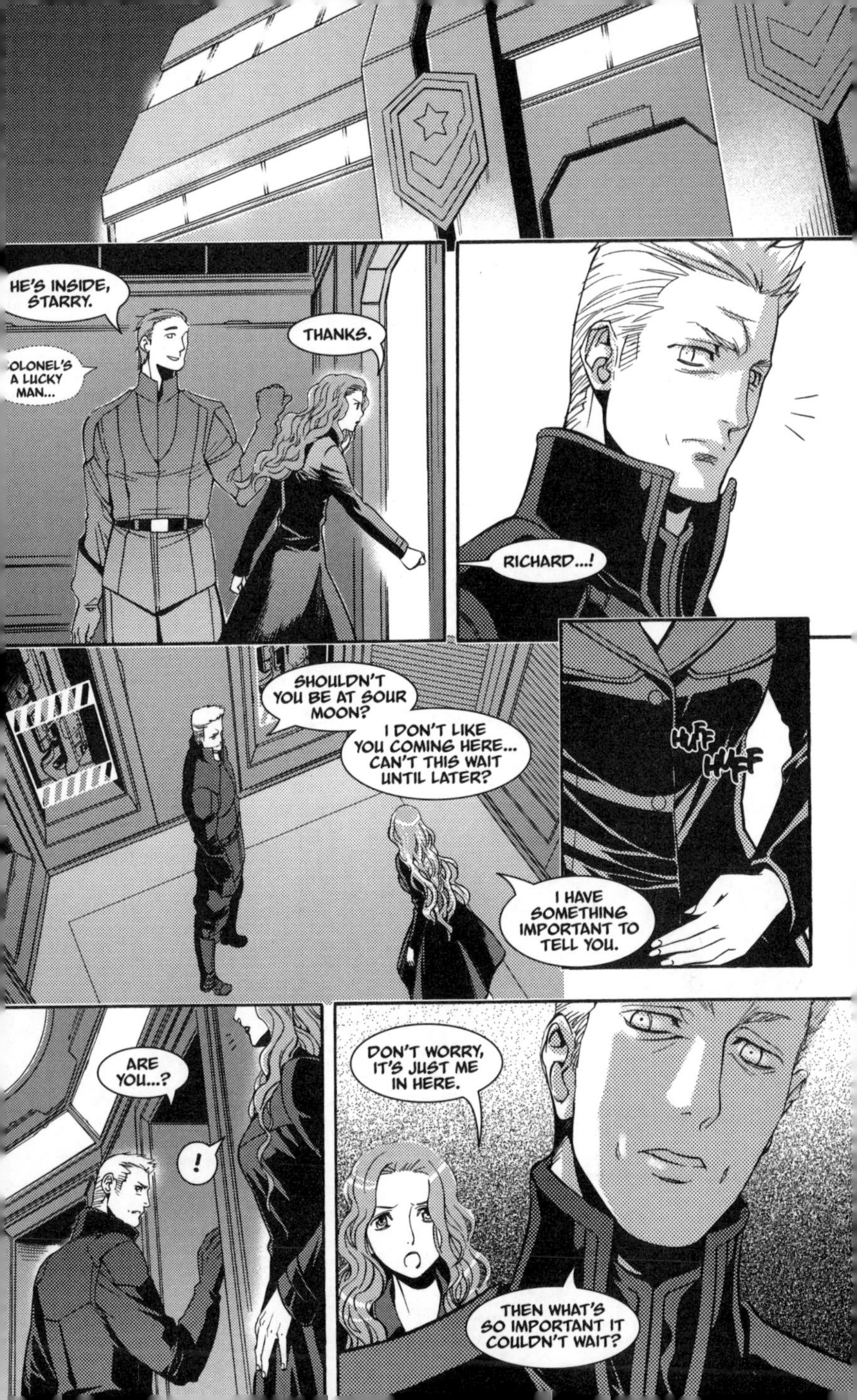
HE'S INSIDE, STARRY.
COLONEL'S A LUCKY MAN...
THANKS.
RICHARD...!
SHOULDN'T YOU BE AT SOUR MOON?
I DON'T LIKE YOU COMING HERE... CAN'T THIS WAIT UNTIL LATER?
HUFF HUFF
I HAVE SOMETHING IMPORTANT TO TELL YOU.
ARE YOU...?
!
DON'T WORRY, IT'S JUST ME IN HERE.
THEN WHAT'S SO IMPORTANT IT COULDN'T WAIT?

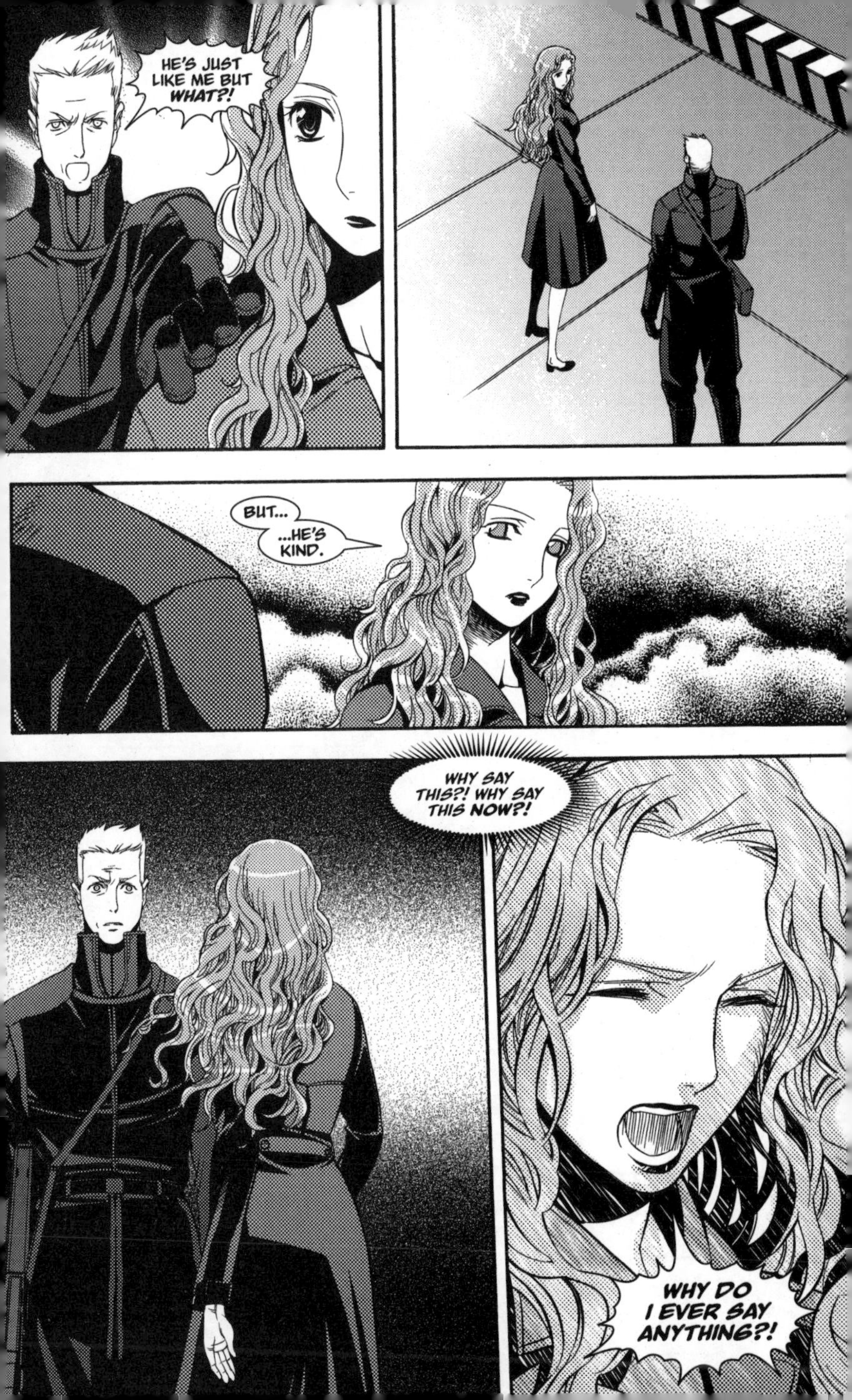
HE'S JUST LIKE ME BUT WHAT?!
BUT...
...HE'S KIND.
WHY SAY THIS?! WHY SAY THIS NOW?!
WHY DO I EVER SAY ANYTHING?!

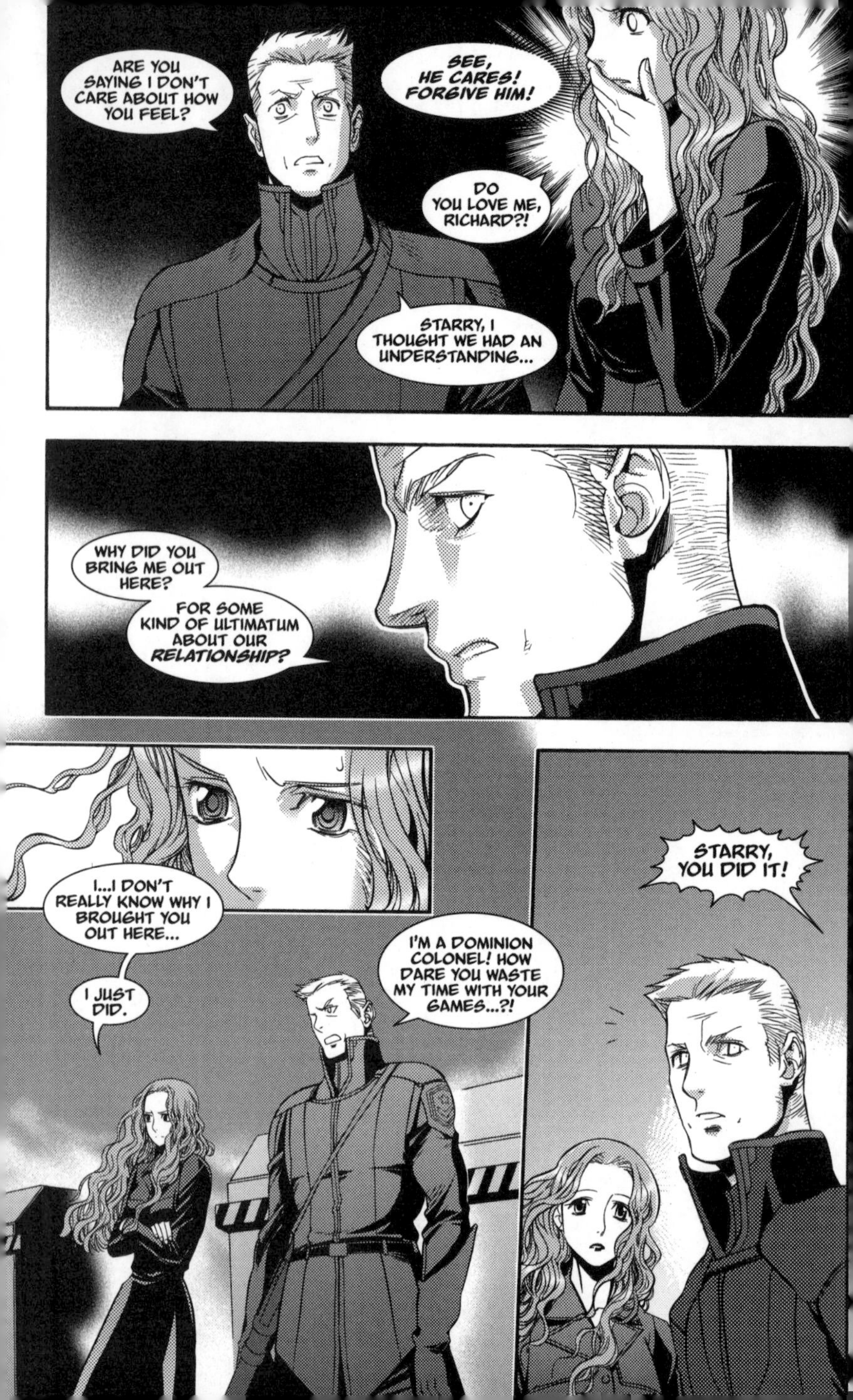
ARE YOU SAYING I DON'T CARE ABOUT HOW YOU FEEL?
SEE, HE CARES! FORGIVE HIM!
DO YOU LOVE ME, RICHARD?!
STARRY, I THOUGHT WE HAD AN UNDERSTANDING...
WHY DID YOU BRING ME OUT HERE?
FOR SOME KIND OF ULTIMATUM ABOUT OUR RELATIONSHIP?
I...I DON'T REALLY KNOW WHY I BROUGHT YOU OUT HERE...
I JUST DID.
I'M A DOMINION COLONEL! HOW DARE YOU WASTE MY TIME WITH YOUR GAMES...?!
STARRY, YOU DID IT!

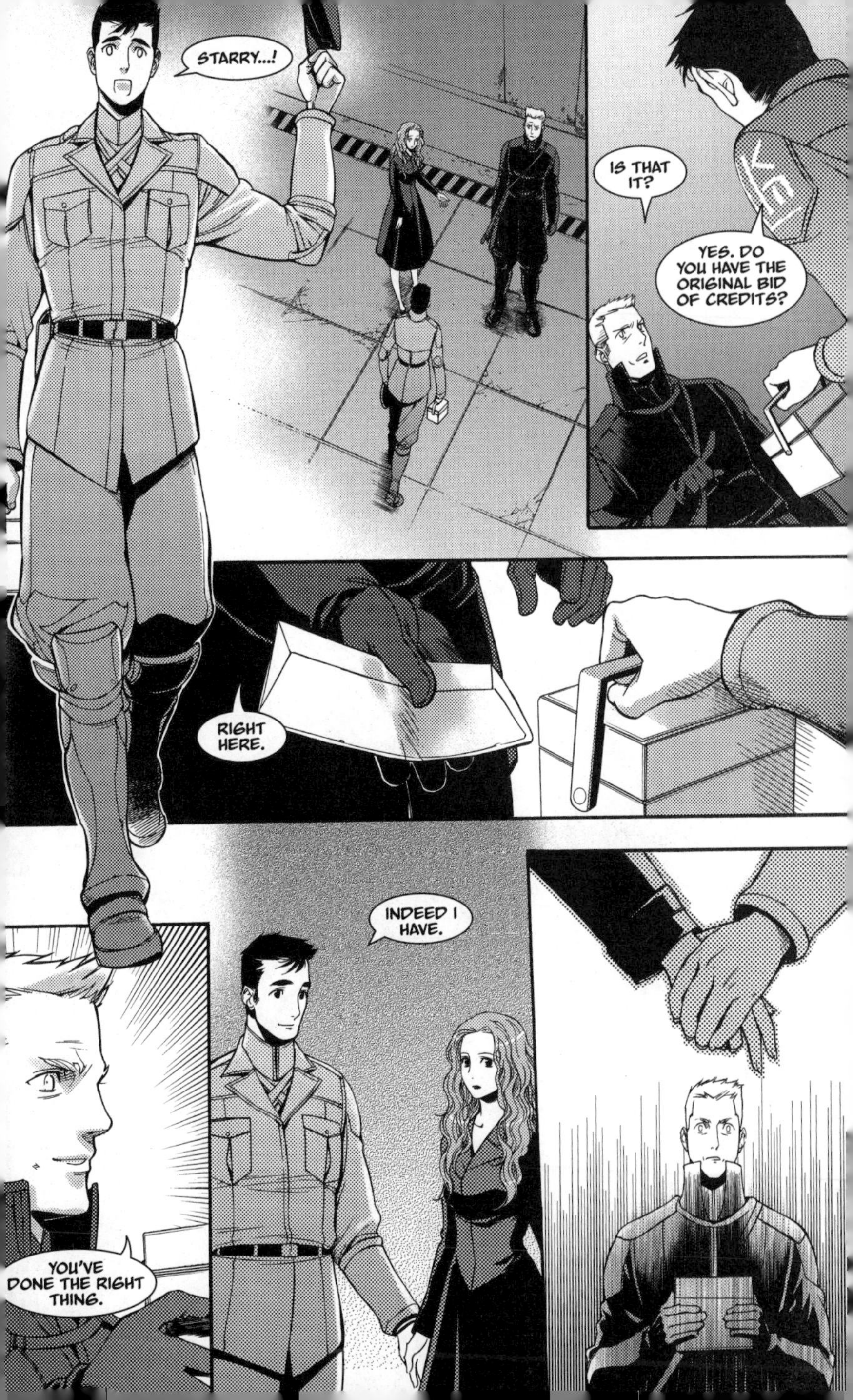
STARRY...!
IS THAT IT?
YES. DO YOU HAVE THE ORIGINAL BID OF CREDITS?
RIGHT HERE.
INDEED I HAVE.
YOU'VE DONE THE RIGHT THING.

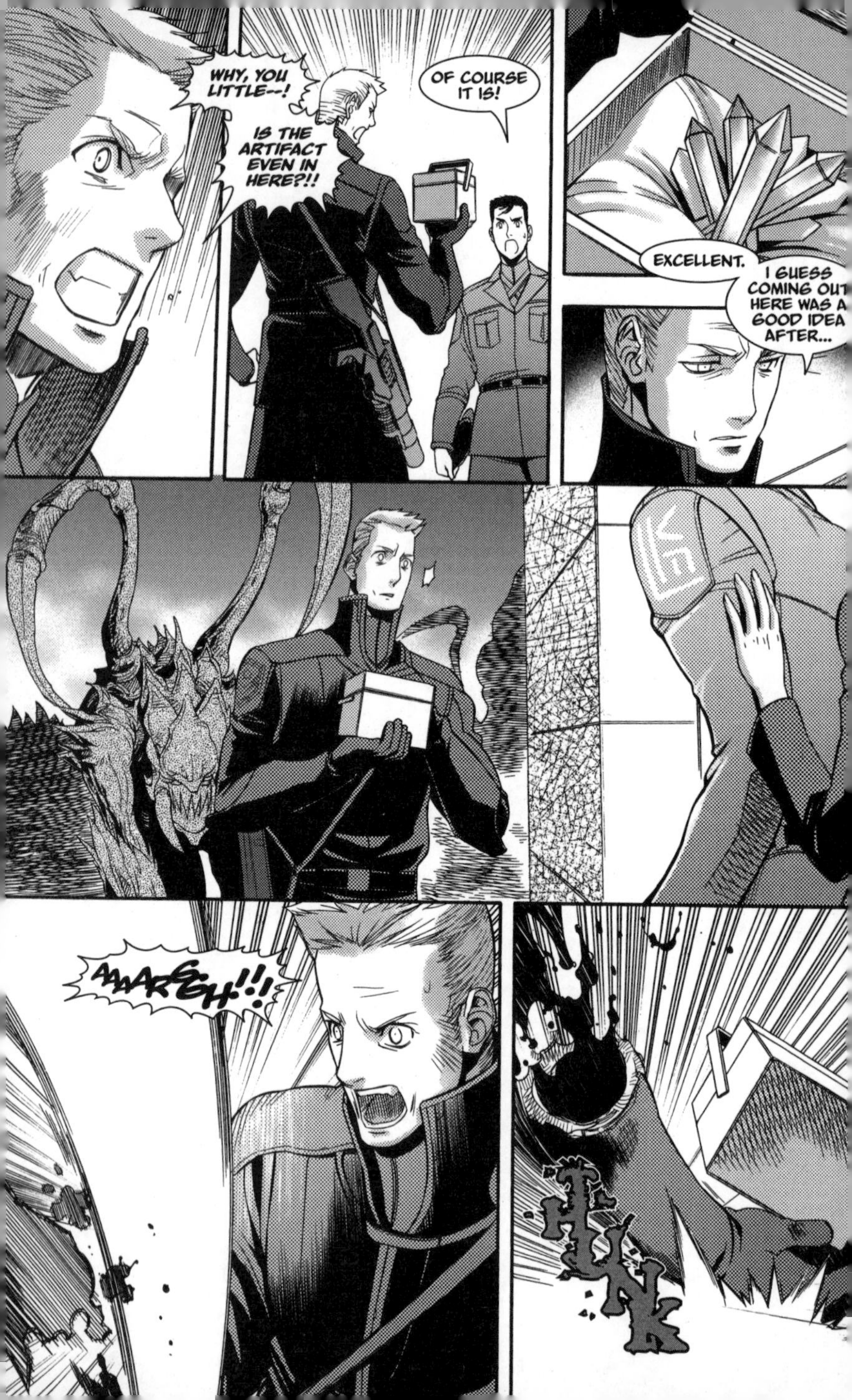
WHY, YOU LITTLE--!
IS THE ARTIFACT EVEN IN HERE?!!
OF COURSE IT IS!
EXCELLENT.
I GUESS COMING OUT HERE WAS A GOOD IDEA AFTER...
AAARGH!!!
HNK

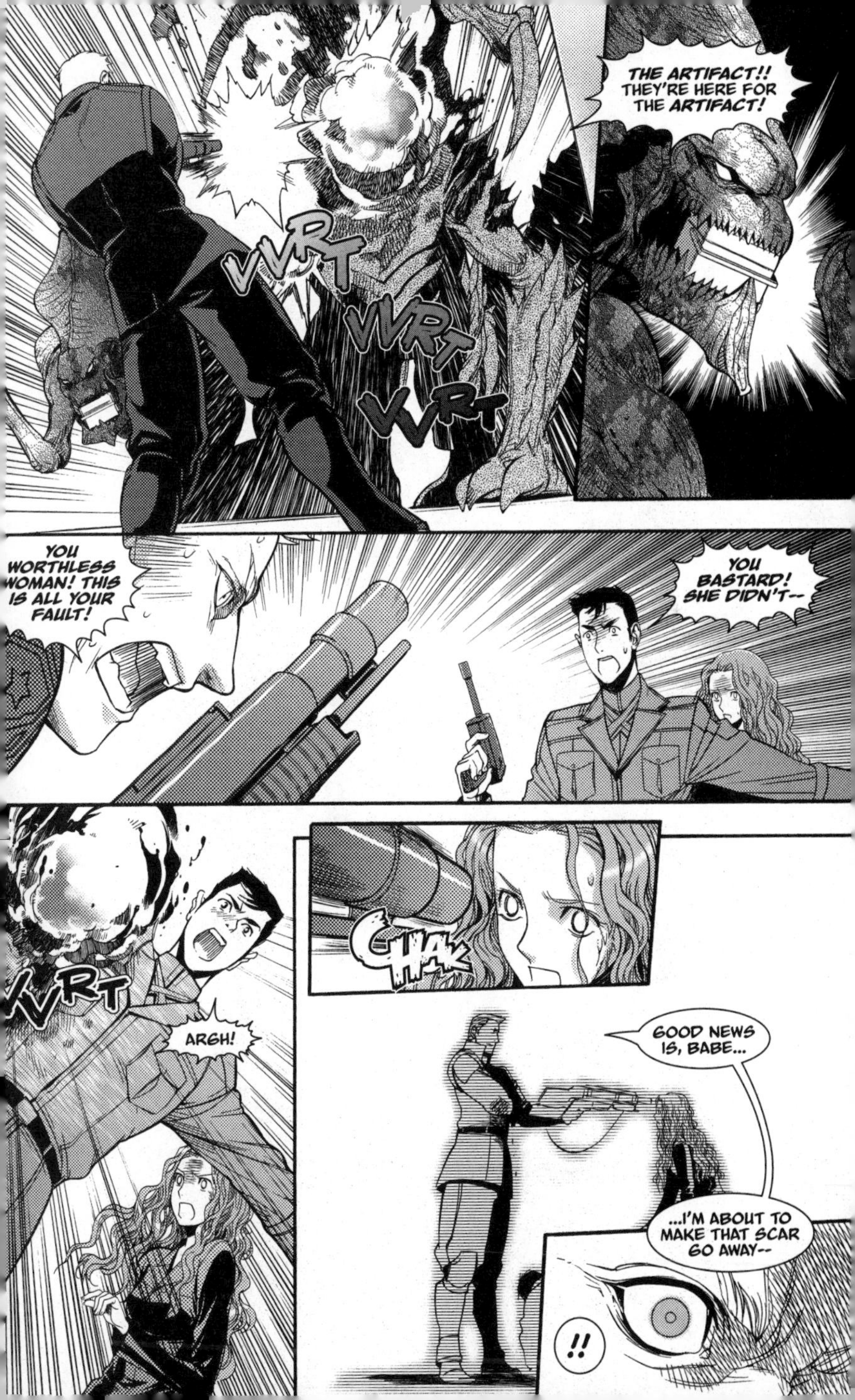
THE ARTIFACT!! THEY'RE HERE FOR THE ARTIFACT!
VVRT
VVRT
VVRT
YOU WORTHLESS WOMAN! THIS IS ALL YOUR FAULT!
YOU BASTARD! SHE DIDN'T--
VVRT
ARGH!
CHAK
GOOD NEWS IS, BABE...
...I'M ABOUT TO MAKE THAT SCAR GO AWAY--
!!

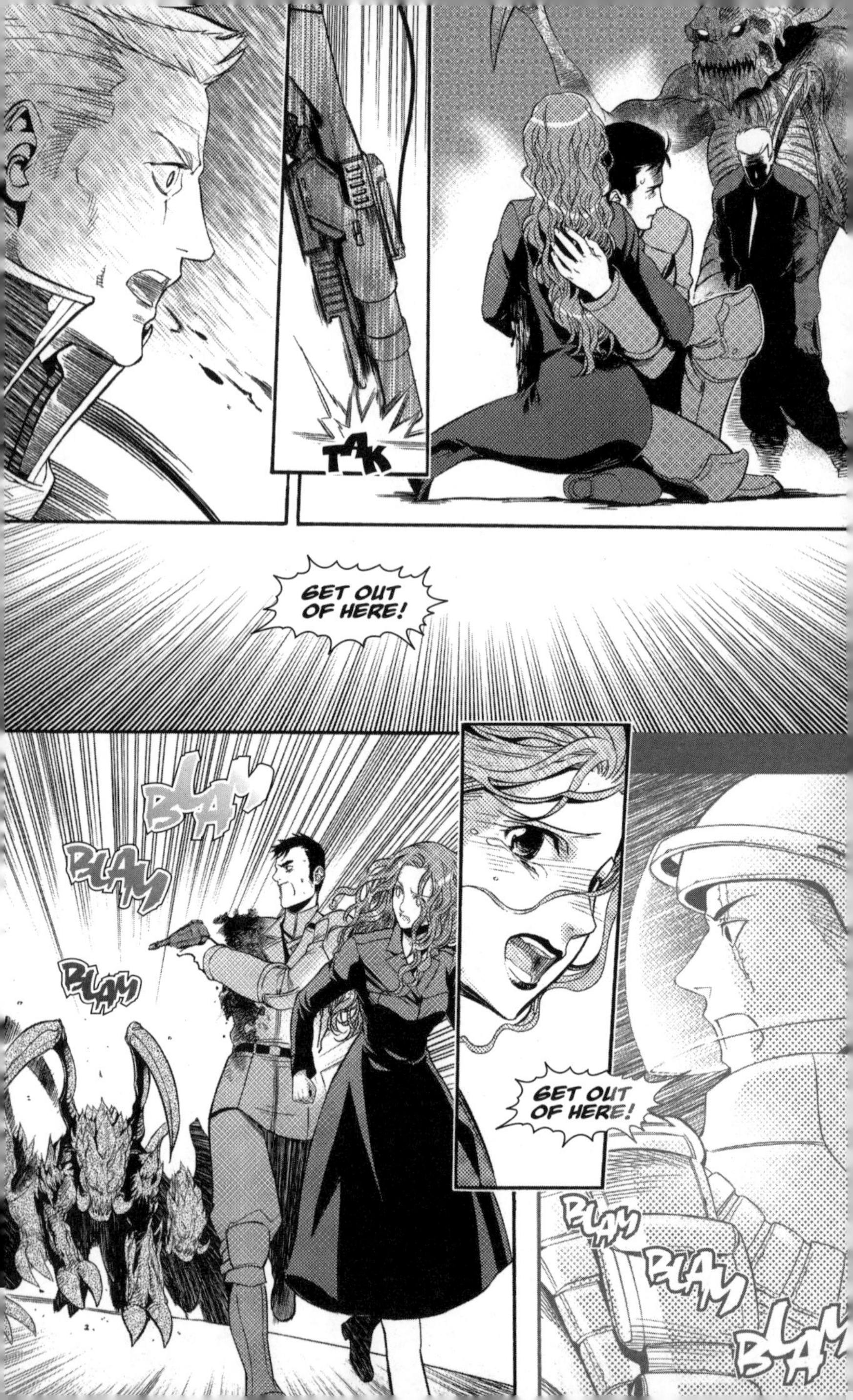
TAK
GET OUT OF HERE!
BLAM
BLAM
BLAM
GET OUT OF HERE!
BLAM
BLAM
BLAM

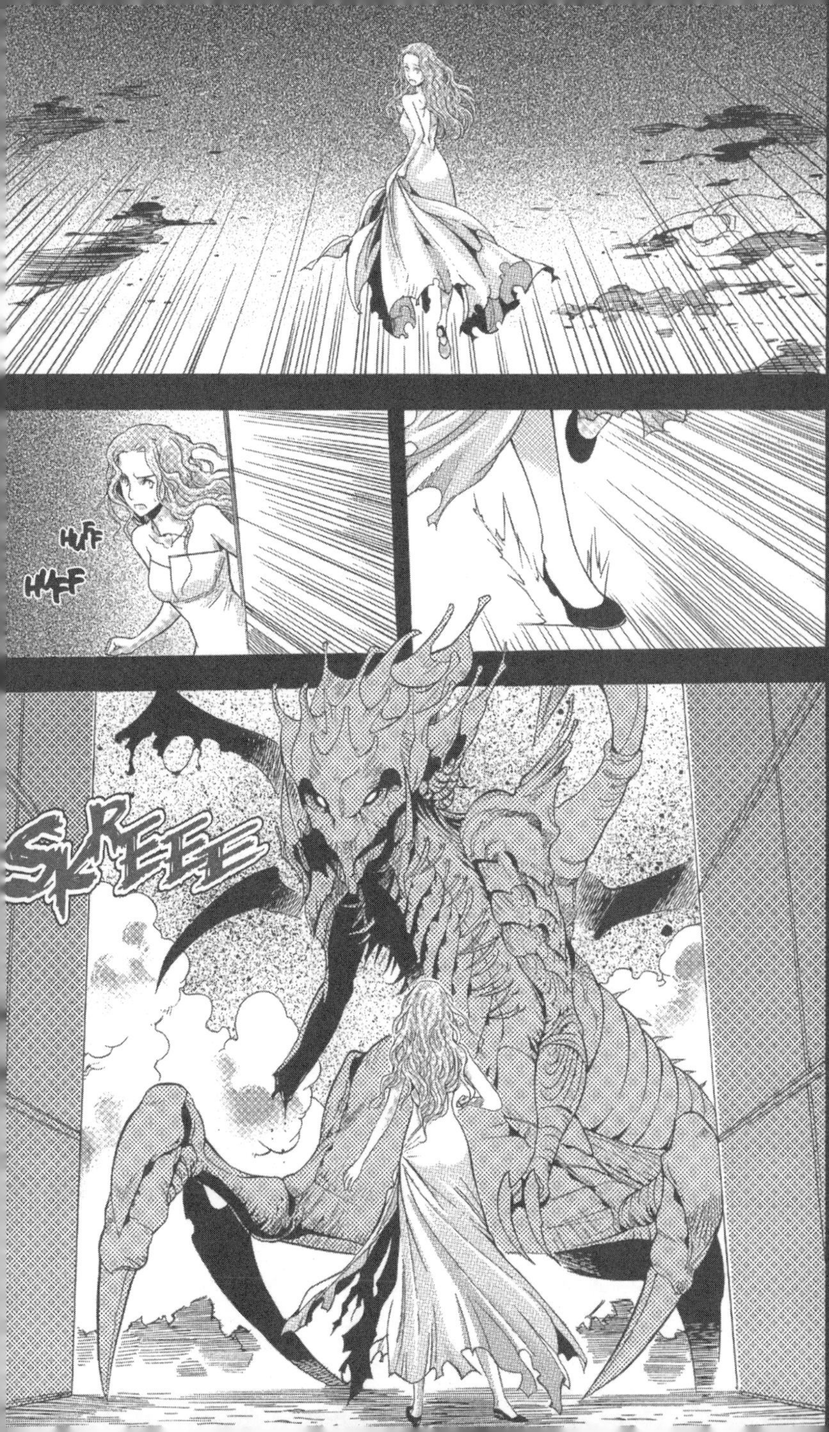
HUFF
HUFF
SKREEE

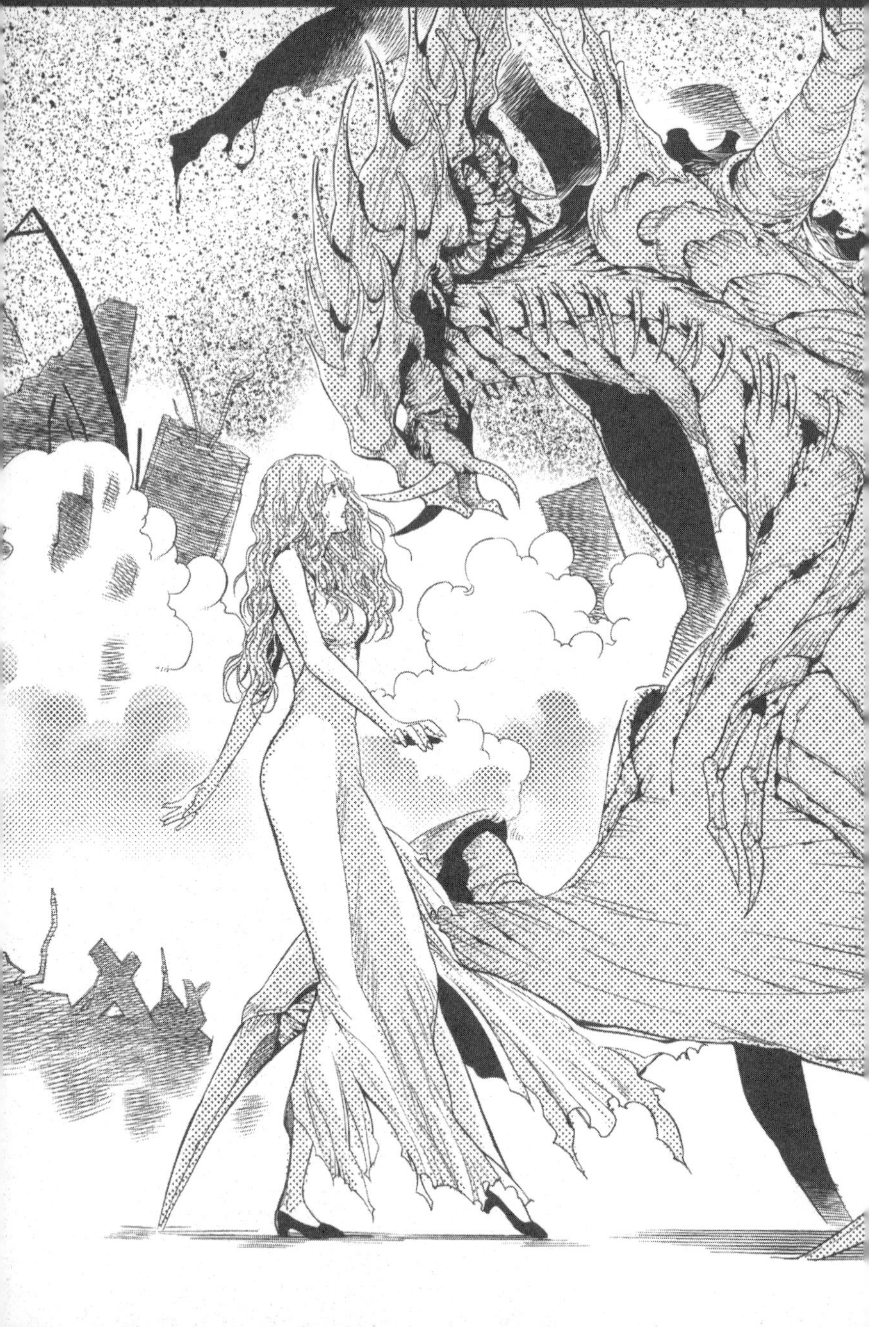

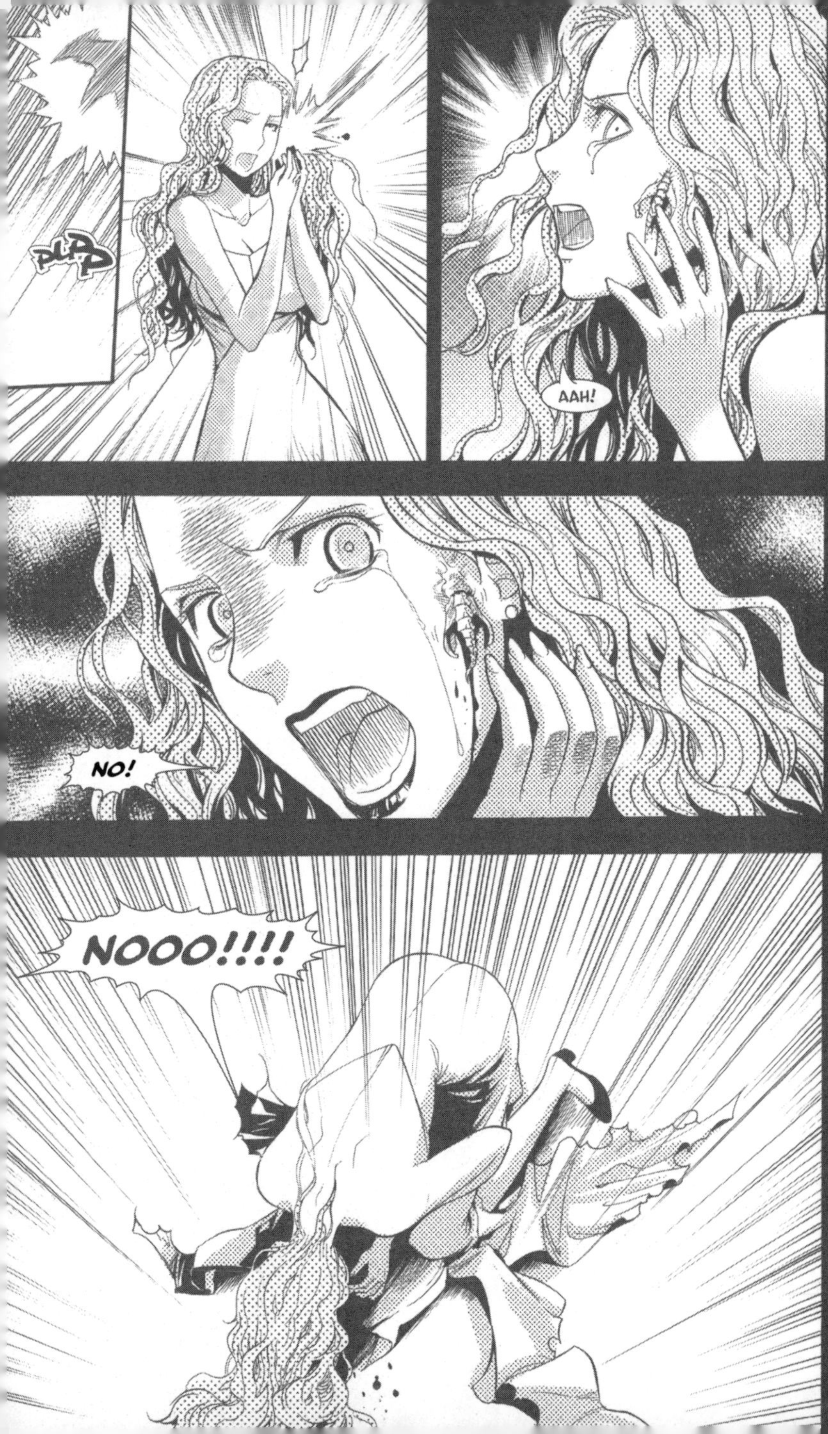
PLIP
AAH!
NO!
NOOO!!!!

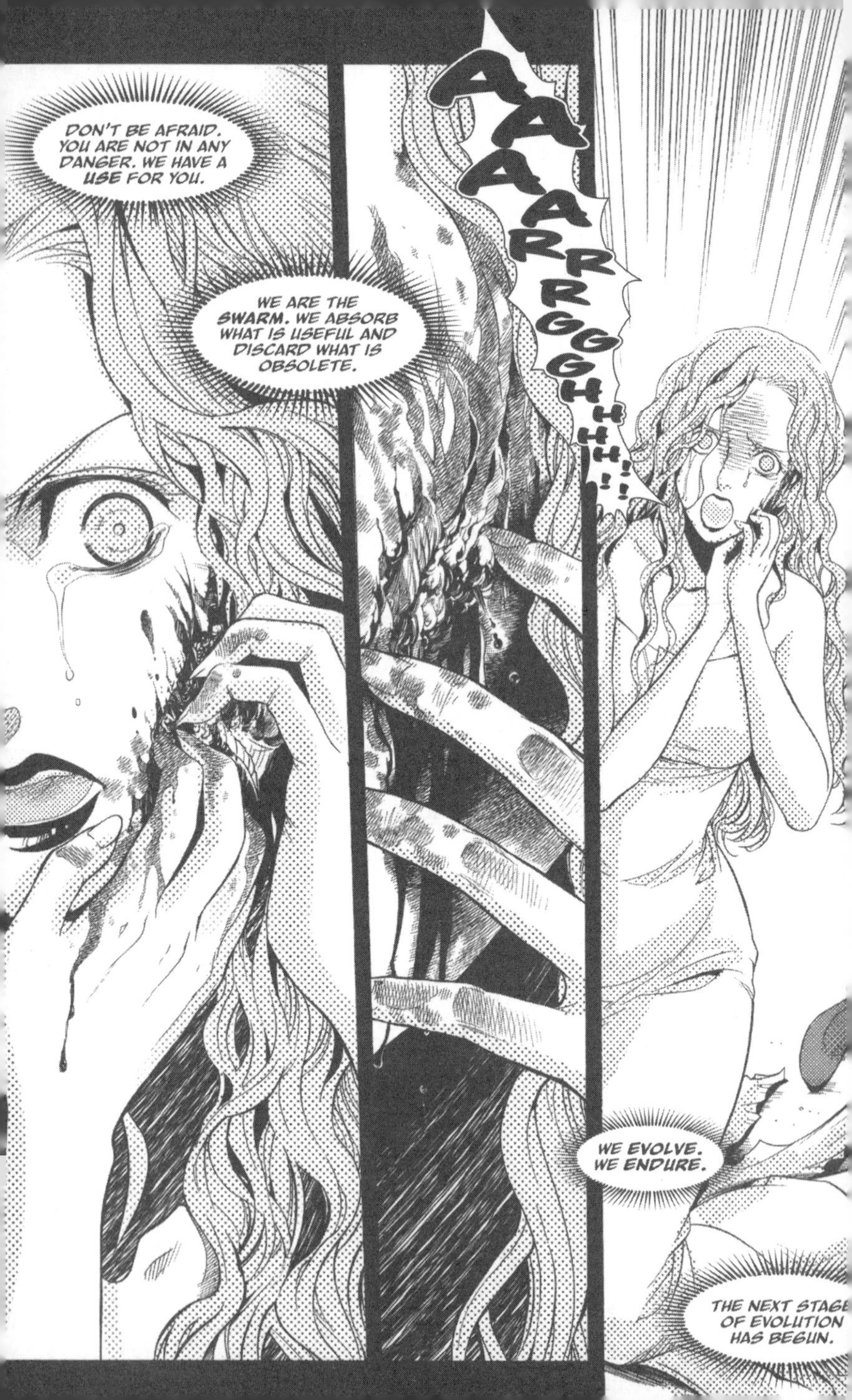
DON'T BE AFRAID. YOU ARE NOT IN ANY DANGER. WE HAVE A USE FOR YOU.
WE ARE THE SWARM. WE ABSORB WHAT IS USEFUL AND DISCARD WHAT IS OBSOLETE.
AAAARRRGGGHHHH!!!
WE EVOLVE. WE ENDURE.
THE NEXT STAGE OF EVOLUTION HAS BEGUN.

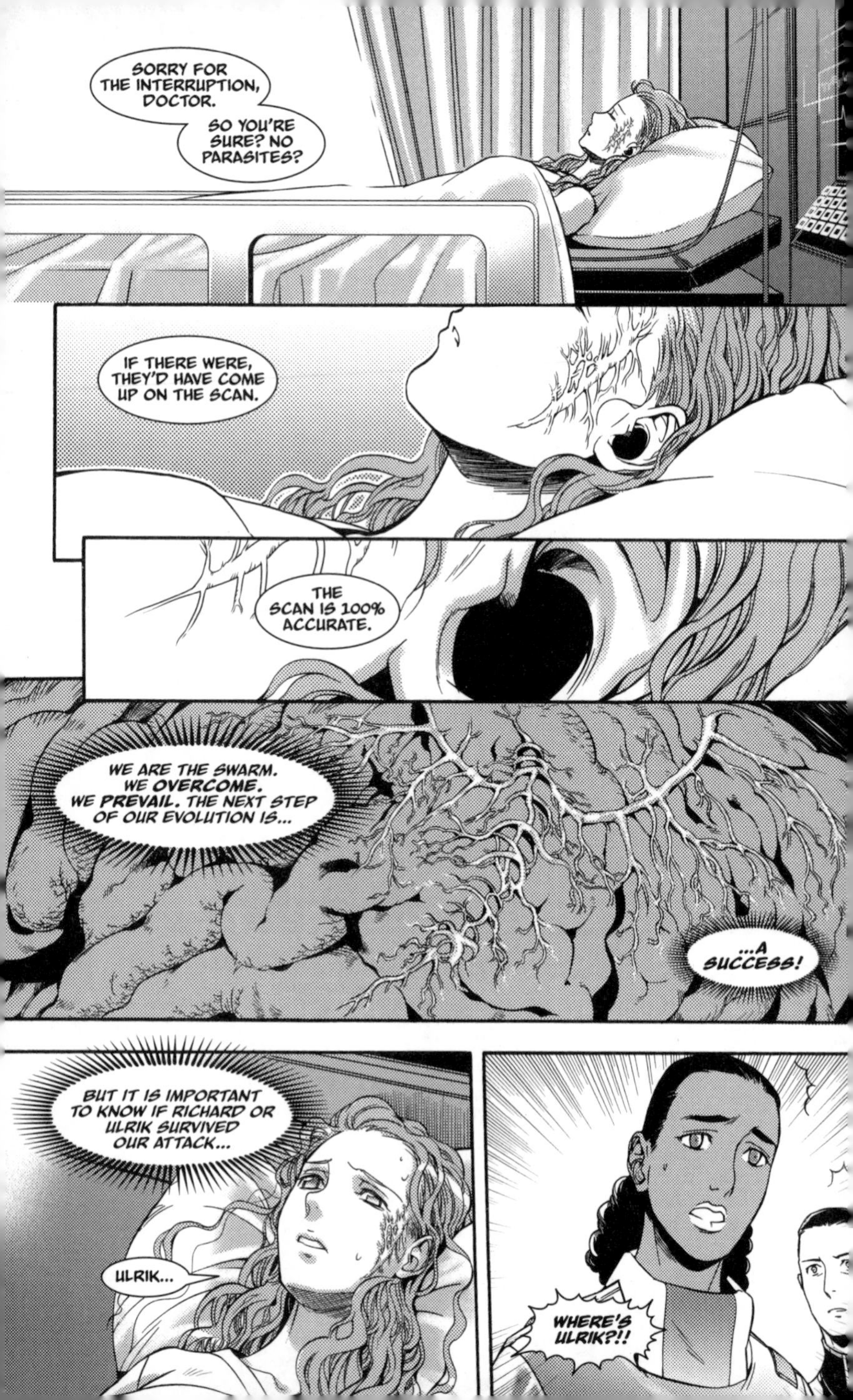
SORRY FOR THE INTERRUPTION, DOCTOR.
SO YOU'RE SURE? NO PARASITES?
IF THERE WERE, THEY'D HAVE COME UP ON THE SCAN.
THE SCAN IS 100% ACCURATE.
WE ARE THE SWARM. WE **OVERCOME**. WE **PREVAIL**. THE NEXT STEP OF OUR EVOLUTION IS...
...A SUCCESS!
BUT IT IS IMPORTANT TO KNOW IF RICHARD OR ULRIK SURVIVED OUR ATTACK...
ULRIK...
WHERE'S ULRIK?!!

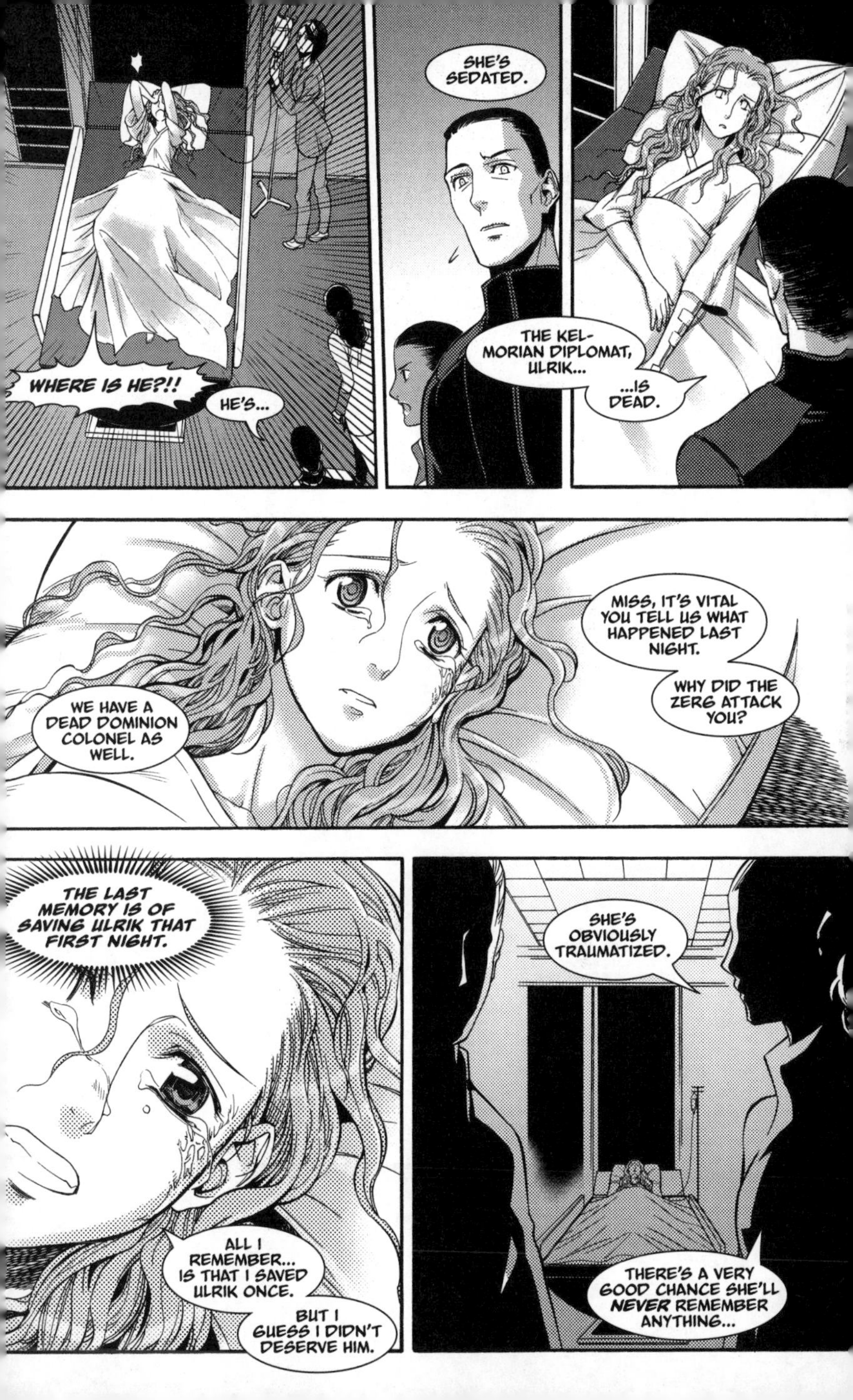
WHERE IS HE?!!
HE'S...
SHE'S SEDATED.
THE KEL-MORIAN DIPLOMAT, ULRIK...
...IS DEAD.
MISS, IT'S VITAL YOU TELL US WHAT HAPPENED LAST NIGHT.
WHY DID THE ZERG ATTACK YOU?
WE HAVE A DEAD DOMINION COLONEL AS WELL.
THE LAST MEMORY IS OF SAVING ULRIK THAT FIRST NIGHT.
ALL I REMEMBER... IS THAT I SAVED ULRIK ONCE.
BUT I GUESS I DIDN'T DESERVE HIM.
SHE'S OBVIOUSLY TRAUMATIZED.
THERE'S A VERY GOOD CHANCE SHE'LL NEVER REMEMBER ANYTHING...

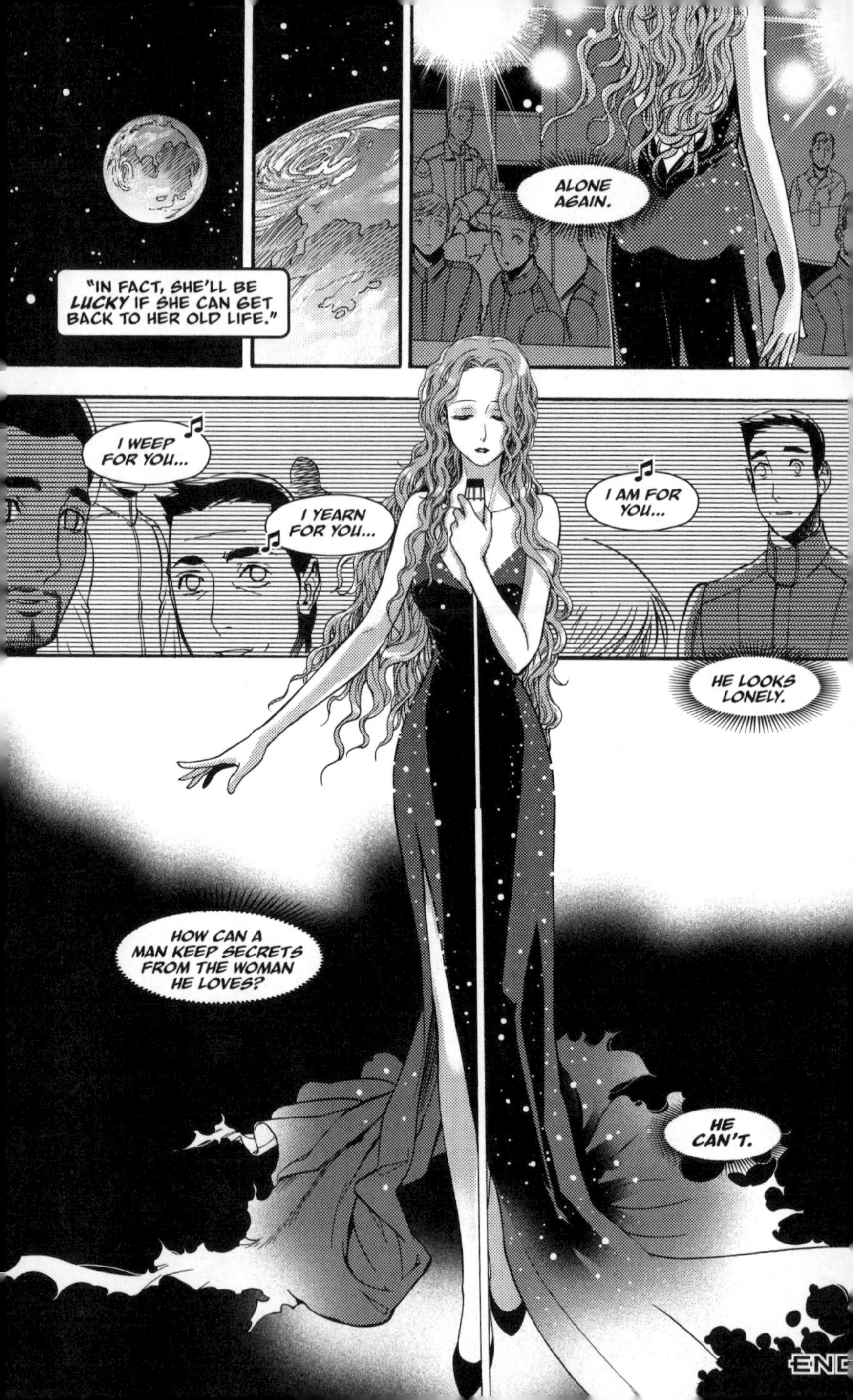
"IN FACT, SHE'LL BE *LUCKY* IF SHE CAN GET BACK TO HER OLD LIFE."
ALONE AGAIN.
I WEEP FOR YOU...
I YEARN FOR YOU...
I AM FOR YOU...
HE LOOKS LONELY.
HOW CAN A MAN KEEP SECRETS FROM THE WOMAN HE LOVES?
HE CAN'T.
END

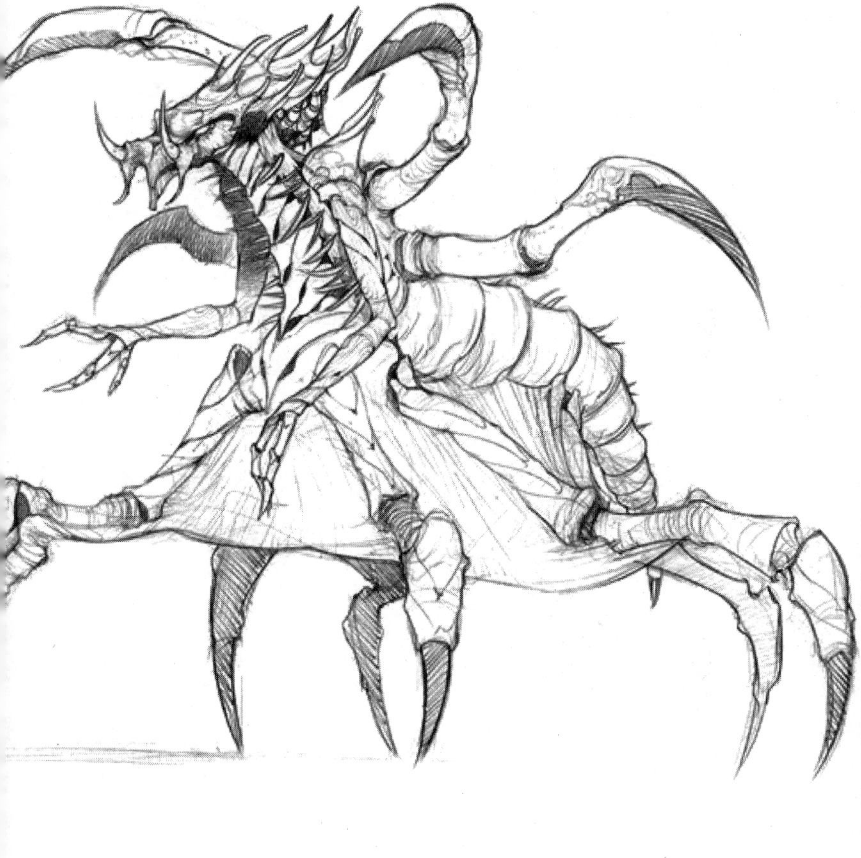

STARCRAFT

FRONTLINE
VOLUME 3

TWILIGHT ARCHON

Written by Ren Zatopek

Pencils and Inks by Noel Rodriguez

Additional Inks by Mel Joy San Juan

Tones by Mara Aum

Letterer: Michael Paolilli

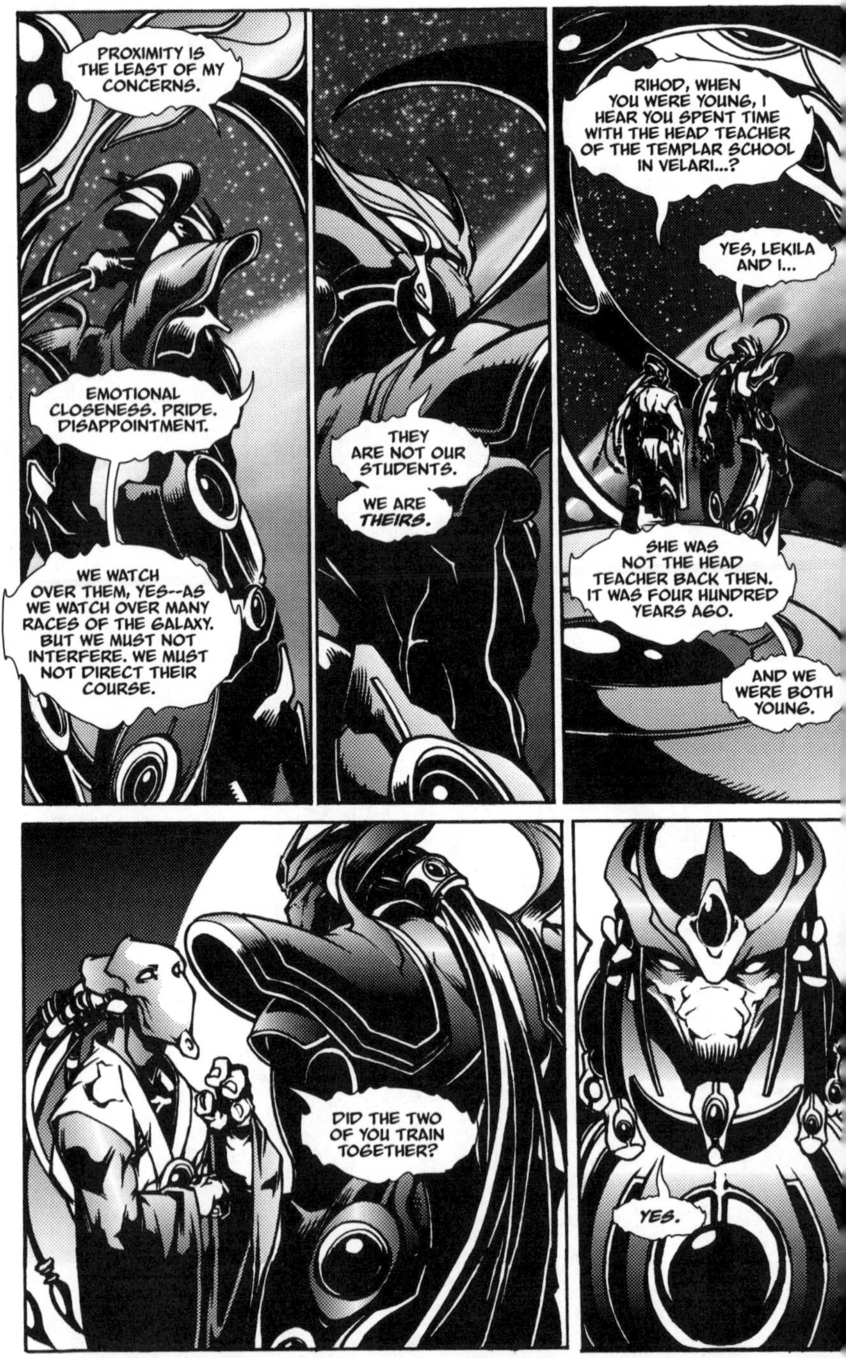
PROXIMITY IS THE LEAST OF MY CONCERNS.
EMOTIONAL CLOSENESS. PRIDE. DISAPPOINTMENT.
WE WATCH OVER THEM, YES--AS WE WATCH OVER MANY RACES OF THE GALAXY. BUT WE MUST NOT INTERFERE. WE MUST NOT DIRECT THEIR COURSE.
THEY ARE NOT OUR STUDENTS.
WE ARE *THEIRS*.
RIHOD, WHEN YOU WERE YOUNG, I HEAR YOU SPENT TIME WITH THE HEAD TEACHER OF THE TEMPLAR SCHOOL IN VELARI...?
YES, LEKILA AND I...
SHE WAS NOT THE HEAD TEACHER BACK THEN. IT WAS FOUR HUNDRED YEARS AGO.
AND WE WERE BOTH YOUNG.
DID THE TWO OF YOU TRAIN TOGETHER?
YES.

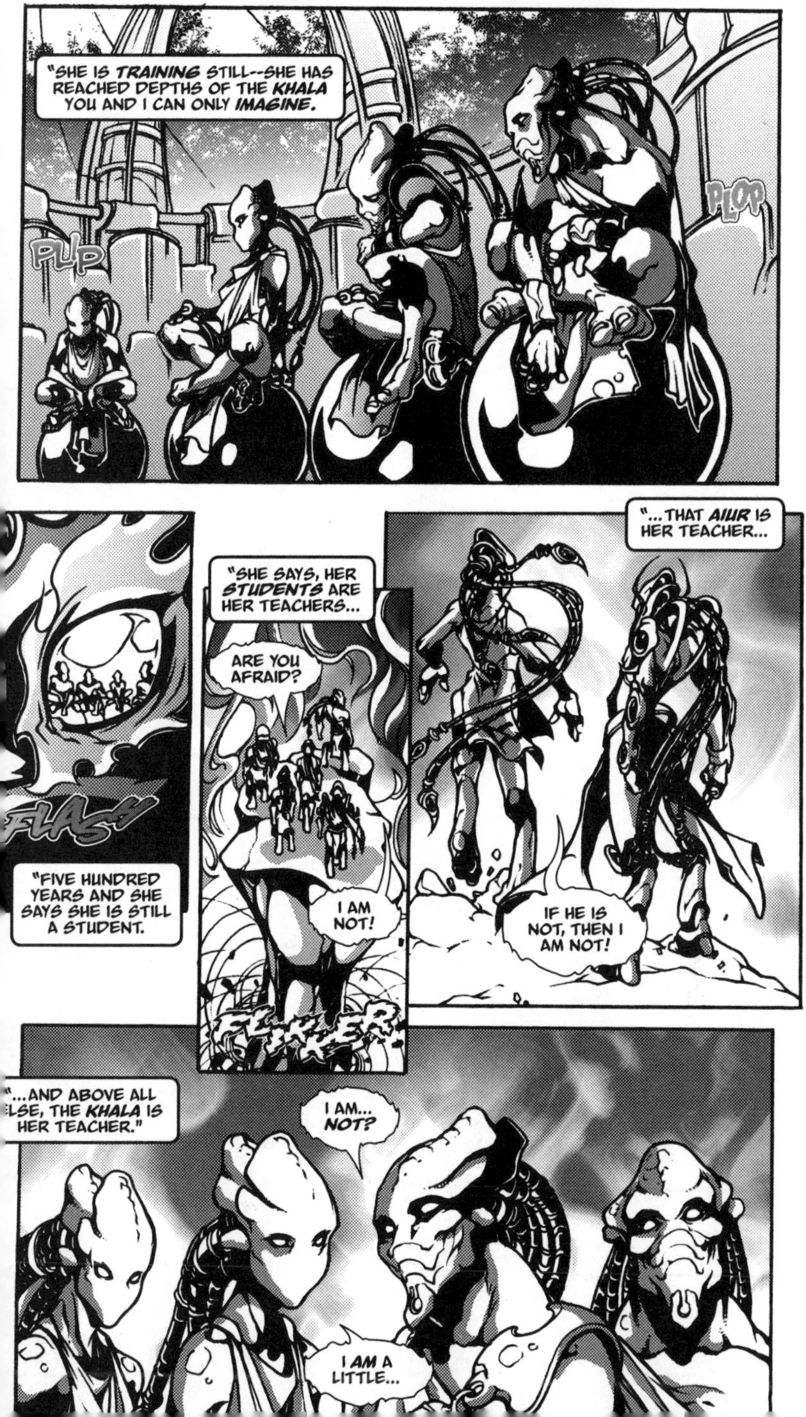

"SHE IS *TRAINING* STILL--SHE HAS REACHED DEPTHS OF THE *KHALA* YOU AND I CAN ONLY *IMAGINE.*
PLIP
PLOP
FLASH
"FIVE HUNDRED YEARS AND SHE SAYS SHE IS STILL A STUDENT.
"SHE SAYS, HER *STUDENTS* ARE HER TEACHERS...
ARE YOU AFRAID?
I AM NOT!
"...THAT *AIUR* IS HER TEACHER...
IF HE IS NOT, THEN I AM NOT!
"...AND ABOVE ALL ELSE, THE *KHALA* IS HER TEACHER."
I AM... *NOT?*
I *AM* A LITTLE...

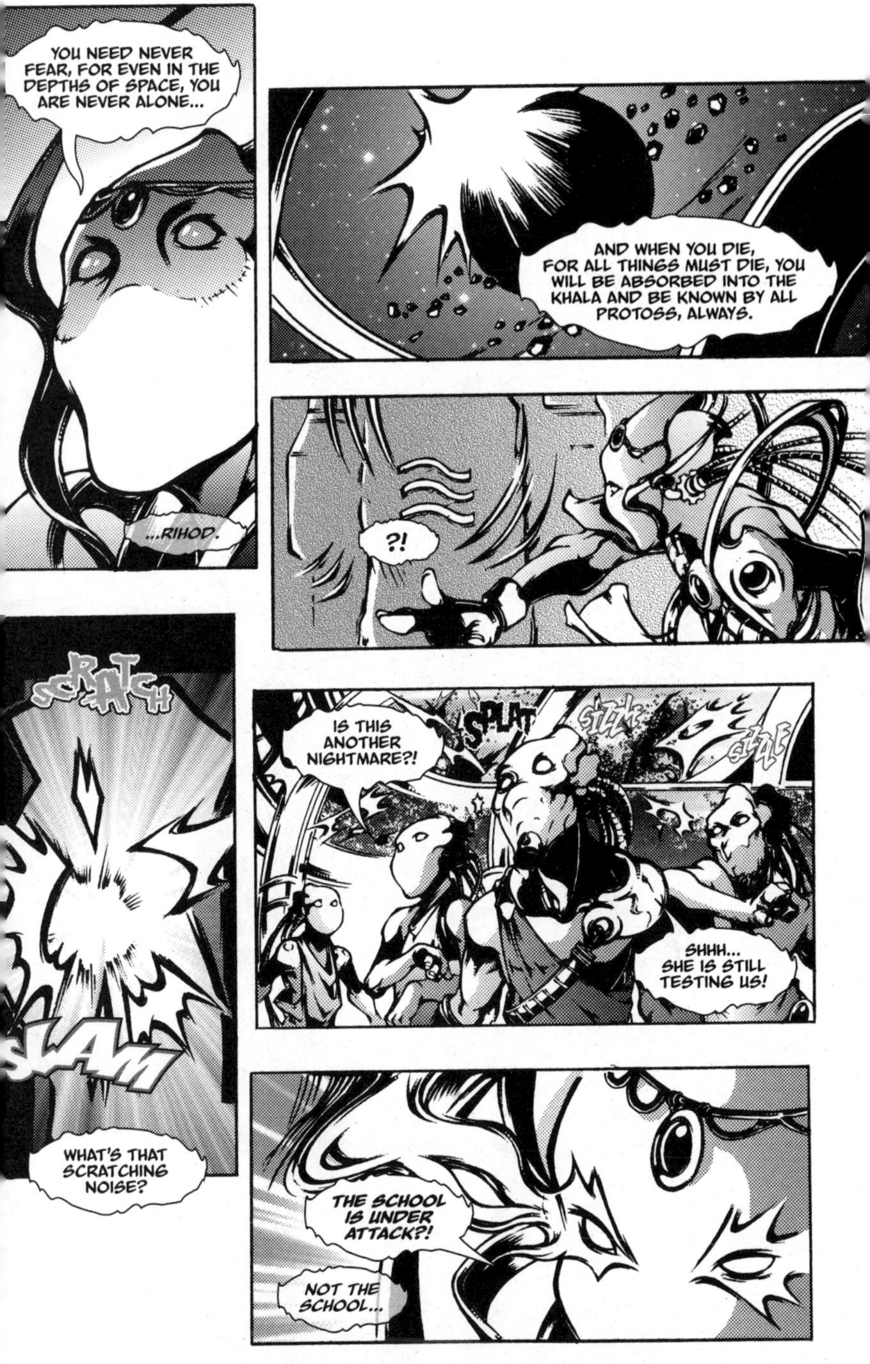
YOU NEED NEVER FEAR, FOR EVEN IN THE DEPTHS OF SPACE, YOU ARE NEVER ALONE...
AND WHEN YOU DIE, FOR ALL THINGS MUST DIE, YOU WILL BE ABSORBED INTO THE KHALA AND BE KNOWN BY ALL PROTOSS, ALWAYS.
...RIHOD.
?!
SCRATCH
SLAM
WHAT'S THAT SCRATCHING NOISE?
IS THIS ANOTHER NIGHTMARE?!
SPLAT
SHHH... SHE IS STILL TESTING US!
THE SCHOOL IS UNDER ATTACK?!
NOT THE SCHOOL...

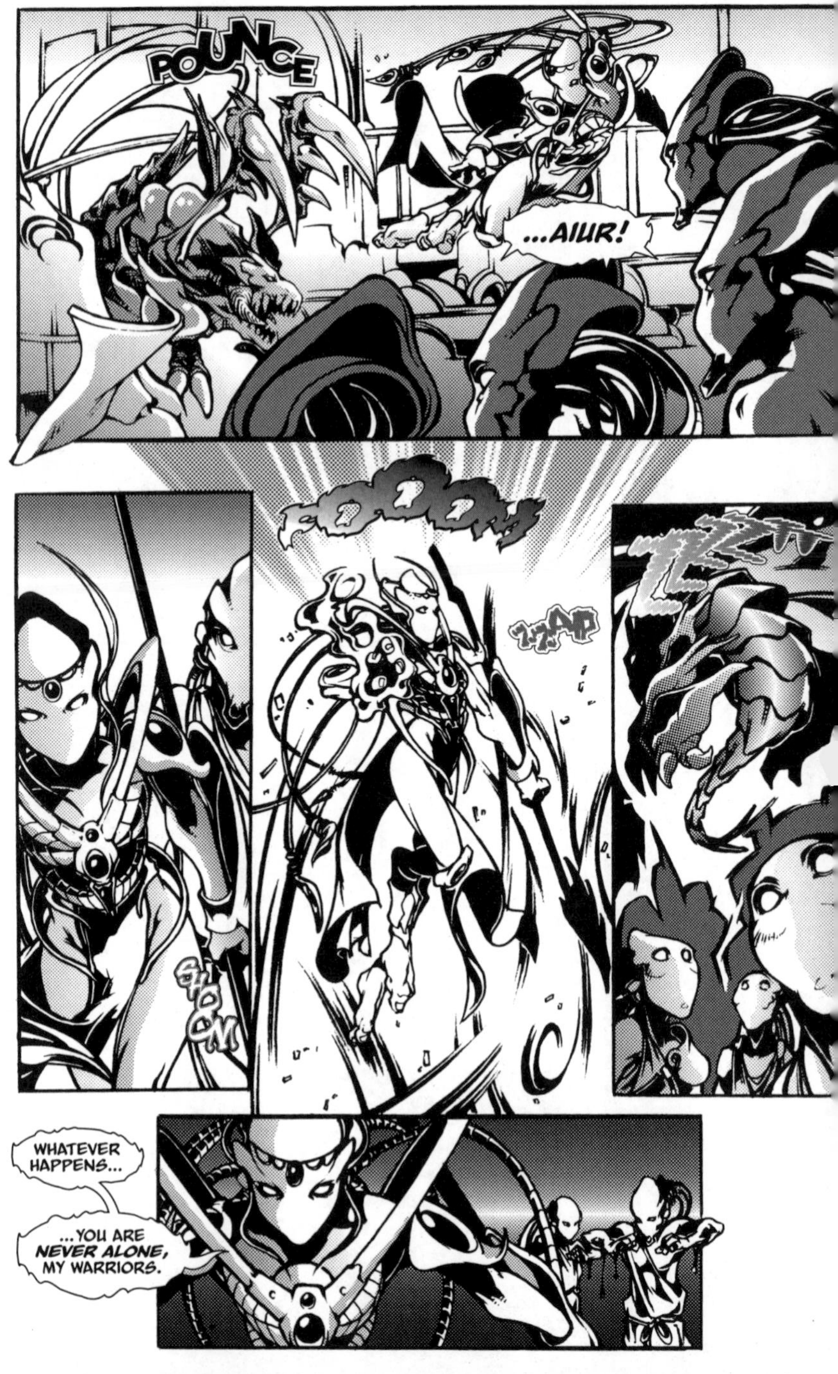
POUNCE
...AIUR!
WHATEVER HAPPENS...
...YOU ARE NEVER ALONE, MY WARRIORS.

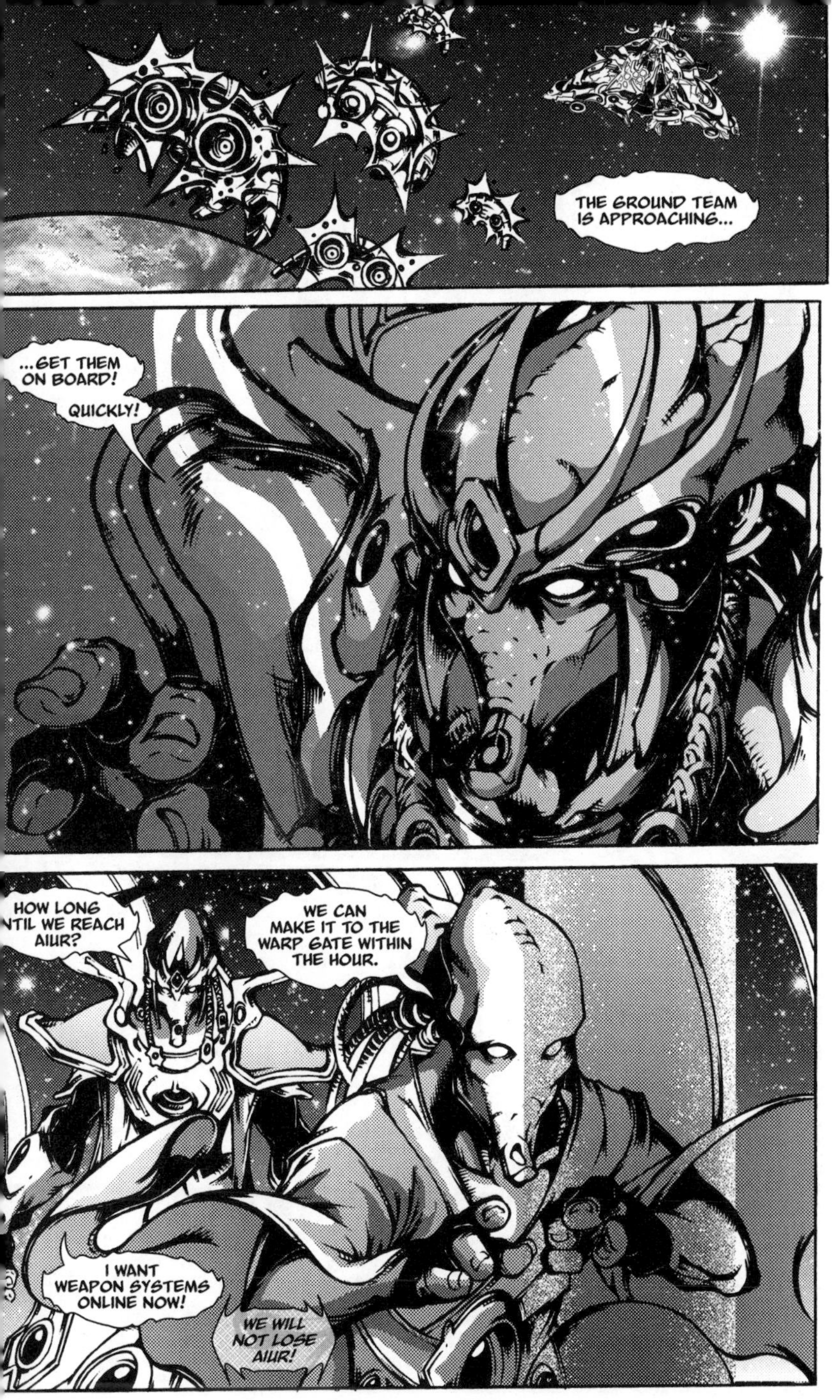
THE GROUND TEAM IS APPROACHING...
...GET THEM ON BOARD!
QUICKLY!
HOW LONG UNTIL WE REACH AIUR?
WE CAN MAKE IT TO THE WARP GATE WITHIN THE HOUR.
I WANT WEAPON SYSTEMS ONLINE NOW!
WE WILL NOT LOSE AIUR!

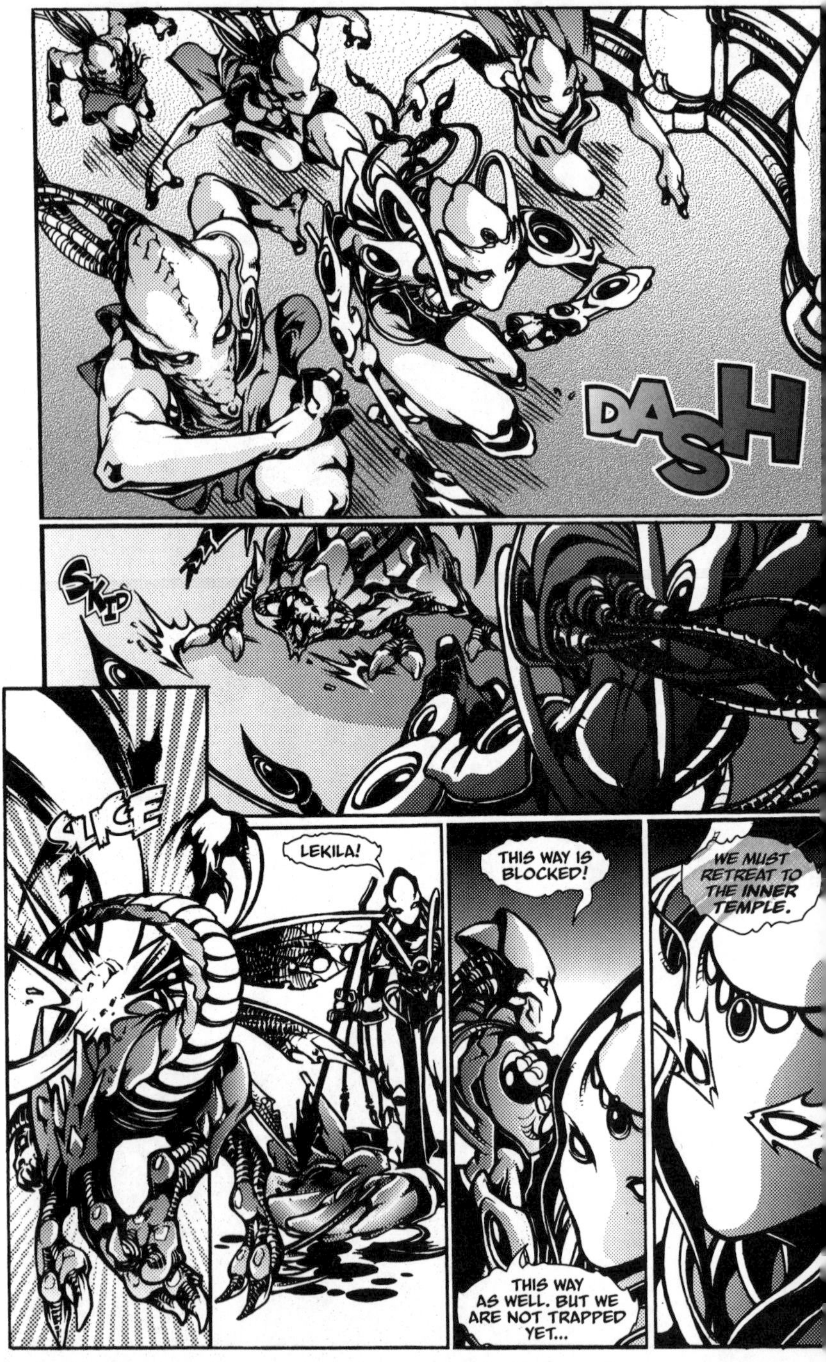
DASH
SKIP
SLICE
LEKILA!
THIS WAY IS BLOCKED!
THIS WAY AS WELL. BUT WE ARE NOT TRAPPED YET...
WE MUST RETREAT TO THE INNER TEMPLE.

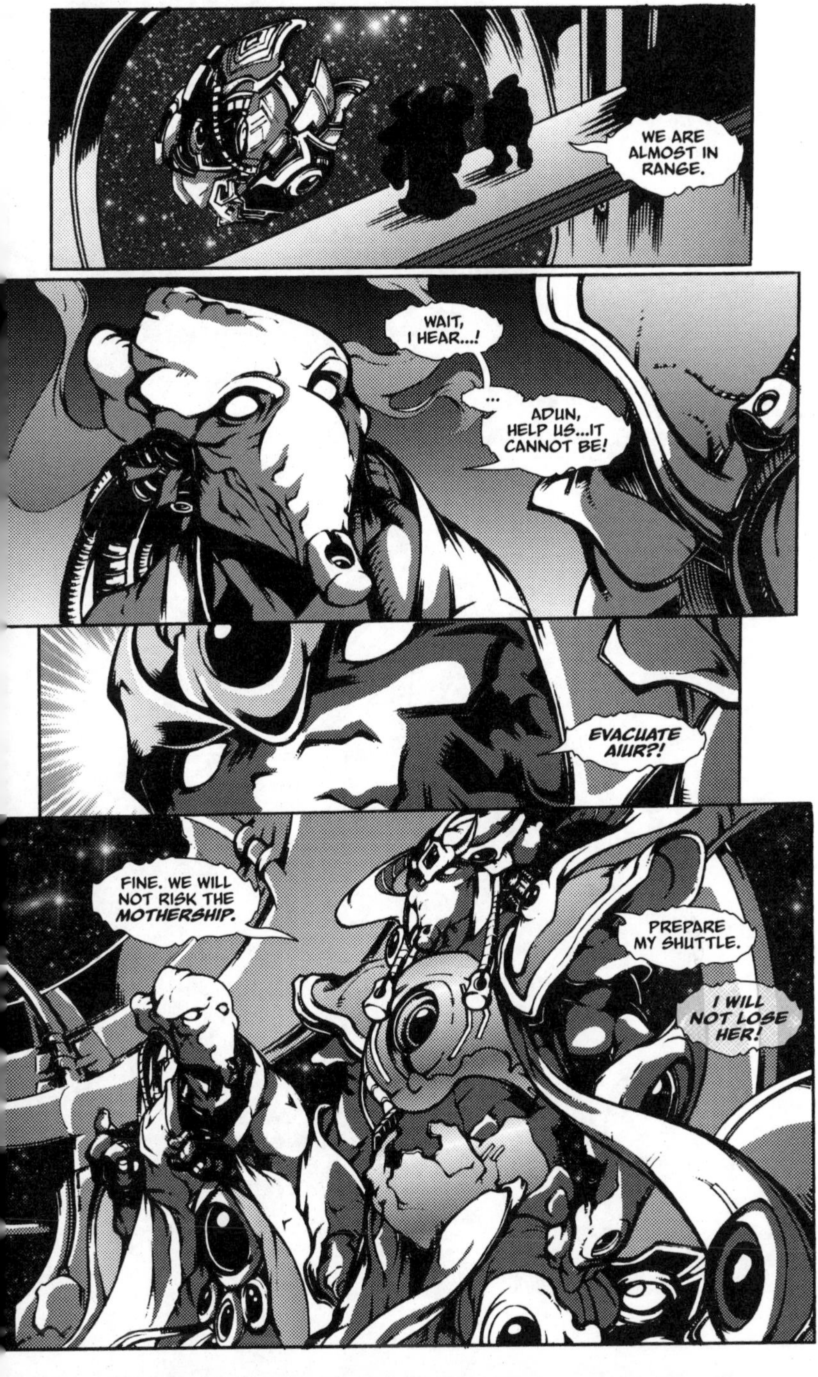
WE ARE ALMOST IN RANGE.
WAIT, I HEAR...!
... ADUN, HELP US...IT CANNOT BE!
EVACUATE AIUR?!
FINE. WE WILL NOT RISK THE *MOTHERSHIP*.
PREPARE MY SHUTTLE.
I WILL NOT LOSE HER!

HERE WE HAVE TEN OF THE FUTURE'S FINEST TEMPLAR.

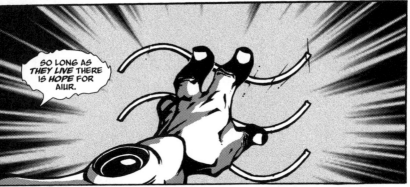

SO LONG AS *THEY LIVE* THERE IS *HOPE* FOR AIUR.

EVERYONE DOWN!

MY FELLOW TEACHERS...

...I *SAID* EVERYONE.

SO LONG AS THEY LIVE...

WFOOOSH

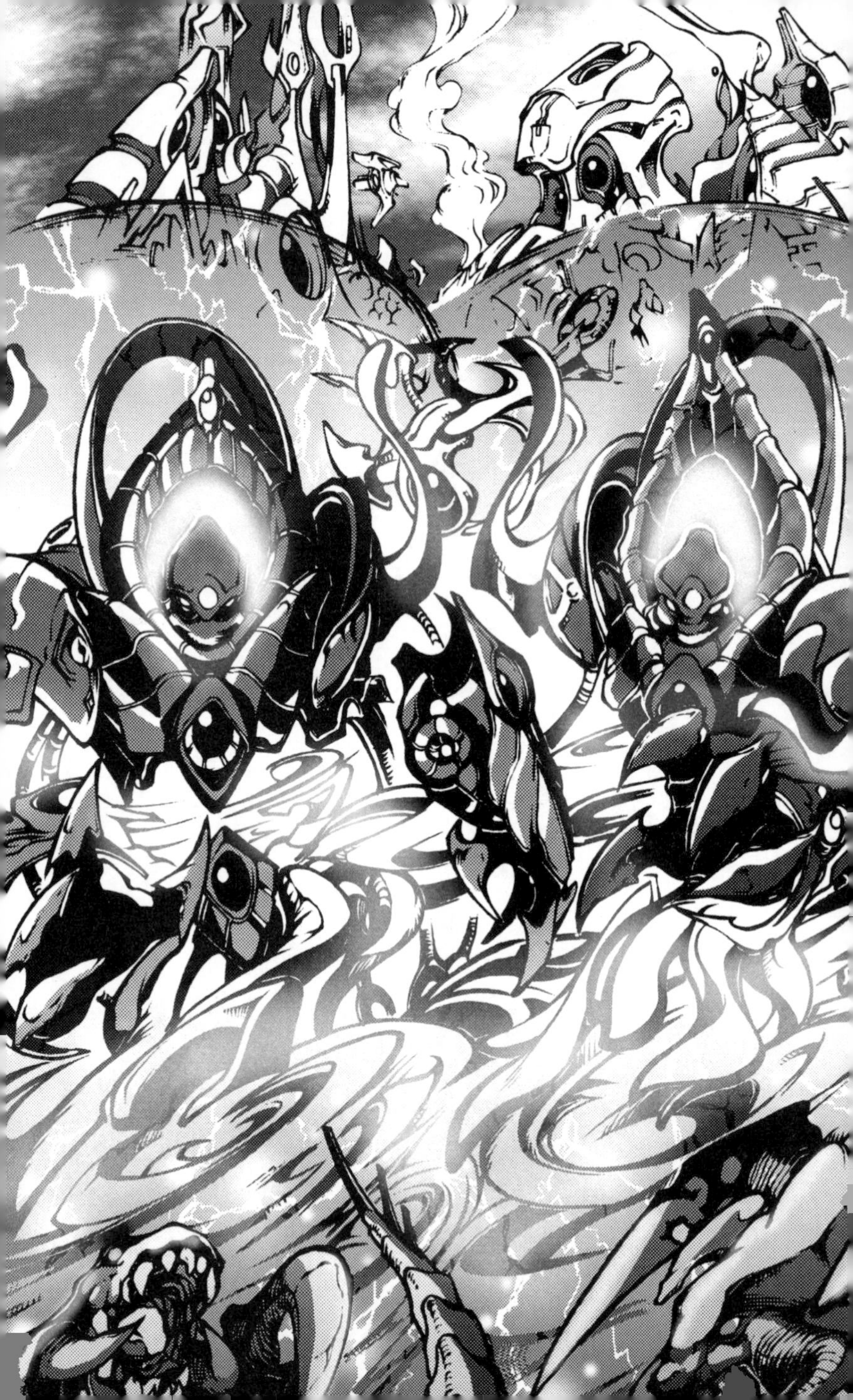

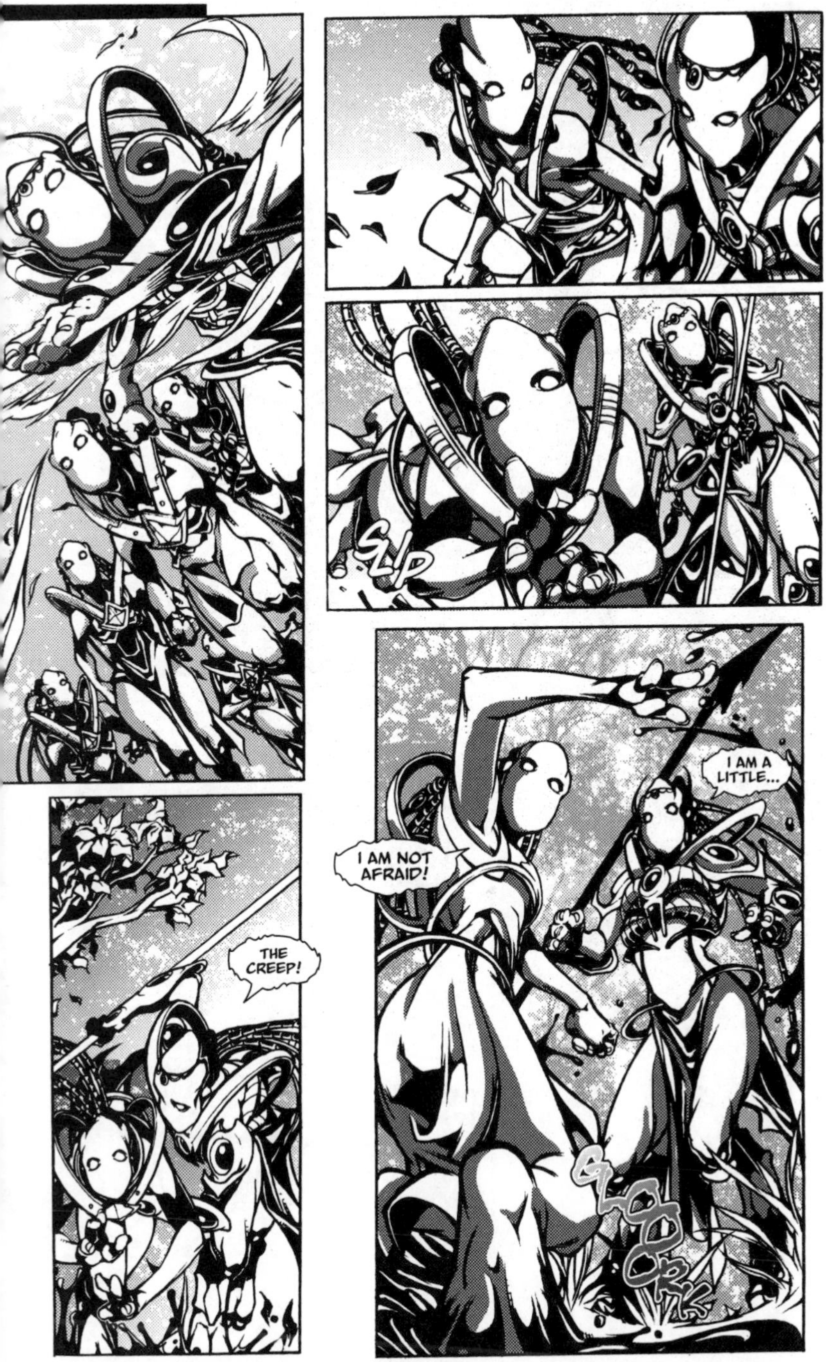
SLIP
THE CREEP!
I AM A LITTLE...
I AM NOT AFRAID!

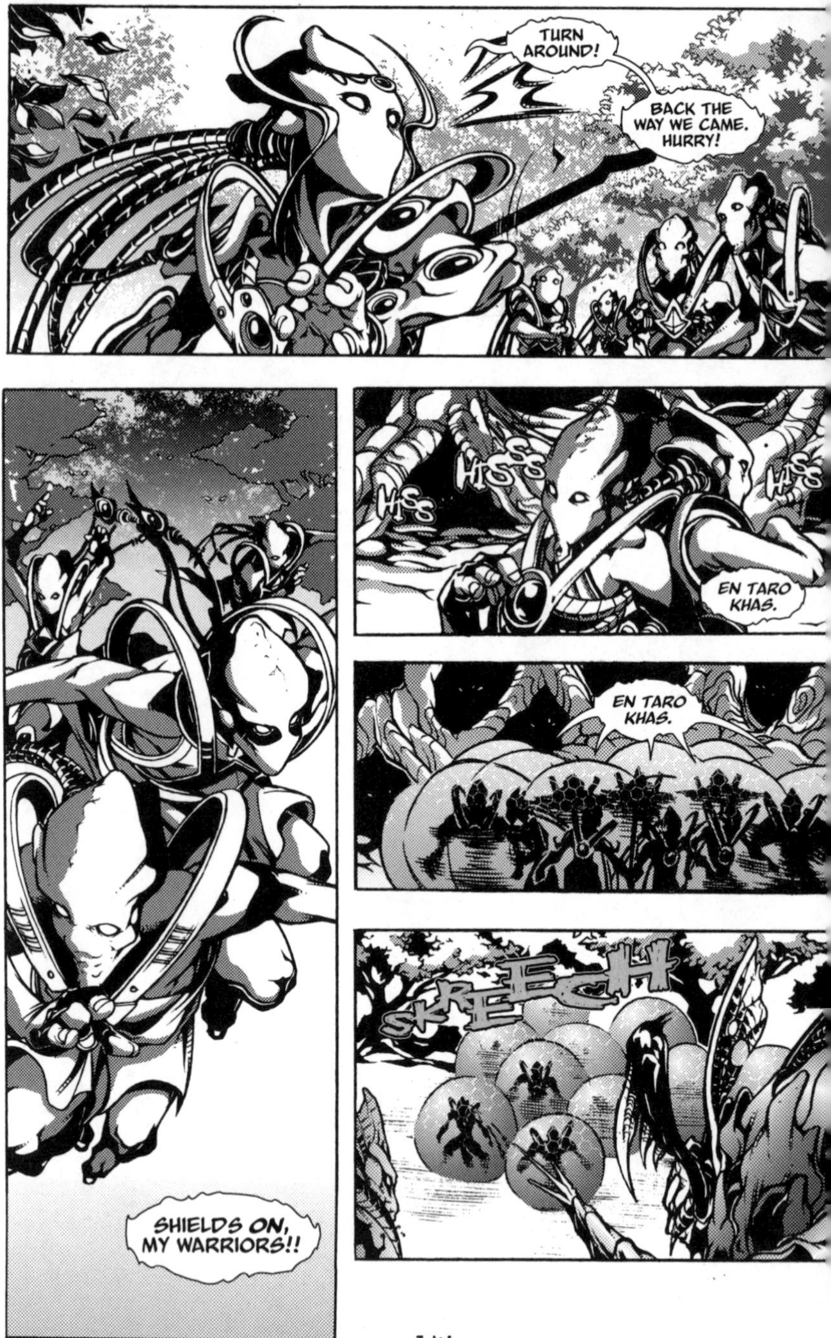
TURN AROUND!
BACK THE WAY WE CAME. HURRY!
SHIELDS ON, MY WARRIORS!!
HISS
HISSS
HISS
EN TARO KHAS.
EN TARO KHAS.
SKREECH

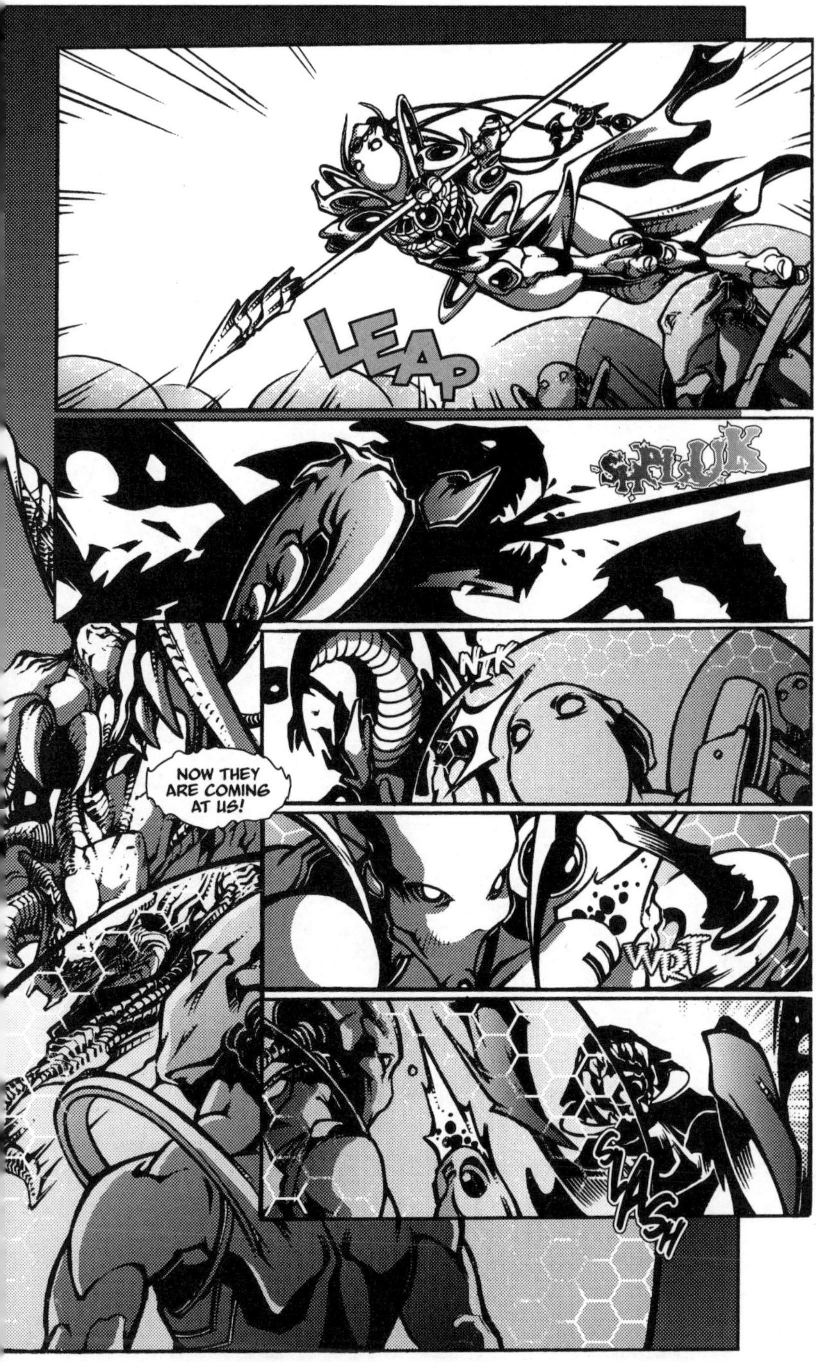
LEAP
SPLUK
NIK
NOW THEY ARE COMING AT US!
WRT
SLASH

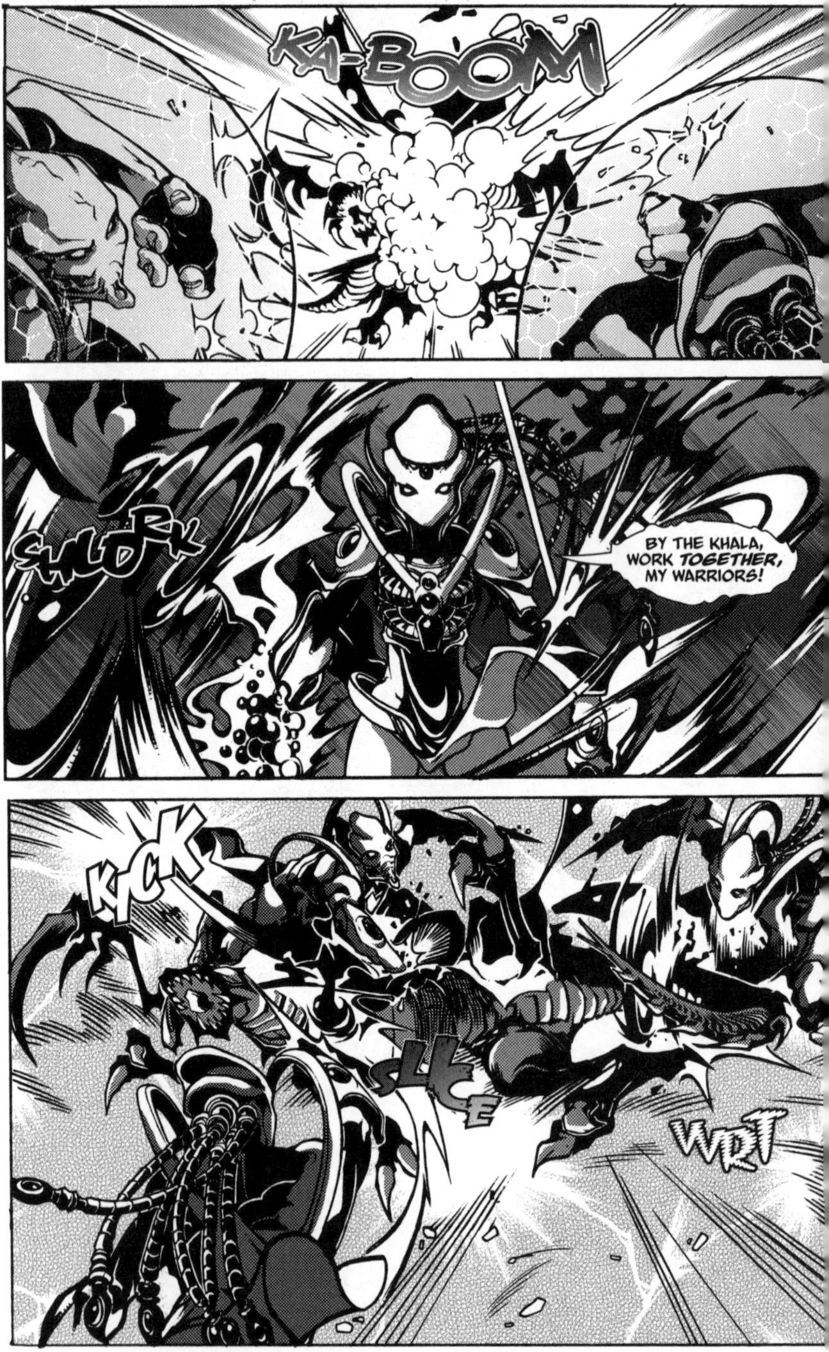
KA-BOOM
BY THE KHALA, WORK *TOGETHER*, MY WARRIORS!
SLICE
VVRT

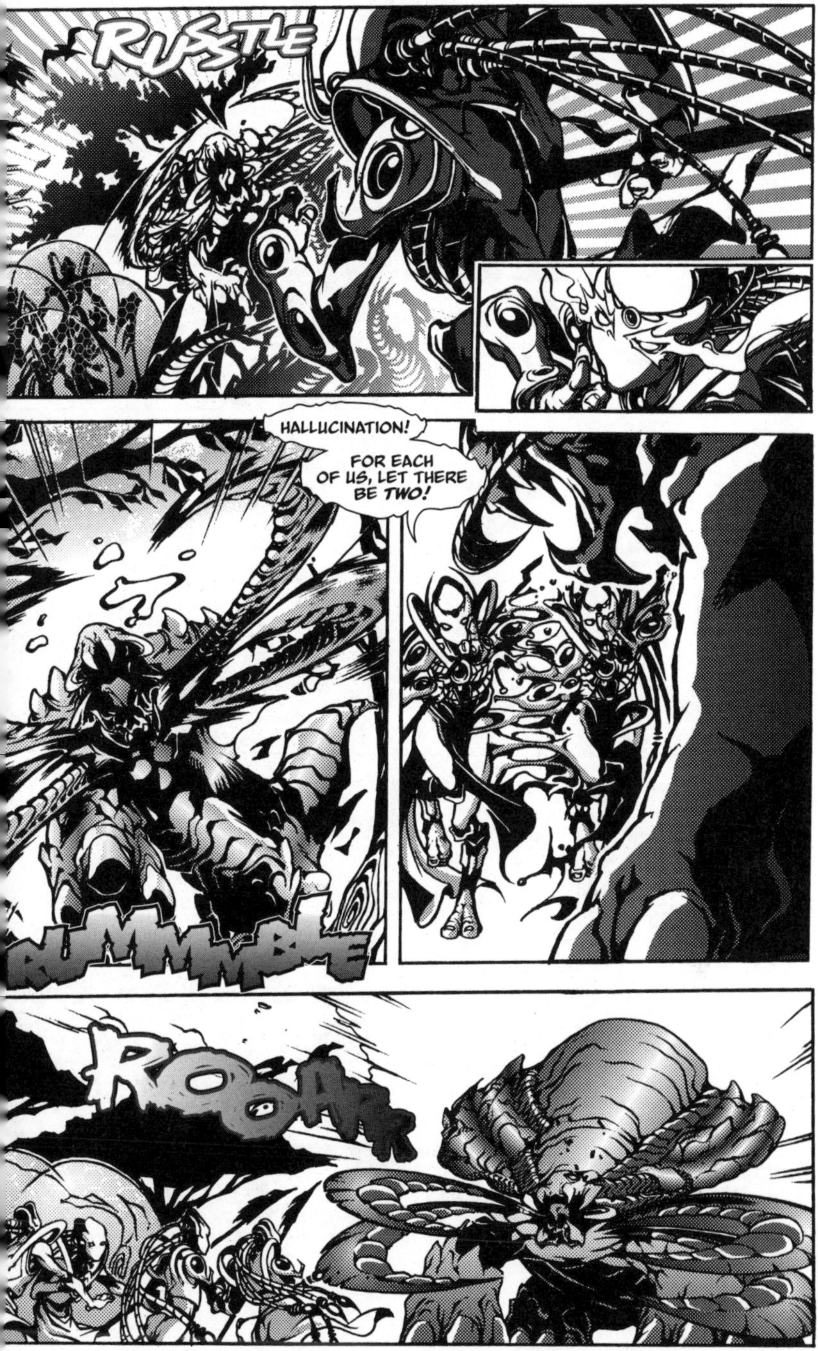
RUSSTLE
HALLUCINATION!
FOR EACH OF US, LET THERE BE *TWO!*
RUMMMBLE
ROOM

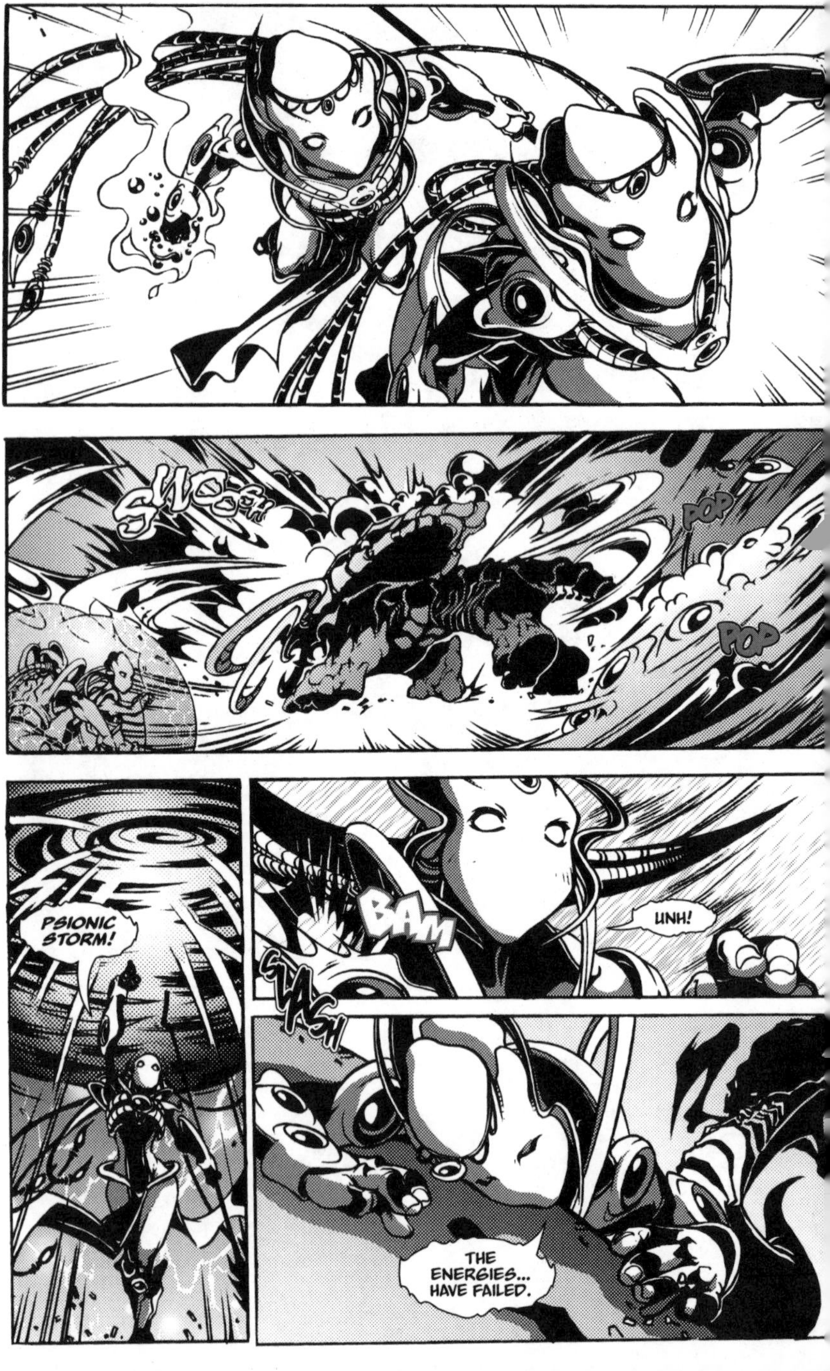

SWOOSH
POP
POP
PSIONIC STORM!
BAM
UNH!
SLASH
THE ENERGIES... HAVE FAILED.

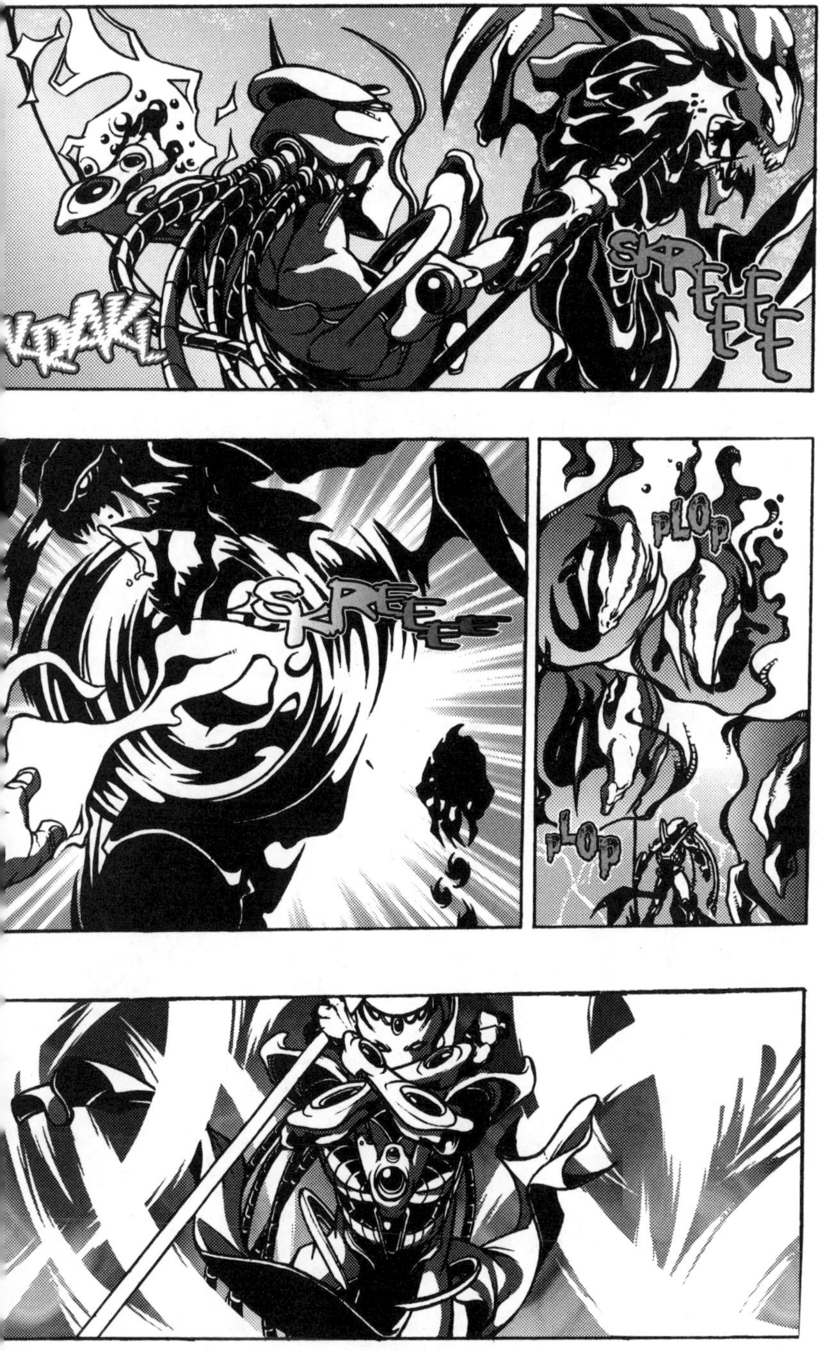
SKREEEEE
SKREEEE
PLOP
PLOP

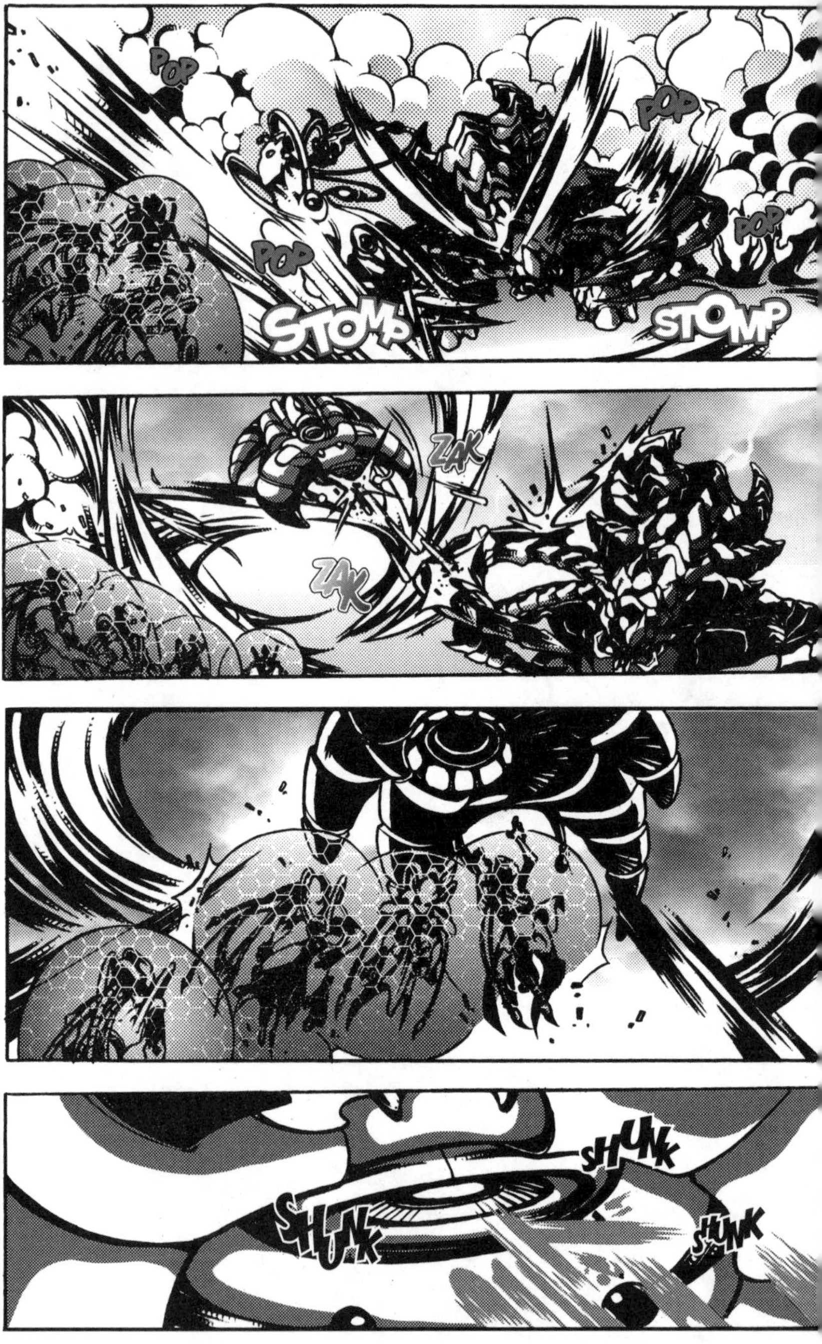
POP
POP
POP
POP
STOMP
STOMP
ZAK
ZAK
SHUNK
SHUNK
SHUNK

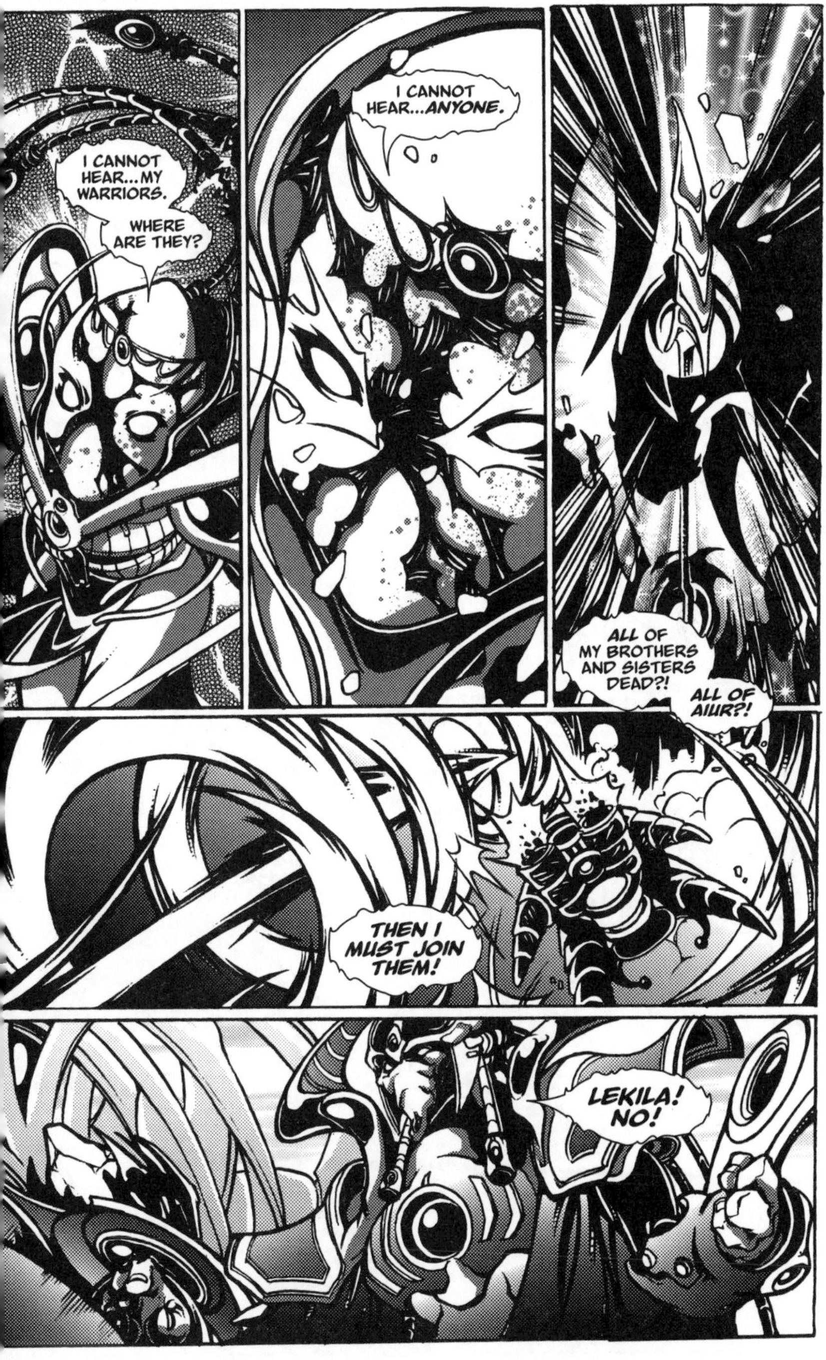
I CANNOT HEAR...MY WARRIORS.
WHERE ARE THEY?
I CANNOT HEAR...ANYONE.
ALL OF MY BROTHERS AND SISTERS DEAD?!
ALL OF AIUR?!
THEN I MUST JOIN THEM!
LEKILA! NO!

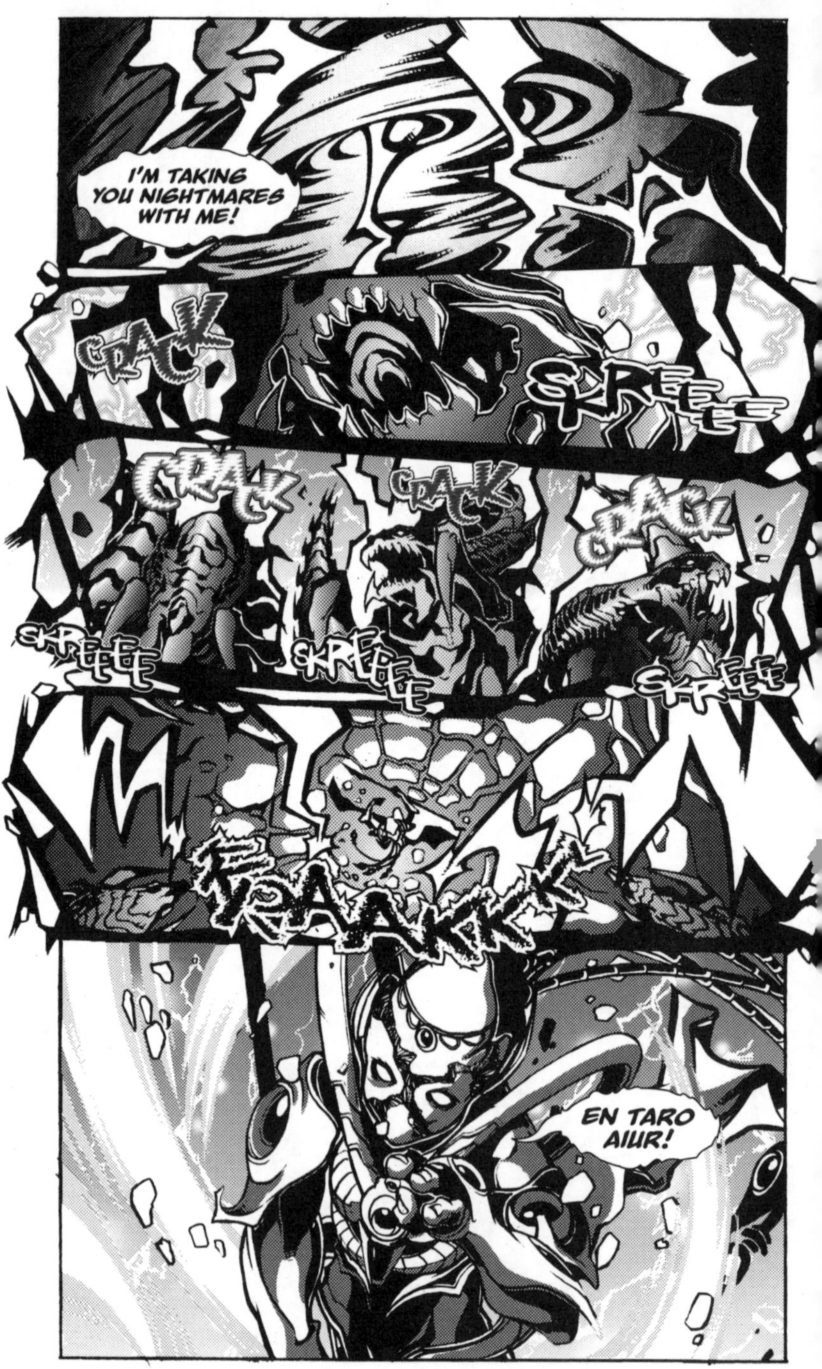
I'M TAKING YOU NIGHTMARES WITH ME!
CRACK
CRACK
CRACK
CRACK
EN TARO AIUR!

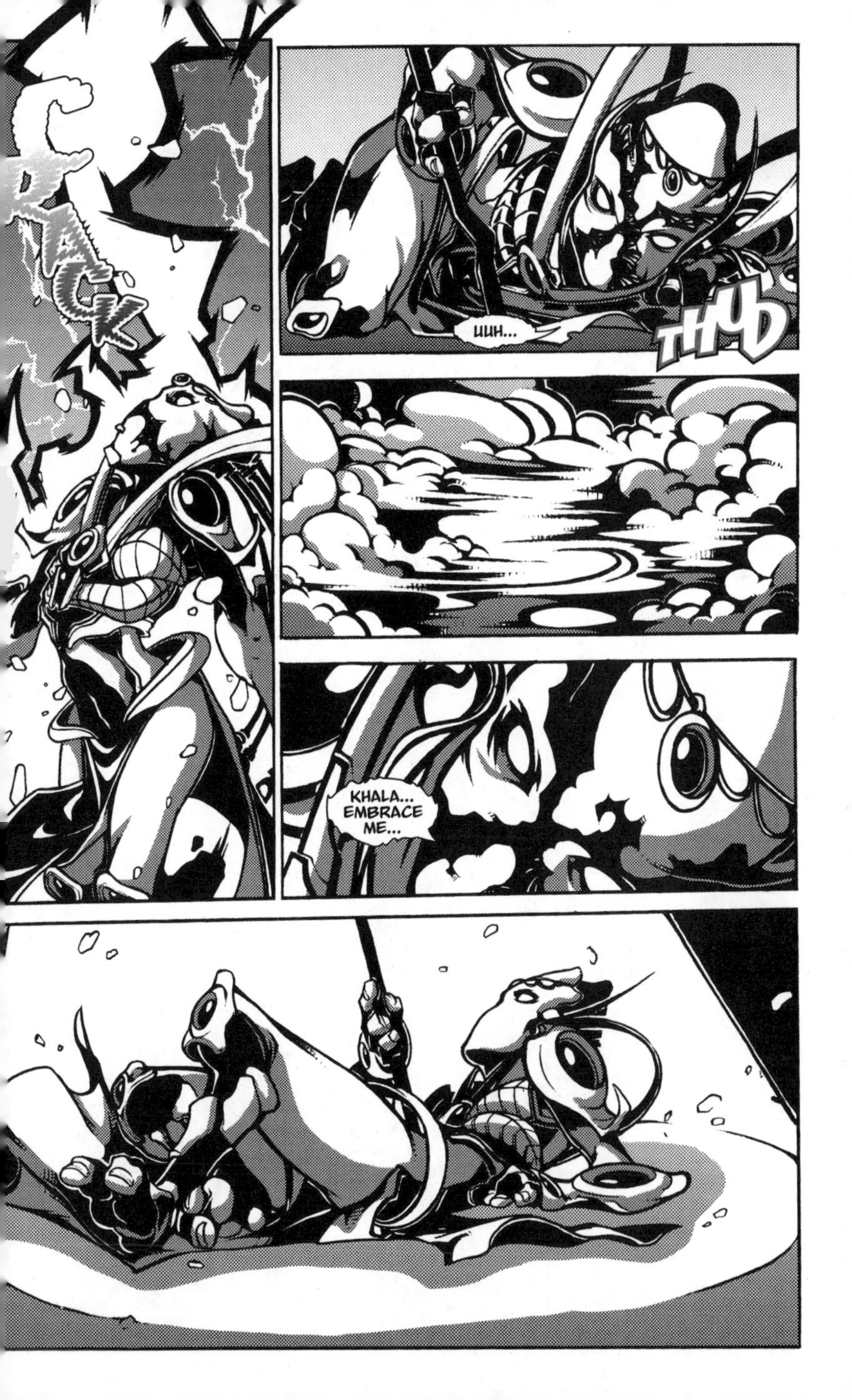
CRACK
UUH...
THUD
KHALA... EMBRACE ME...

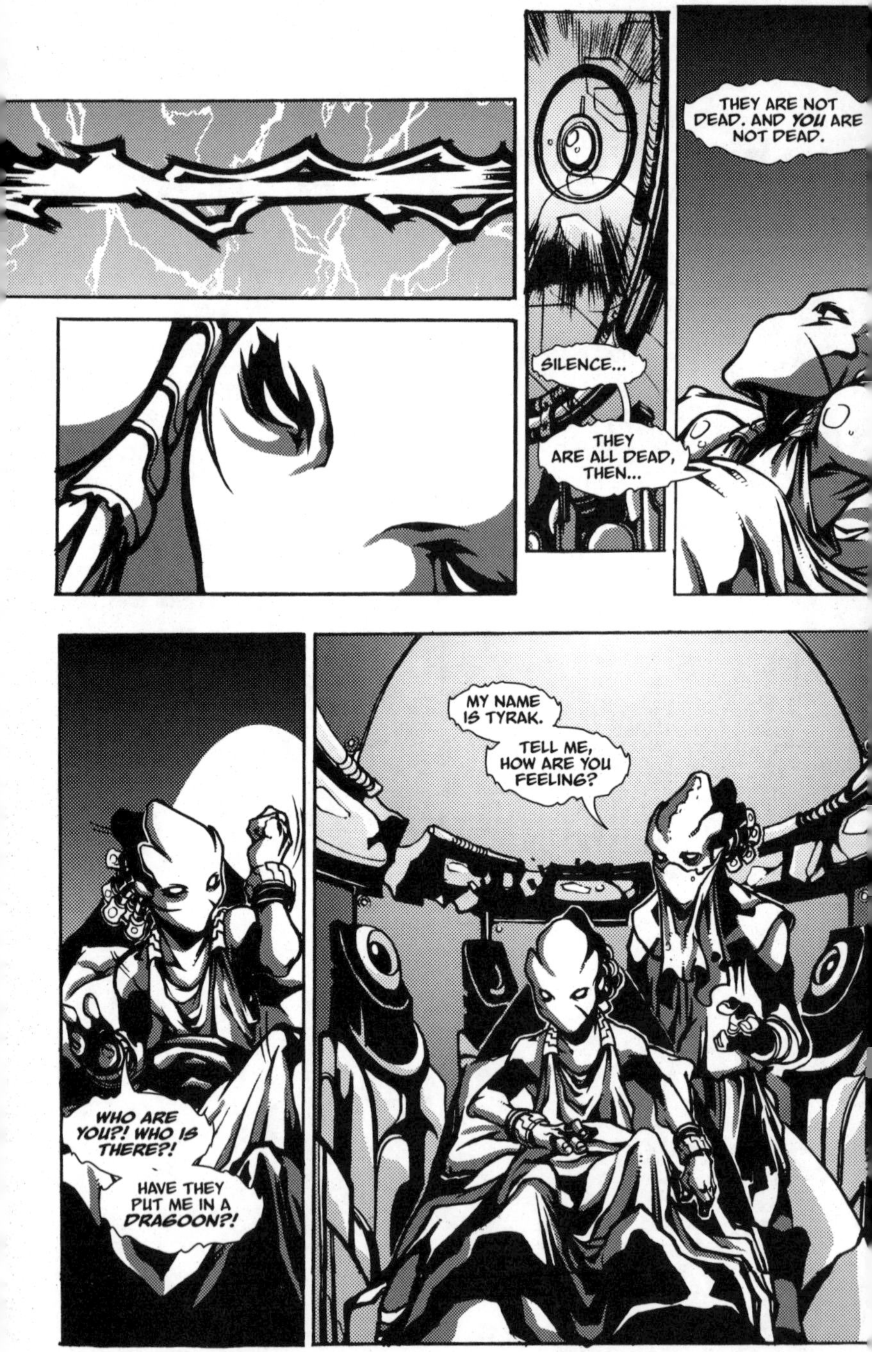
SILENCE...
THEY ARE ALL DEAD, THEN...
THEY ARE NOT DEAD. AND YOU ARE NOT DEAD.
WHO ARE YOU?! WHO IS THERE?!
HAVE THEY PUT ME IN A DRAGOON?!
MY NAME IS TYRAK.
TELL ME, HOW ARE YOU FEELING?

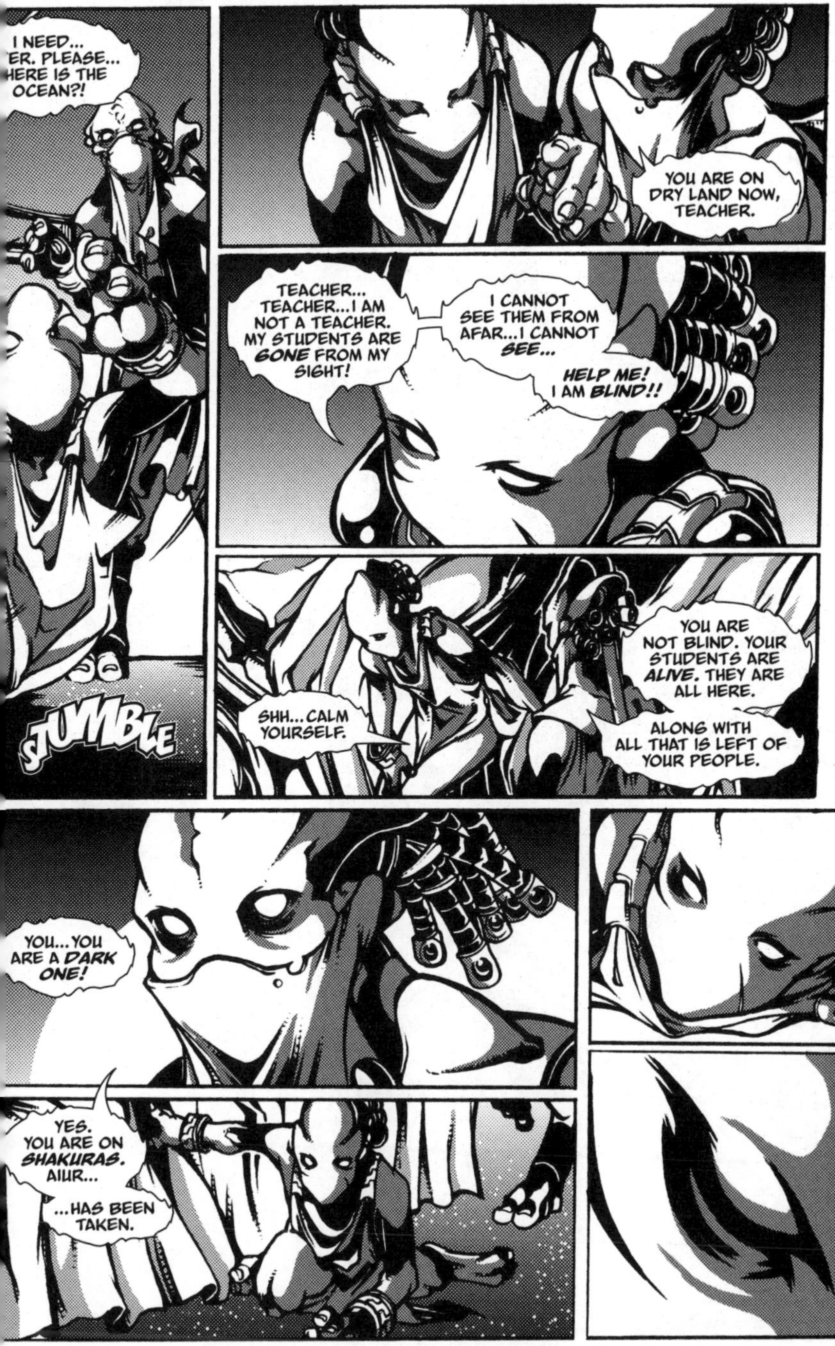
I NEED...
ER. PLEASE...
HERE IS THE
OCEAN?!
STUMBLE
YOU ARE ON
DRY LAND NOW,
TEACHER.
TEACHER...
TEACHER...I AM
NOT A TEACHER.
MY STUDENTS ARE
GONE FROM MY
SIGHT!
I CANNOT
SEE THEM FROM
AFAR...I CANNOT
SEE...
HELP ME!
I AM BLIND!!
SHH...CALM
YOURSELF.
YOU ARE
NOT BLIND. YOUR
STUDENTS ARE
ALIVE. THEY ARE
ALL HERE.
ALONG WITH
ALL THAT IS LEFT OF
YOUR PEOPLE.
YOU...YOU
ARE A DARK
ONE!
YES.
YOU ARE ON
SHAKURAS.
AIUR...
...HAS BEEN
TAKEN.

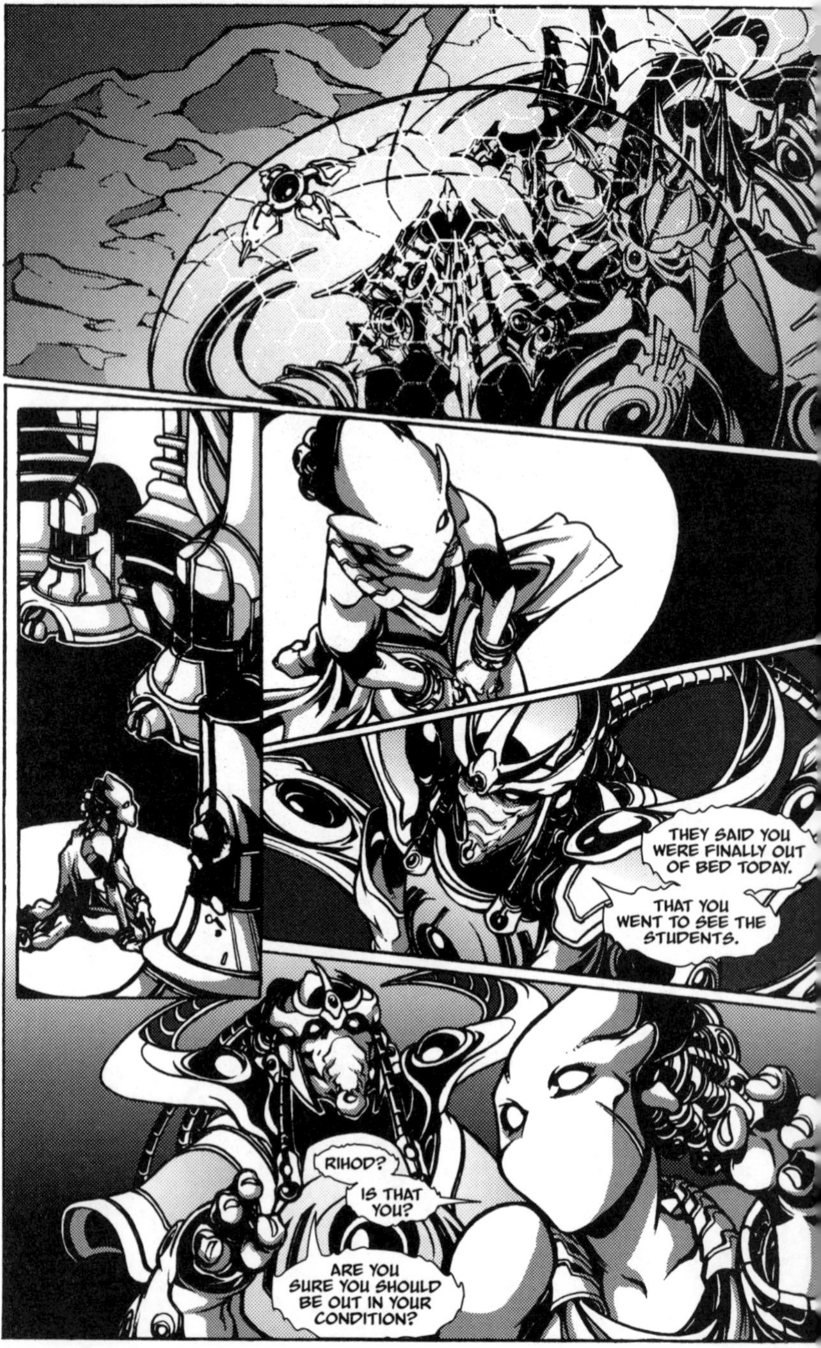
THEY SAID YOU WERE FINALLY OUT OF BED TODAY.
THAT YOU WENT TO SEE THE STUDENTS.
RIHOD?
IS THAT YOU?
ARE YOU SURE YOU SHOULD BE OUT IN YOUR CONDITION?

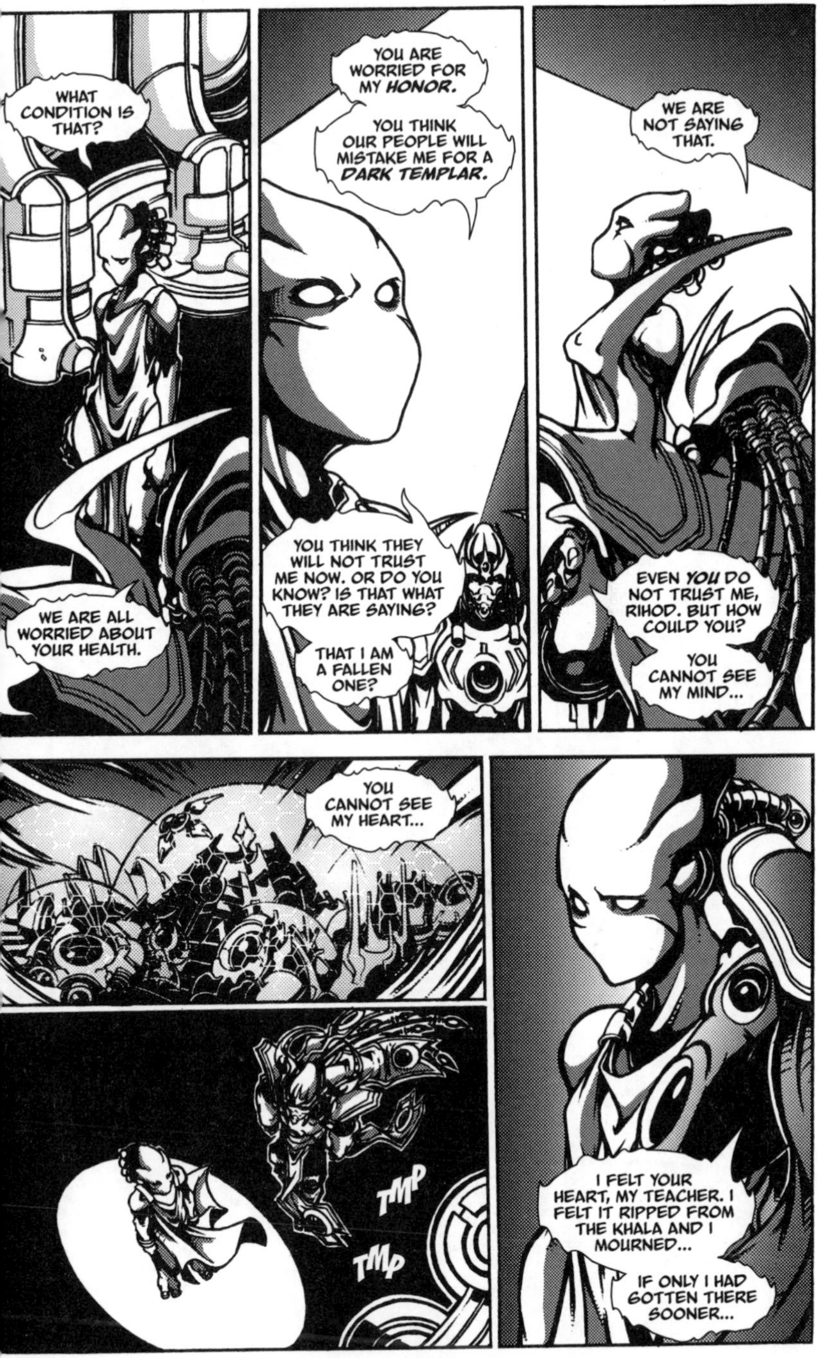
WHAT CONDITION IS THAT?
WE ARE ALL WORRIED ABOUT YOUR HEALTH.
YOU ARE WORRIED FOR MY HONOR.
YOU THINK OUR PEOPLE WILL MISTAKE ME FOR A DARK TEMPLAR.
YOU THINK THEY WILL NOT TRUST ME NOW. OR DO YOU KNOW? IS THAT WHAT THEY ARE SAYING?
THAT I AM A FALLEN ONE?
WE ARE NOT SAYING THAT.
EVEN YOU DO NOT TRUST ME, RIHOD. BUT HOW COULD YOU?
YOU CANNOT SEE MY MIND...
YOU CANNOT SEE MY HEART...
TMP
TMP
I FELT YOUR HEART, MY TEACHER. I FELT IT RIPPED FROM THE KHALA AND I MOURNED...
IF ONLY I HAD GOTTEN THERE SOONER...

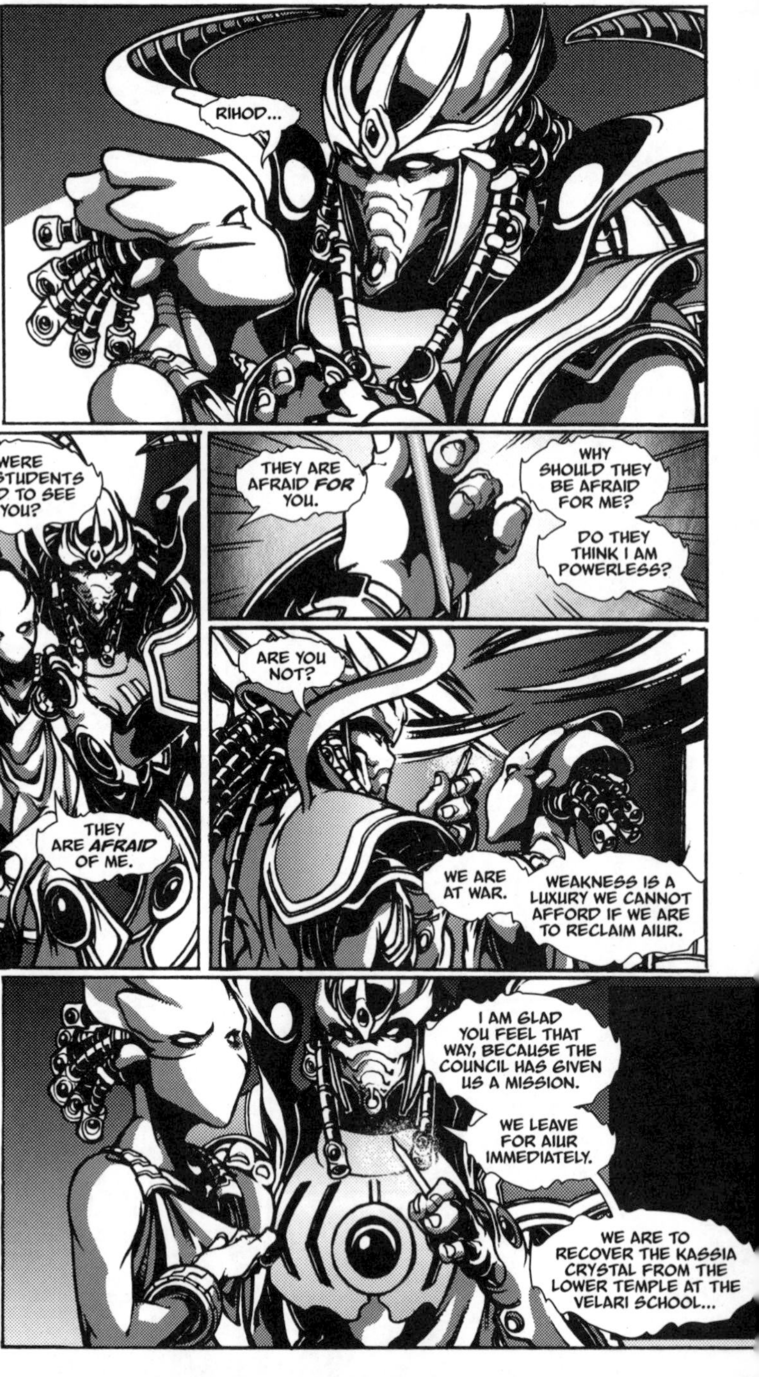
RIHOD...
WERE THE STUDENTS GLAD TO SEE YOU?
THEY ARE AFRAID OF ME.
THEY ARE AFRAID *FOR* YOU.
WHY SHOULD THEY BE AFRAID FOR ME?
DO THEY THINK I AM POWERLESS?
ARE YOU NOT?
WE ARE AT WAR.
WEAKNESS IS A LUXURY WE CANNOT AFFORD IF WE ARE TO RECLAIM AIUR.
I AM GLAD YOU FEEL THAT WAY, BECAUSE THE COUNCIL HAS GIVEN US A MISSION.
WE LEAVE FOR AIUR IMMEDIATELY.
WE ARE TO RECOVER THE KASSIA CRYSTAL FROM THE LOWER TEMPLE AT THE VELARI SCHOOL...

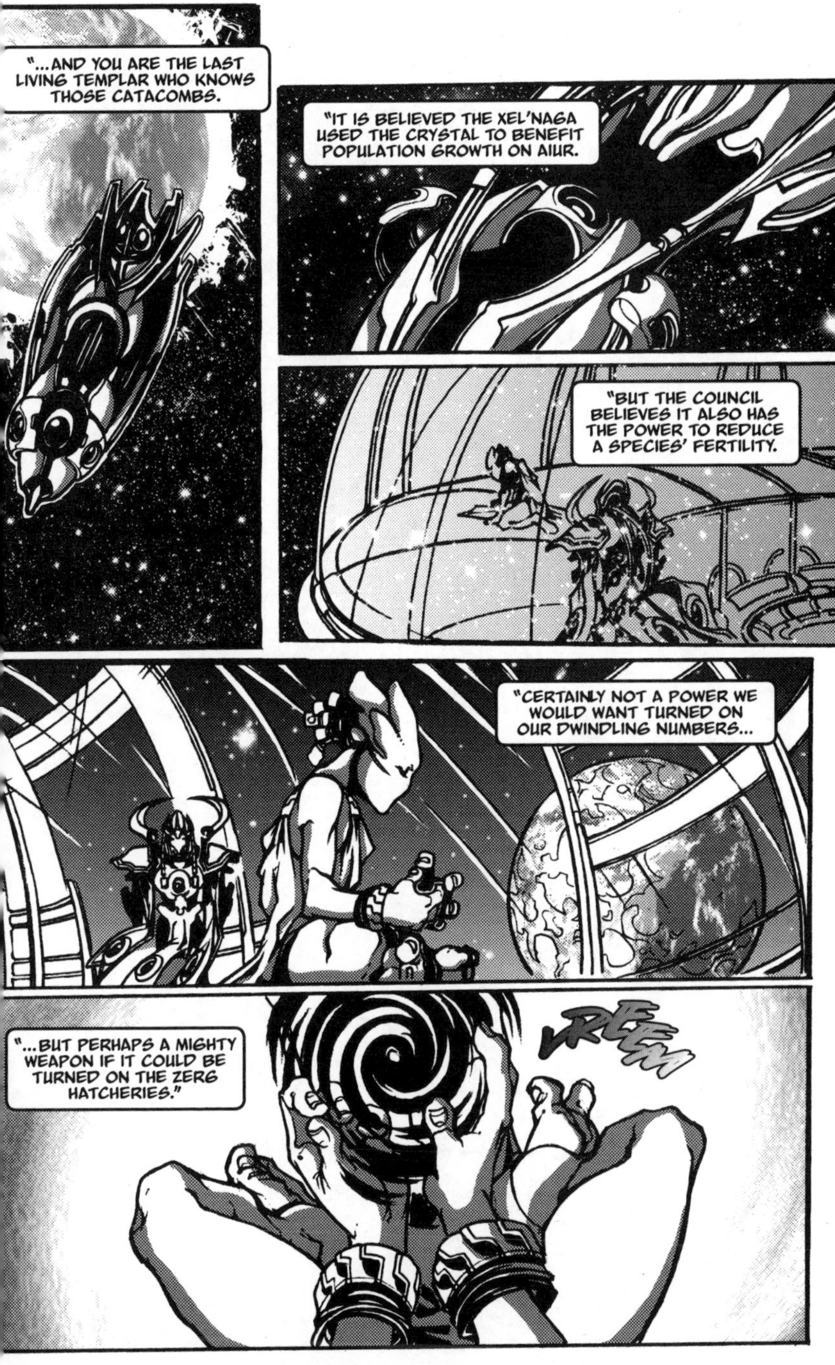
"...AND YOU ARE THE LAST LIVING TEMPLAR WHO KNOWS THOSE CATACOMBS.
"IT IS BELIEVED THE XEL'NAGA USED THE CRYSTAL TO BENEFIT POPULATION GROWTH ON AIUR.
"BUT THE COUNCIL BELIEVES IT ALSO HAS THE POWER TO REDUCE A SPECIES' FERTILITY.
"CERTAINLY NOT A POWER WE WOULD WANT TURNED ON OUR DWINDLING NUMBERS...
"...BUT PERHAPS A MIGHTY WEAPON IF IT COULD BE TURNED ON THE ZERG HATCHERIES."
VREEEM

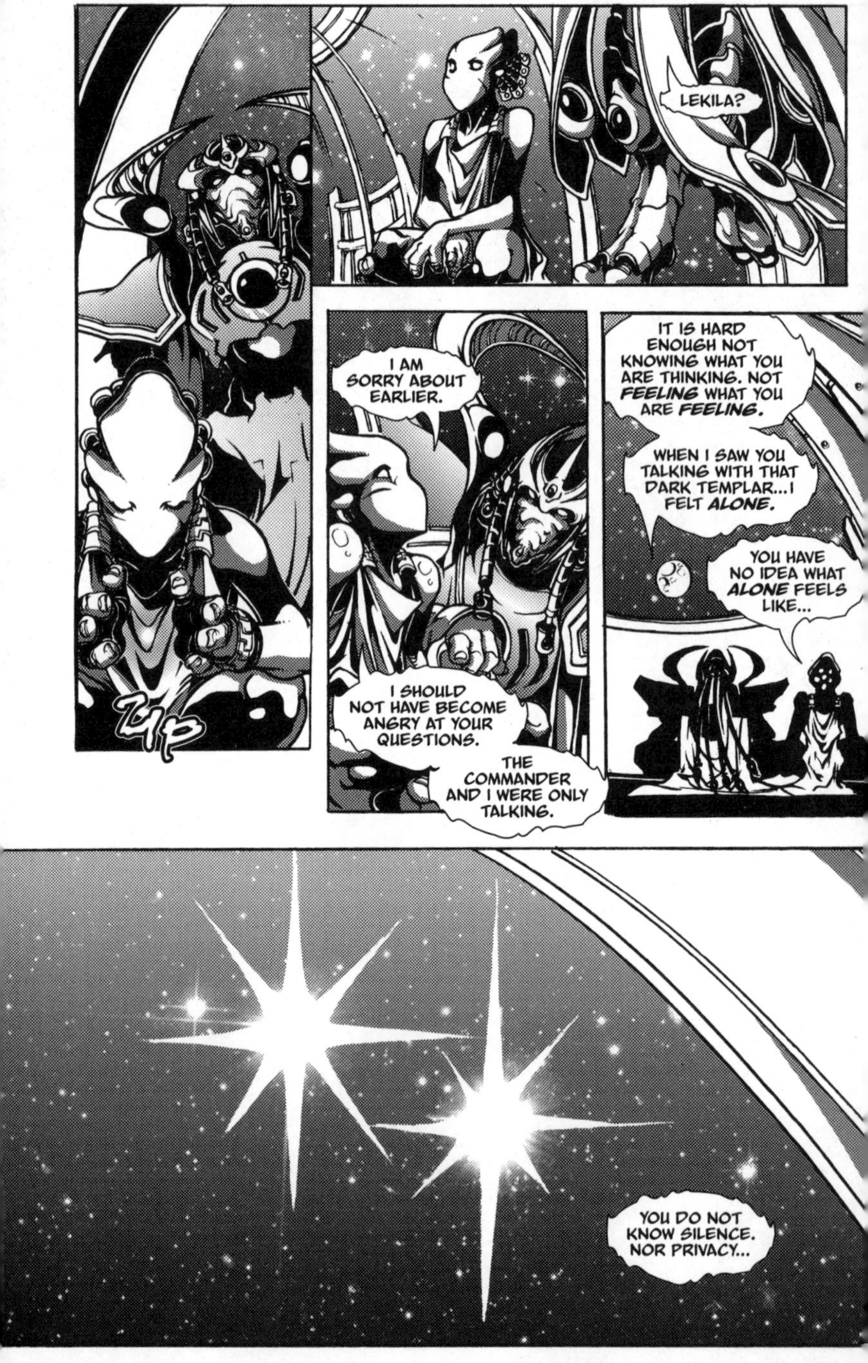
LEKILA?
ZIP
I AM SORRY ABOUT EARLIER.
I SHOULD NOT HAVE BECOME ANGRY AT YOUR QUESTIONS.
THE COMMANDER AND I WERE ONLY TALKING.
IT IS HARD ENOUGH NOT KNOWING WHAT YOU ARE THINKING. NOT FEELING WHAT YOU ARE FEELING.
WHEN I SAW YOU TALKING WITH THAT DARK TEMPLAR...I FELT ALONE.
YOU HAVE NO IDEA WHAT ALONE FEELS LIKE...
YOU DO NOT KNOW SILENCE. NOR PRIVACY...

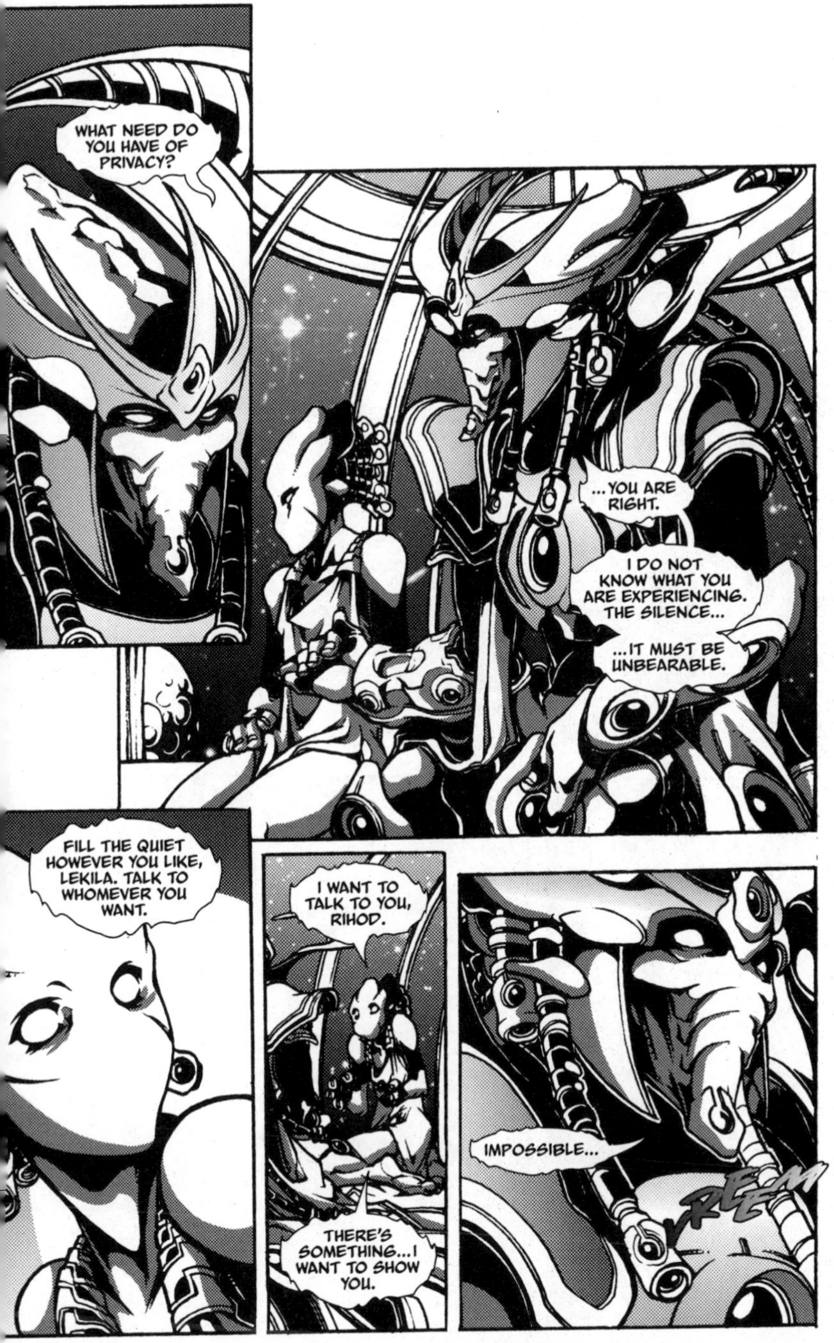
WHAT NEED DO YOU HAVE OF PRIVACY?
...YOU ARE RIGHT.
I DO NOT KNOW WHAT YOU ARE EXPERIENCING. THE SILENCE...
...IT MUST BE UNBEARABLE.
FILL THE QUIET HOWEVER YOU LIKE, LEKILA. TALK TO WHOMEVER YOU WANT.
I WANT TO TALK TO YOU, RIHOD.
THERE'S SOMETHING...I WANT TO SHOW YOU.
IMPOSSIBLE...
VREEEM

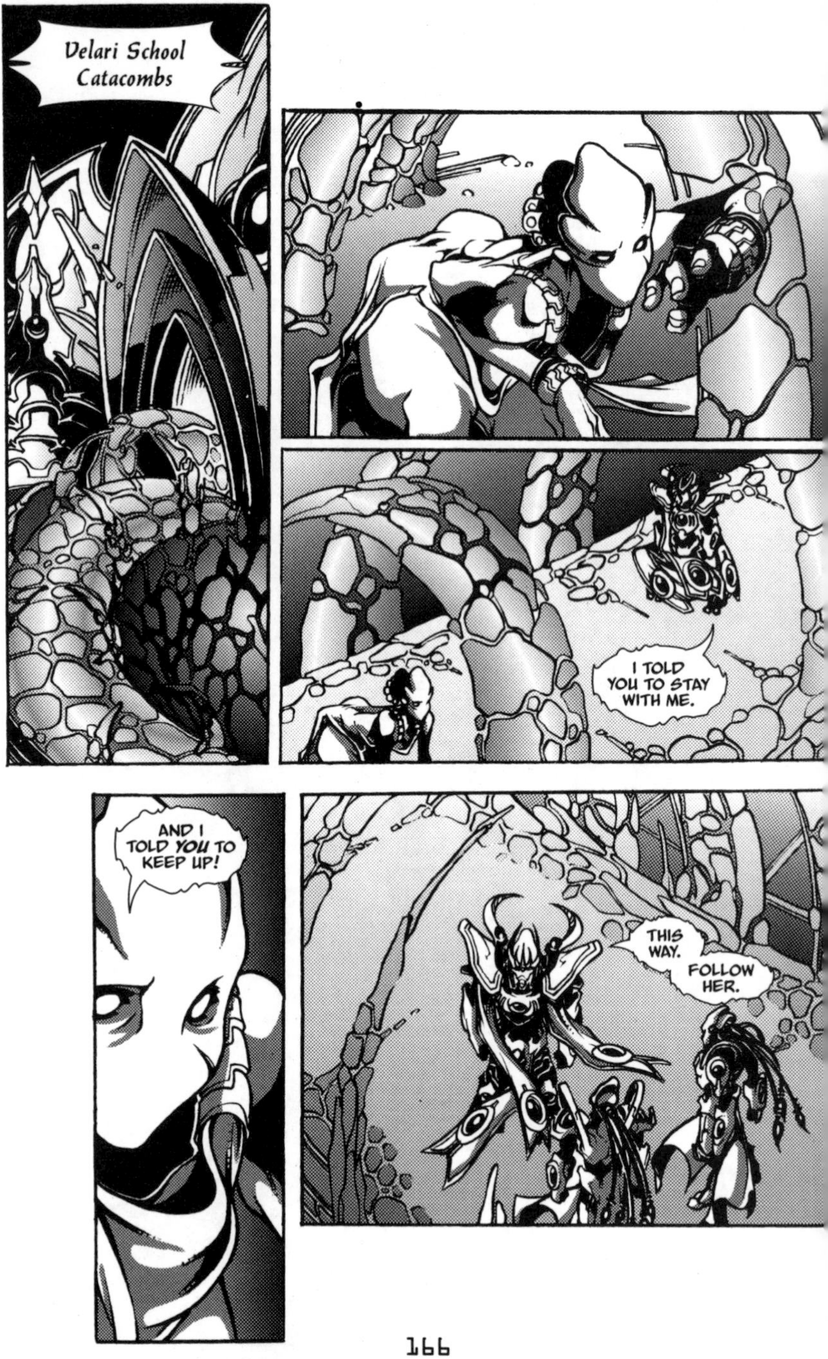
Velari School Catacombs
I TOLD YOU TO STAY WITH ME.
AND I TOLD *YOU* TO KEEP UP!
THIS WAY.
FOLLOW HER.

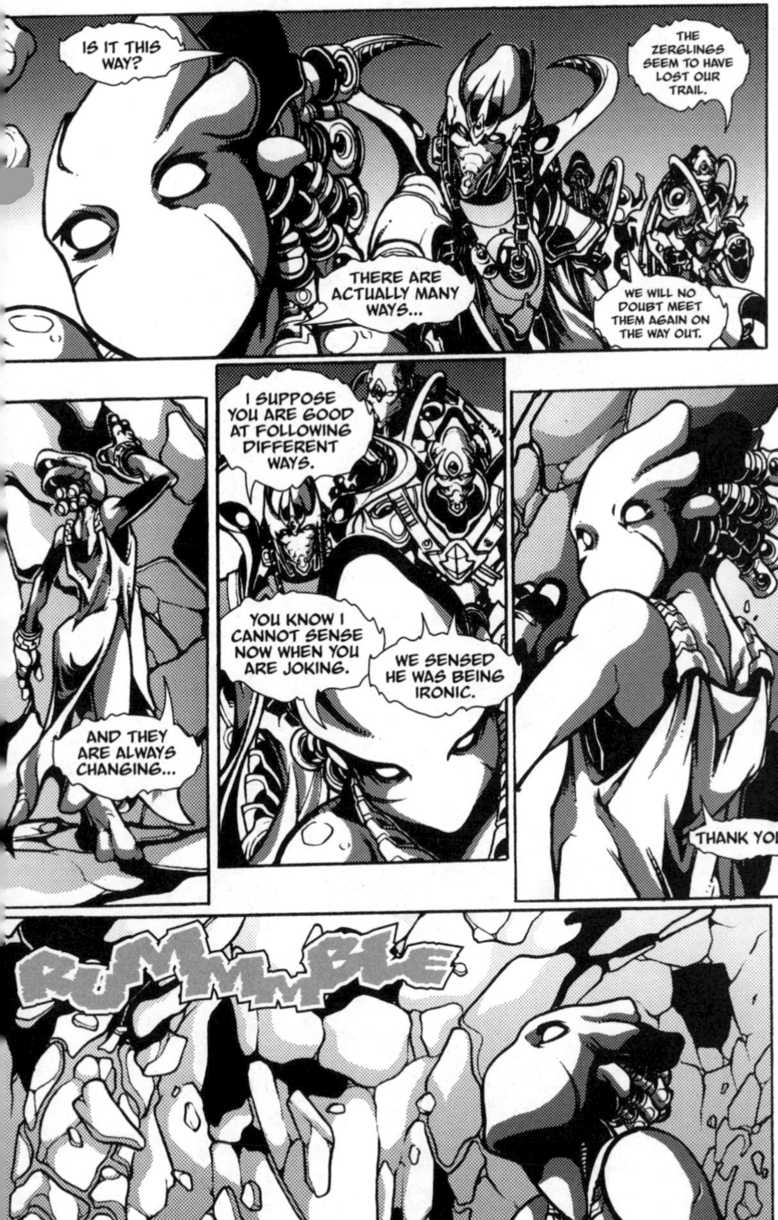
IS IT THIS WAY?
THE ZERGLINGS SEEM TO HAVE LOST OUR TRAIL.
THERE ARE ACTUALLY MANY WAYS...
WE WILL NO DOUBT MEET THEM AGAIN ON THE WAY OUT.
AND THEY ARE ALWAYS CHANGING...
I SUPPOSE YOU ARE GOOD AT FOLLOWING DIFFERENT WAYS.
YOU KNOW I CANNOT SENSE NOW WHEN YOU ARE JOKING.
WE SENSED HE WAS BEING IRONIC.
THANK YOU...
RUMMMBLE

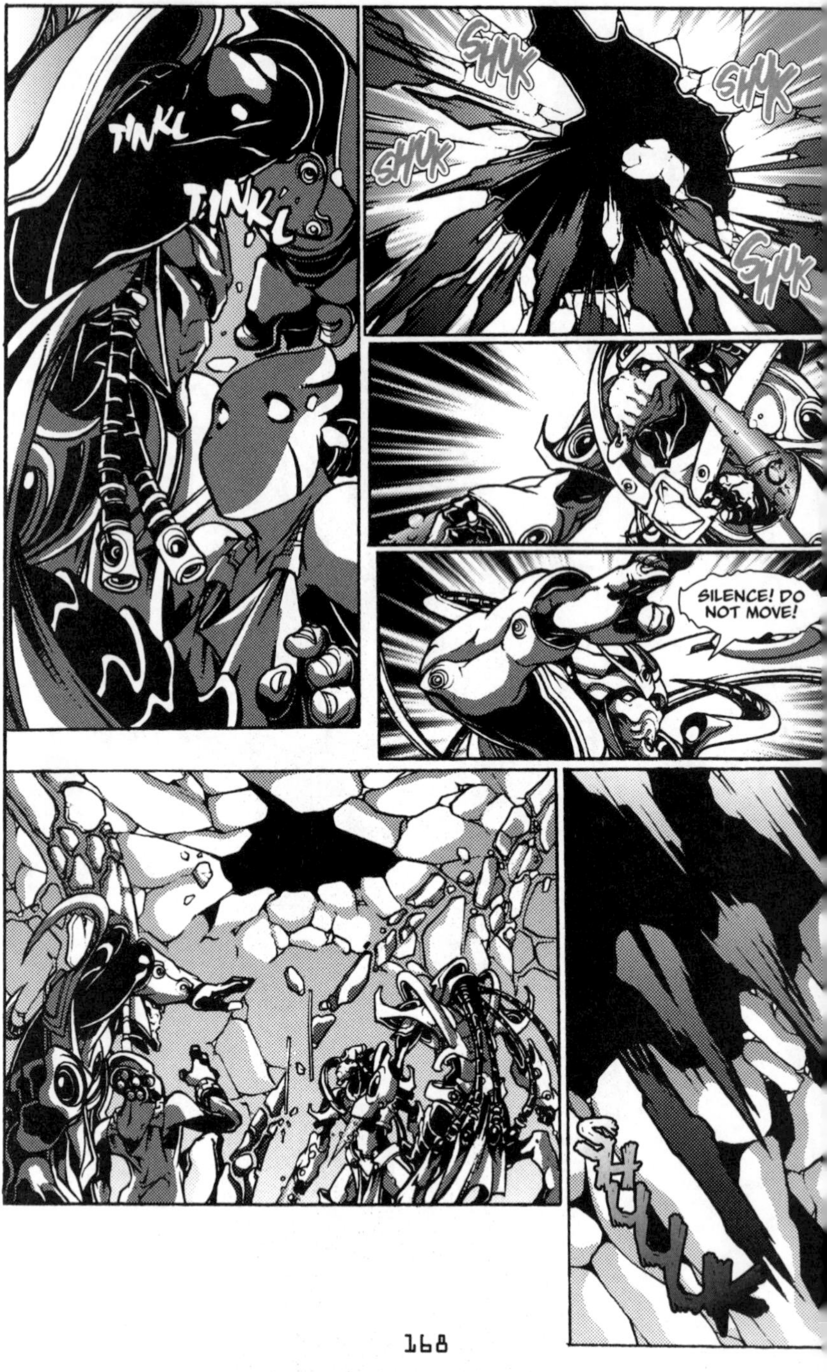
TINKL
TINKL
SHUK
SHUK
SHUK
SHUK
SILENCE! DO NOT MOVE!
SHUUK

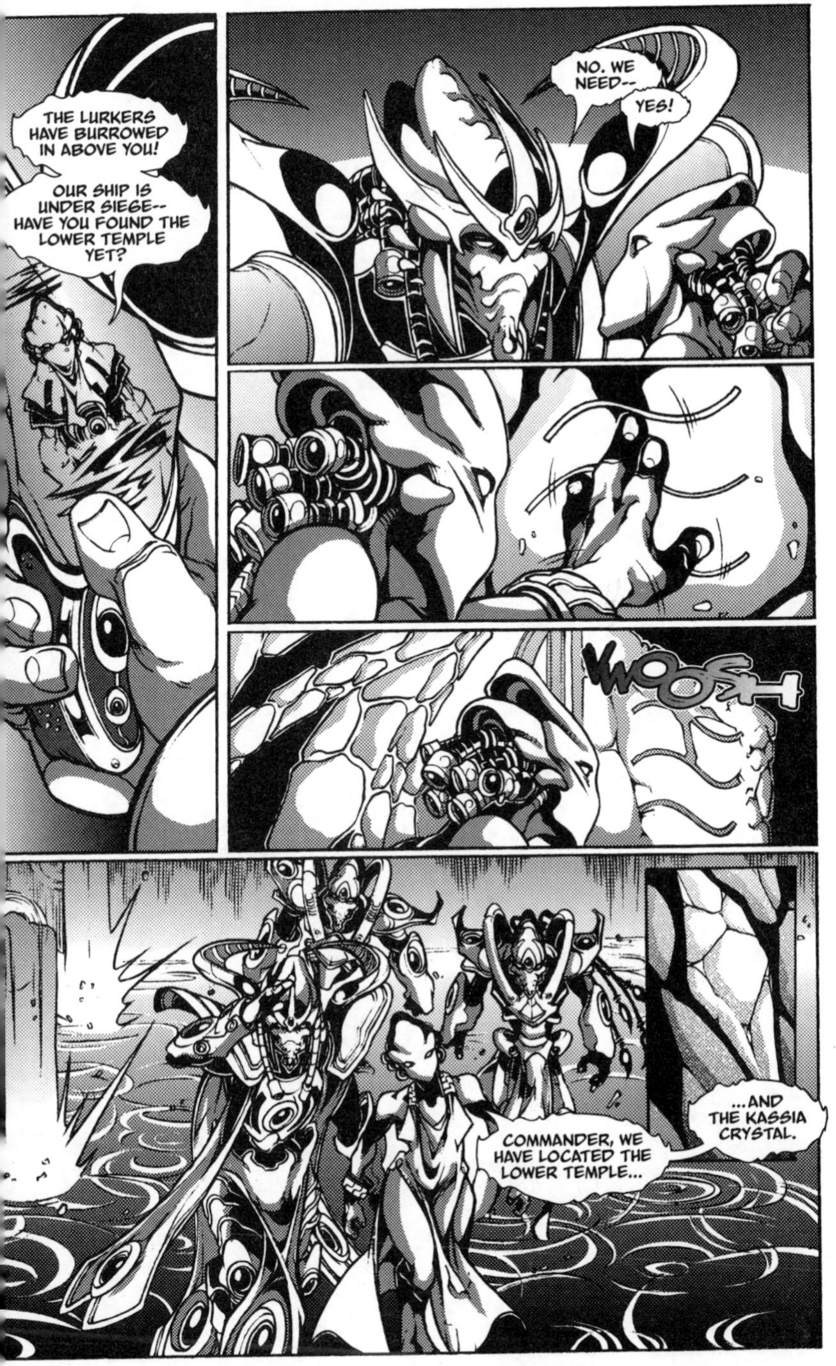
THE LURKERS HAVE BURROWED IN ABOVE YOU!
OUR SHIP IS UNDER SIEGE-- HAVE YOU FOUND THE LOWER TEMPLE YET?
NO. WE NEED--
YES!
WHOOSH
COMMANDER, WE HAVE LOCATED THE LOWER TEMPLE...
...AND THE KASSIA CRYSTAL.

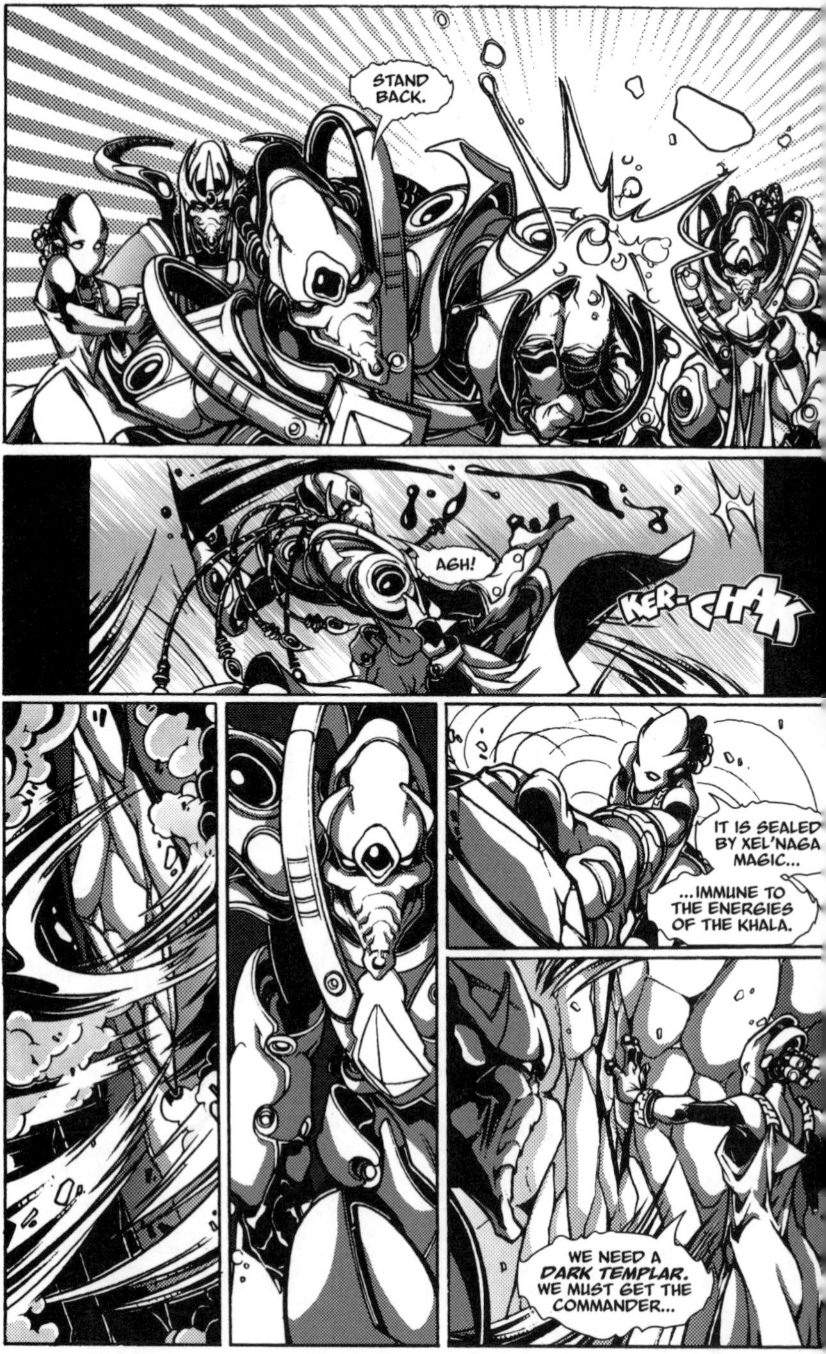
STAND BACK.
AGH!
KER-CHAK
IT IS SEALED BY XEL'NAGA MAGIC...
...IMMUNE TO THE ENERGIES OF THE KHALA.
WE NEED A *DARK TEMPLAR.* WE MUST GET THE COMMANDER...

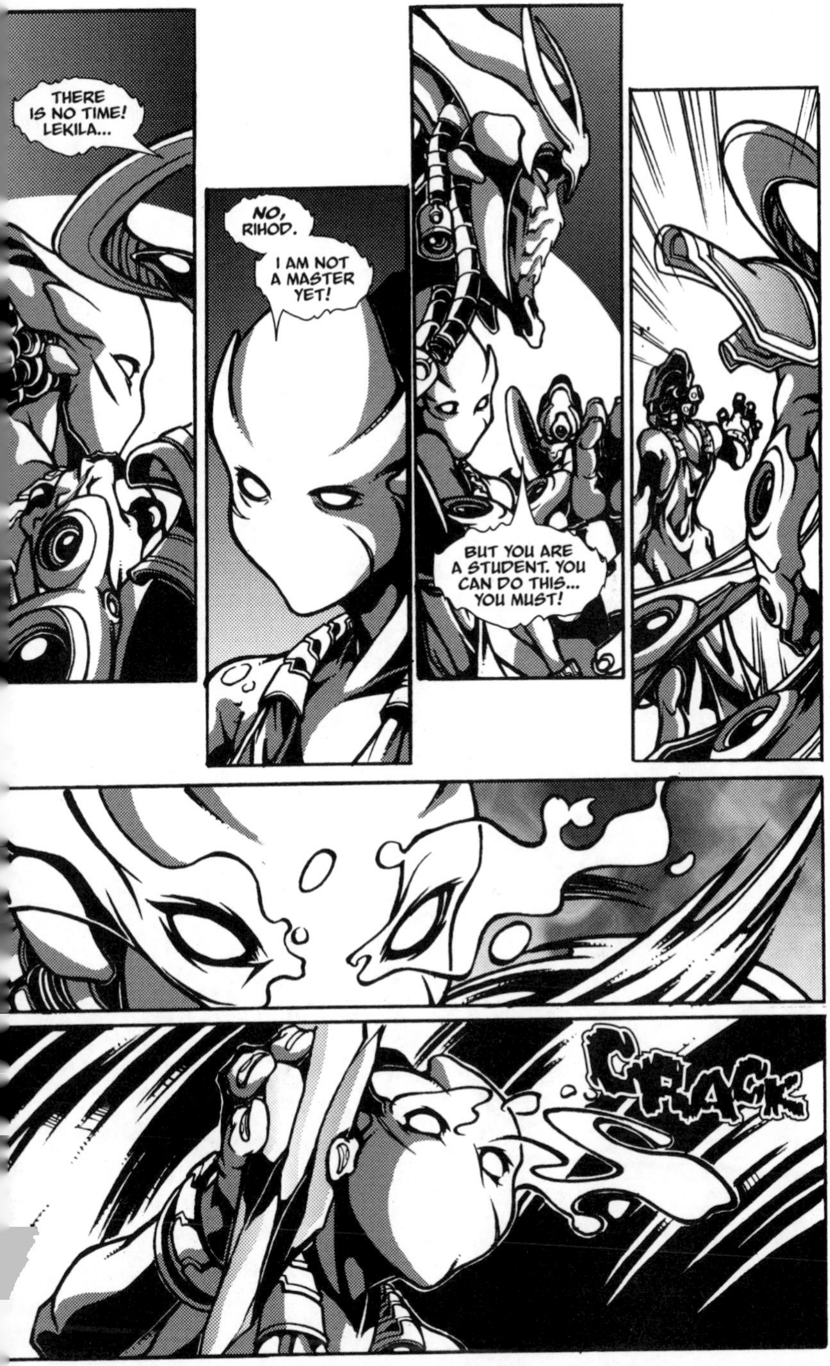
THERE IS NO TIME! LEKILA...
NO, RIHOD.
I AM NOT A MASTER YET!
BUT YOU ARE A STUDENT. YOU CAN DO THIS... YOU MUST!
CRACK

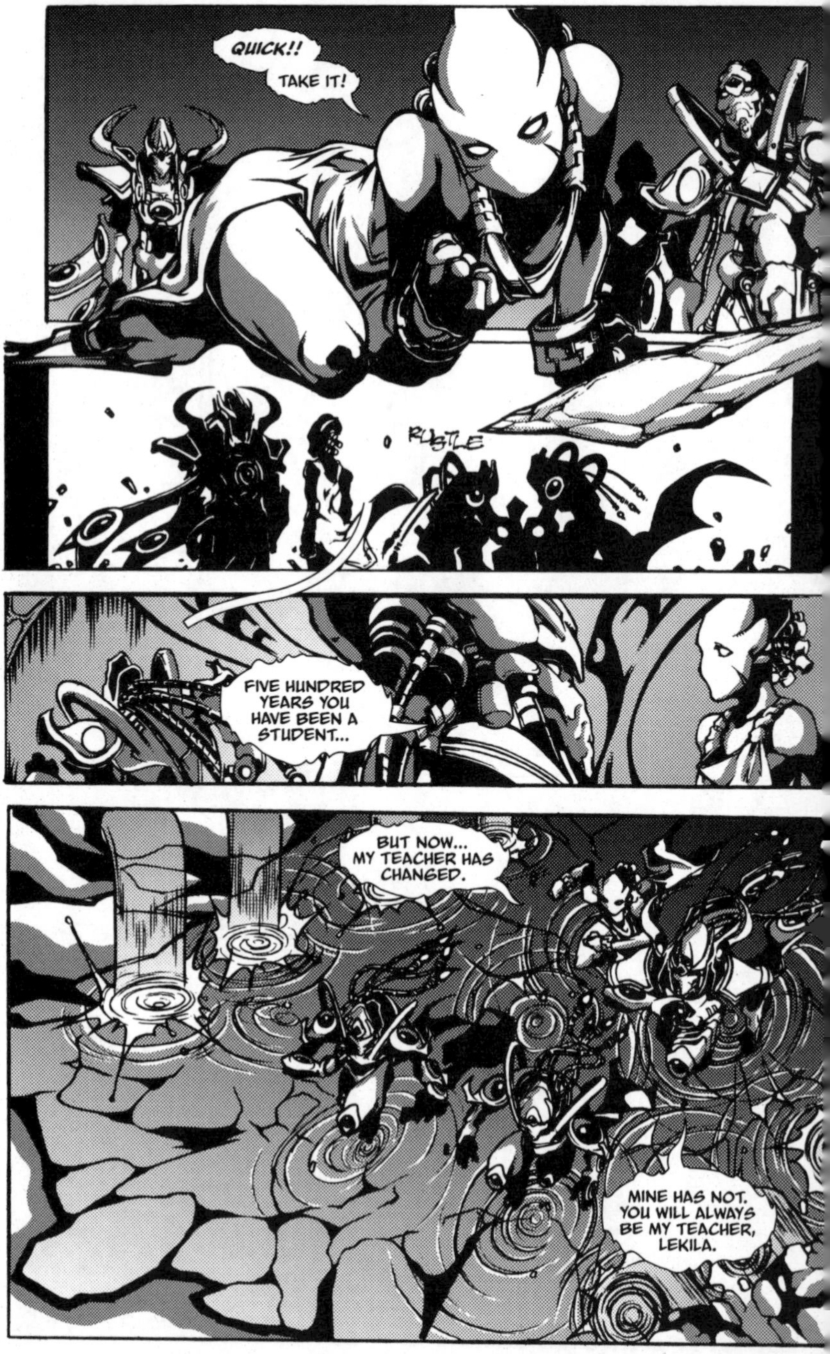
QUICK!!
TAKE IT!
RUSTLE
FIVE HUNDRED YEARS YOU HAVE BEEN A STUDENT...
BUT NOW... MY TEACHER HAS CHANGED.
MINE HAS NOT. YOU WILL ALWAYS BE MY TEACHER, LEKILA.

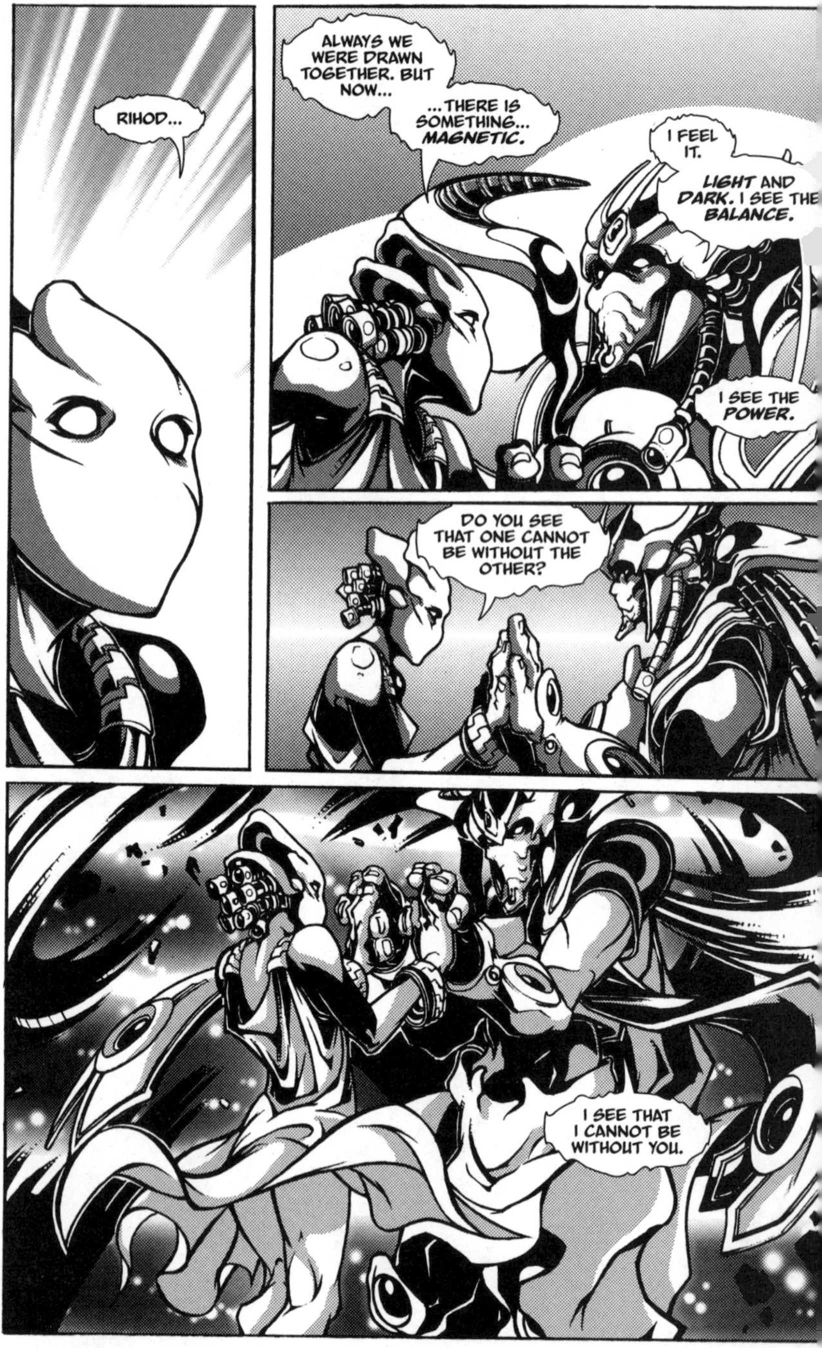
RIHOD...
ALWAYS WE WERE DRAWN TOGETHER. BUT NOW...
...THERE IS SOMETHING... MAGNETIC.
I FEEL IT.
LIGHT AND DARK. I SEE THE BALANCE.
I SEE THE POWER.
DO YOU SEE THAT ONE CANNOT BE WITHOUT THE OTHER?
I SEE THAT I CANNOT BE WITHOUT YOU.

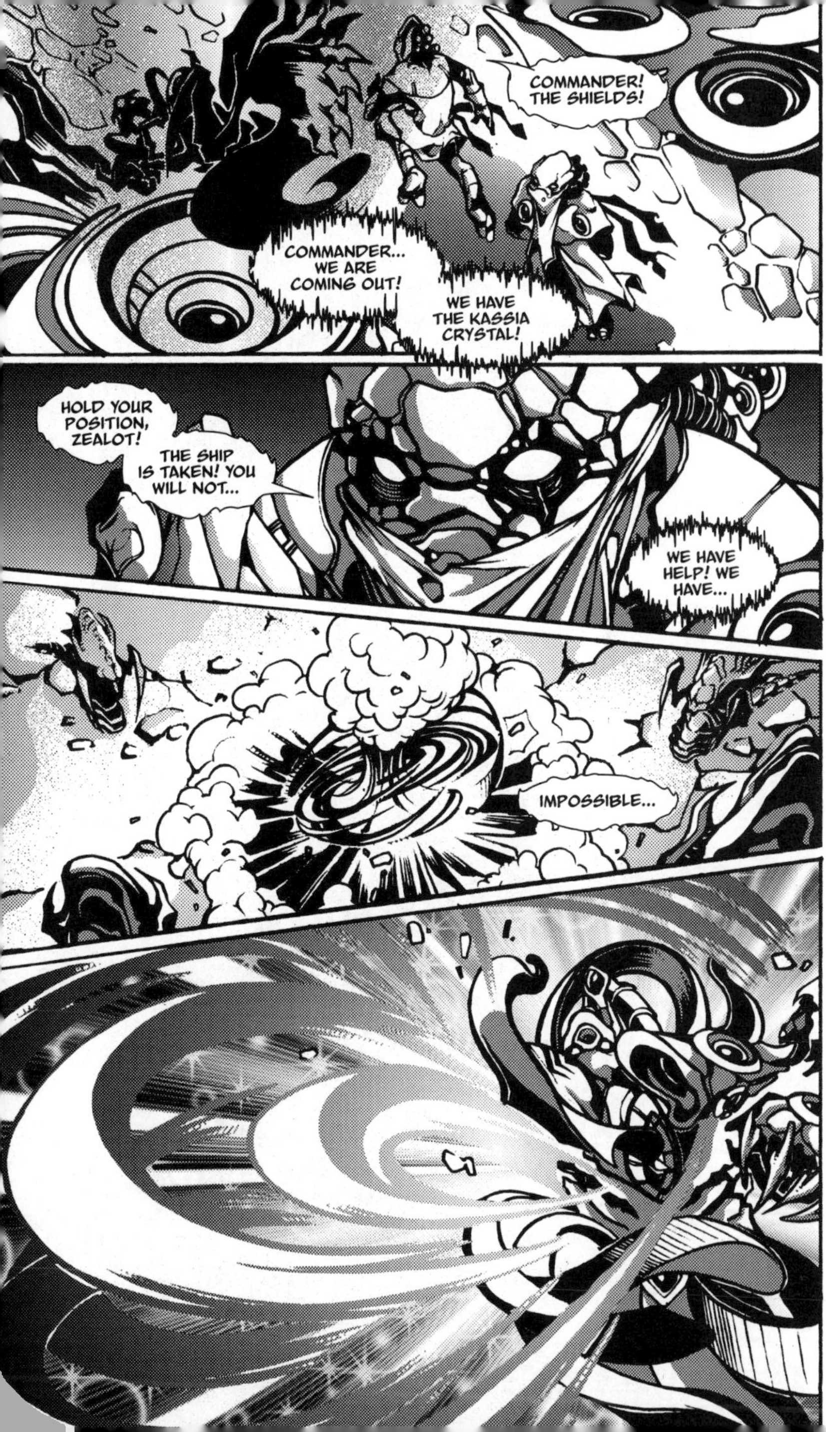
COMMANDER! THE SHIELDS!
COMMANDER... WE ARE COMING OUT!
WE HAVE THE KASSIA CRYSTAL!
HOLD YOUR POSITION, ZEALOT!
THE SHIP IS TAKEN! YOU WILL NOT...
WE HAVE HELP! WE HAVE...
IMPOSSIBLE...

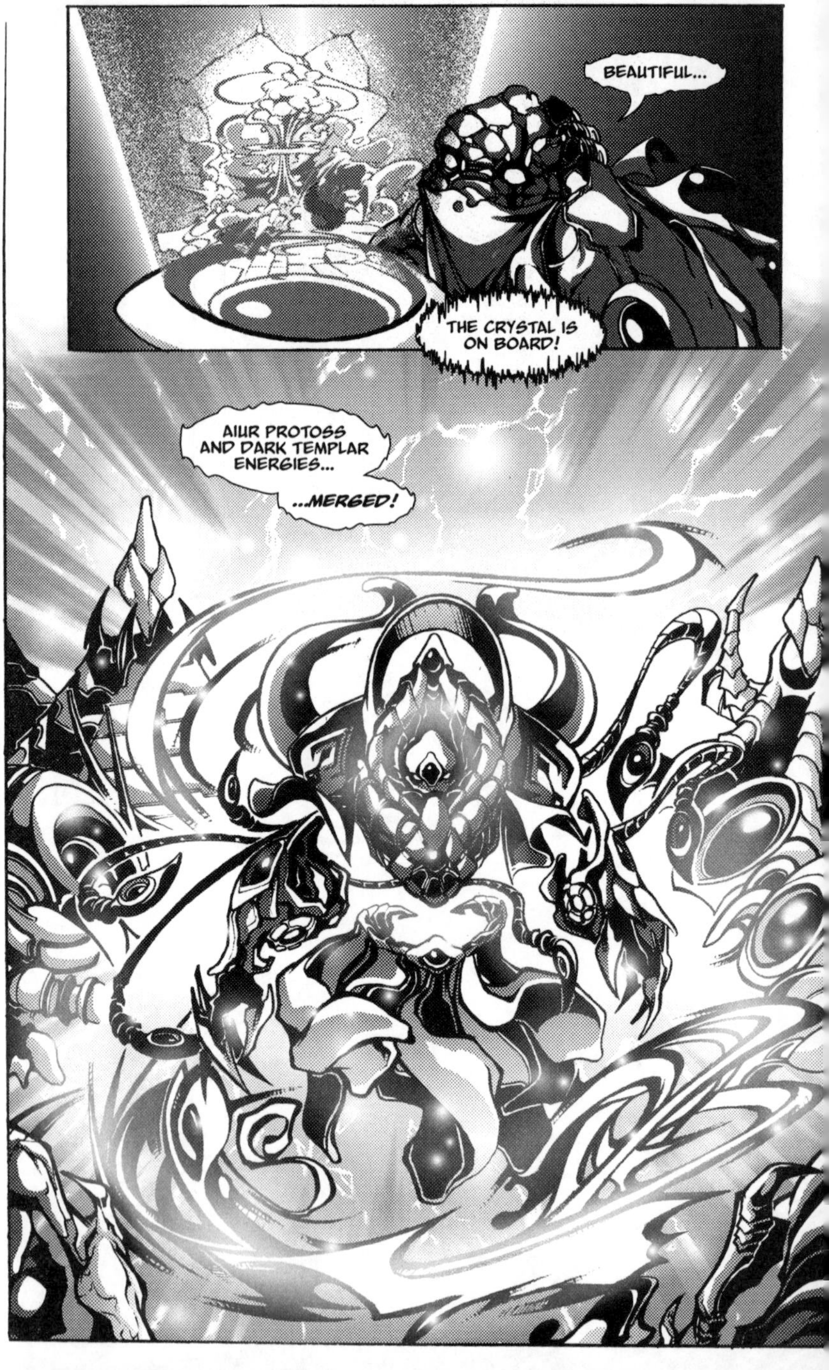
BEAUTIFUL...
THE CRYSTAL IS ON BOARD!
AIUR PROTOSS AND DARK TEMPLAR ENERGIES...
...MERGED!

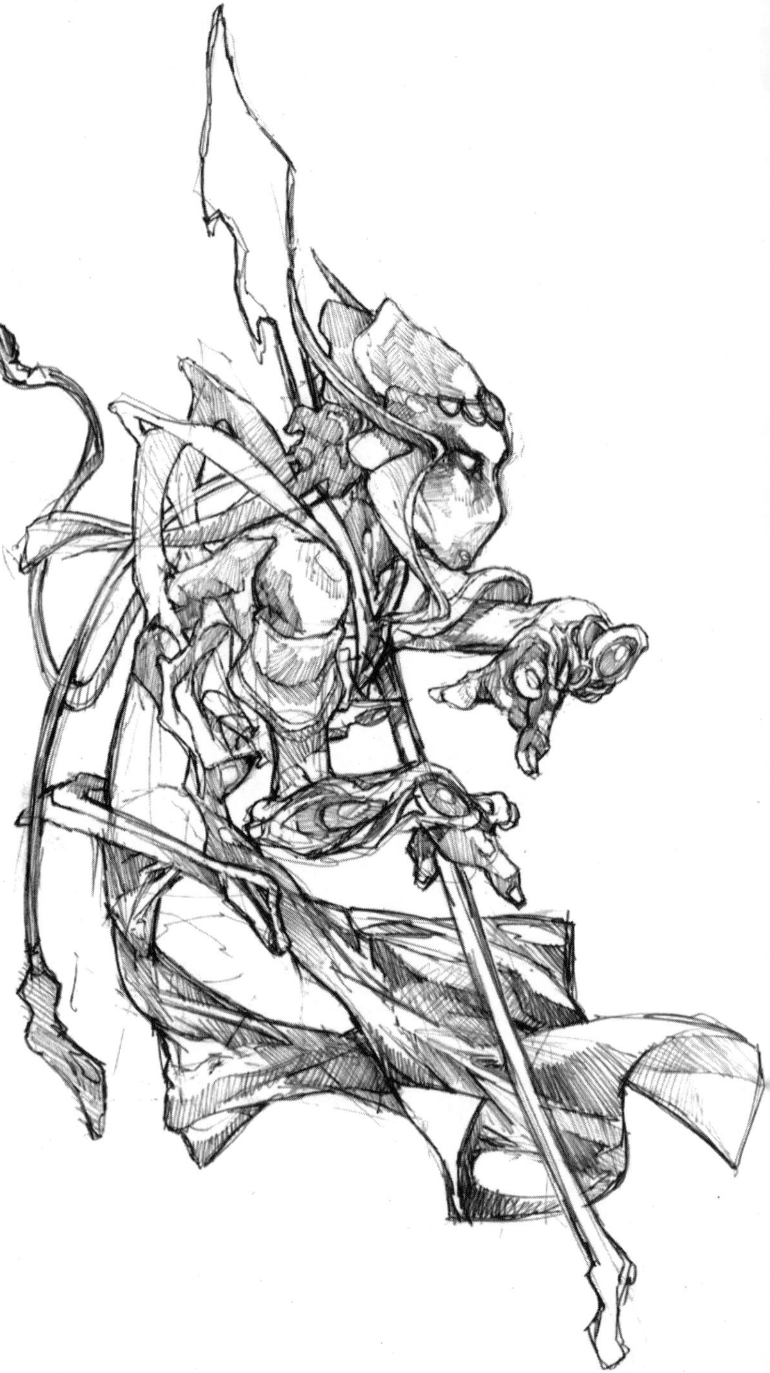

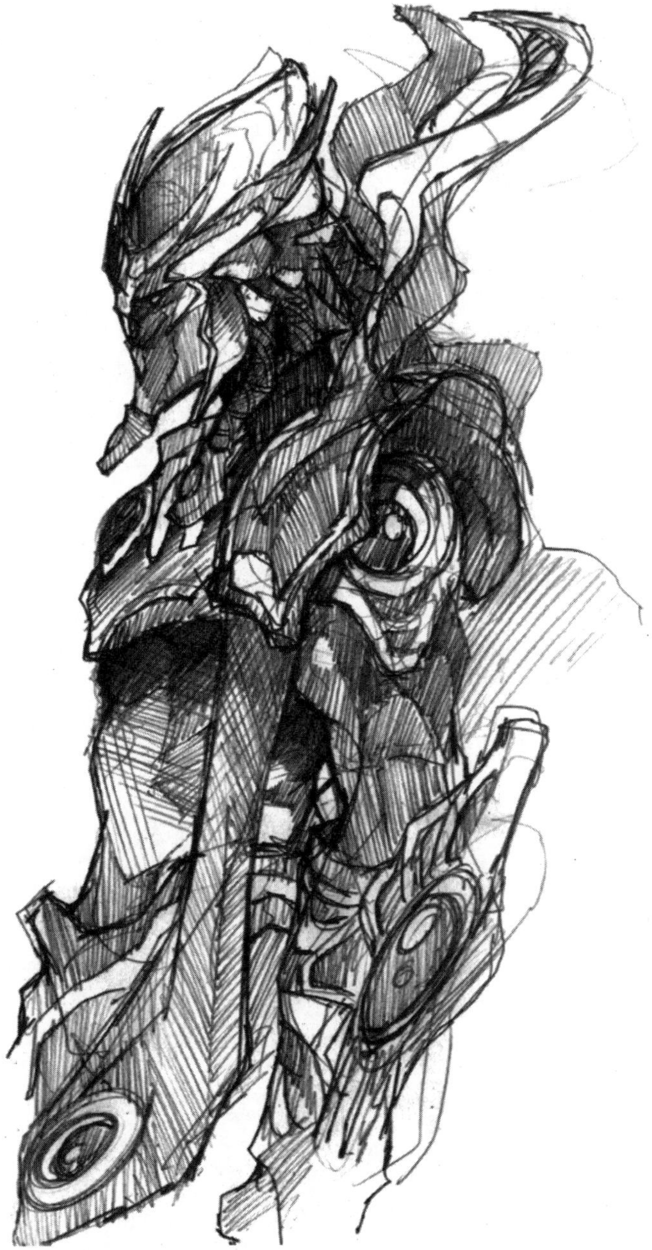

WRITERS:

PAUL BENJAMIN

Paul Benjamin is a writer, editor, supermodel, video game writer, and producer based in Austin, Texas. His comic book and graphic novel work ranges from his original manga series *Pantheon High* to *Marvel Adventures: Hulk* and *Marvel Adventures: Spider-Man*. His stories have appeared in numerous other Marvel titles as well as *Star Trek: The Manga* and *StarCraft: Frontline* series. Paul's video game writing and producing credits include Sega's *The Incredible Hulk* and Activision's *Spider-Man: Web of Shadows* for the Nintendo DS as well as *X-Men Origins: Wolverine* for Wii and PlayStation 2 and Electronic Arts's *G.I. JOE: The Rise of COBRA* for many platforms.

DAVE SHRAMEK

Dave Shramek is a game designer and writer in Austin, Texas. As is so often the case, he settled there after graduating from the University of Texas with a degree in radio, television, and film. Much to the delight of his parents, he was able to turn this normally unemployable degree into an actual profession with regular employment opportunities in the game-development-rich environment of Austin. He currently resides there with his ambitions of global dominance and an unhealthy addiction to Tex-Mex.

JOSH ELDER

Josh Elder is the handsome and brilliant writer of *Mail Order Ninja*, which he's pretty sure has been acclaimed by some critic, somewhere. A graduate of Northwestern University with a degree in film, Joshua currently resides in the quaint, little midwestern town of Chicago, Illinois. A longtime *StarCraft* fanboy, Josh is still geek-gasming over the fact that he got to write for *Frontline*. But Josh also played football, so he isn't a total dork. But he also played Dungeons & Dragons. So yeah, he kind of is a total dork.

GRACE RANDOLPH

Grace Randolph is a comedic actor and writer born and raised in New York City. Previously she's written *Justice League Unlimited #41* for DC Comics plus "Newsworthy" for *StarCraft: Frontline* and "Warrior: Divided" for *Warcraft: Legends*. Outside of comics, Grace is the host, writer, and producer of the webshow *Beyond the Trailer*, which is distributed by Next New Networks. Grace also studies at the Upright Citizens Brigade Theatre (UCB) where she has written, performed and produced the shows "Situation: Awkward" and "Igor On Strike."

REN ZATOPEK

Ren Zatopek is a medicine woman by day and a screenwriter and story analyst by night. She first worked on writingt he English adaptation of Youn In-Wan's *Deja Vu*. She was asked to create a story for the *StarCraft* anthology because of her physical similarities to the protoss: long hair, psionic powers, and knees that bend backwards. Ren knows there is no cow level.

HECTOR SEVILLA

Hector Sevilla hails from Chihuahua, Mexico. He is a huge fan of **StarCraft**, and never imagined he would help create a part of the **StarCraft** universe. He thanks Kathy Schilling, Paul Morrissey, and Blizzard Entertainment for the wonderful opportunity--and Hope Donovan for her great patience. In addition, Hector has created **Lullaby**, and worked on **Leviticus Cross** and Konami's **Lunar Knights**. He dedicates this manga to his parents for all the love and support they show each day to him.

RAMANDA KAMARGA

Like a superhero, **Ramanda Kamarga** holds a regular job during the day and draws comics at night. An avid gamer, he shares his free time with his wife and his PSP. Ramanda's previous works include **G.I. JOE: Sigma Six, Bristol Board Jungle, Psy*Comm** volumes 2 & 3, and of course **StarCraft: Frontline**.

SEUNG-HUI KYE

After publishing thirteen manwha and illustrating two light novels in South Korea, **Seung-hui Kye** decided to move on. In 2008, she made her Japanese manga debut with the one-shot story "Kuroi Ude" in **MiChao!** magazine, published through Kodansha. And now she has made her English-language debut in **StarCraft: Frontline**.

NOEL RODRIGUEZ

Noel Rodriguez began drawing, inking, and coloring manga at age seventeen in his native Philippines for the local market. Before long, he was discovered by Glass House Graphics. Noel began working out of their Manila officesonsuchWesternmangaprojects as **Dream Knight** and his own co-creation, **Warlords of Oz**. He is happiest drawing **StarCraft** and only recently discovered food.

Deception, betrayal, hubris, cruelty . . . and that was just getting the creative teams for this anthology signed up! I kid. The **StarCraft** world may be brutal, but you couldn't ask for a crackier team of minutemen . . . er, I mean, a finer team of manga creators!

First, a big congratulations to those on their second **Frontline** tour of duty: writers Paul Benjamin, Dave Shramek, Grace Randolph, Josh Elder, and artist Ramanda Kamarga. And also thanks to our most decorated veteran, Hector Sevilla, on his third story in as many volumes. Last but not least, a little fresh blood never hurt a campaign, and commendable rookies Ren Zatopek, Noel Rodriguez, and Seung-hui Kye shocked our system into high gear with the rocket-like force of their incredible craft.

As always, our deepest thanks goes to the guiding forces at Blizzard Entertainment. I'd like to thank our immediate contacts for their ongoing support of our soldiers on the **Frontline.** You keep us reaching for the stars—and upon missing, we still end up on motherships.

And speaking of stars, the star-studded fourth installment of **StarCraft: Frontline** is upon us—featuring the iconic Jim Raynor in a story written by Chris Metzen himself. And you faithful readers will also be treated to David Gerrold's (the writer of **Star Trek's** "Trouble with Tribbles") first foray into the **StarCraft** universe.

And very lastly, thanks to my fellow squad members, editor Troy Lewter and layout artist and **StarCraft** expert Michael "I Can Do It" Paolilli. Rock and roll!

Hope Donovan
Editor

STARCRAFT

FRONTLINE

IN THE NEXT VOLUME...

You've just read four stories of isolation, courage, despair, and redemption . . . but still you look toward the future, fixing your eyes upon further *StarCraft* adventures that await you on the near horizon...

Chris Metzen, the former senior vice president of Blizzard Entertainment's Creative Development team, brings you a never-before-seen story of Jim Raynor's past that leads directly into StarCraft II: Wings of Liberty...

Colin Phash is inducted into the Ghost Academy while his father Corbin runs for his life from that which Colin is to become . . .

Follow a rogue reaper in a tale of revenge that explodes across the StarCraft universe and invites the wrath of a protoss dark templar...

A brave team of protoss dark templar face down an ancient evil threatening to envelop the Koprulu sector in madness...

So suit up in your CMC armor, get on the FRONTLINE, and prepare yourself for another intense barrage of *StarCraft* stories!

STARCRAFT: FRONTLINE VOLUME 4